Scottish
Hill Names

Scottish Hill Names

*The origin and meaning of the names of
Scotland's hills and mountains*

Peter Drummond

drawings by
John Mitchell

SCOTTISH MOUNTAINEERING TRUST

Published in Great Britain by the Scottish Mountaineering Trust, 2010

First Edition 1991
Reprinted 1992
Second Edition 2007
Revised and reprinted 2010

ISBN 978-0-907521-95-2
A catalogue record for this book is available from the British Library

This book is published by the Scottish Mountaineering Trust, a charitable trust. Revenue from all books published by the Trust is used for the continuation of its publishing programme and for charitable purposes associated with Scottish mountains and mountaineering. For more information see <www.smc.org.uk/trust/trust.htm>

Illustrations
Front cover: Extract from Blaeu's map, 1654. Area around Ben Nevis, The Mamores and Glen Coe (including Buachaille Etive Mòr).

Back cover: Extract from Pont's map, c.1590s. Area around Arrochar, including Suy Arthire (Ben Arthur, i.e. The Cobbler), Ben Vane and Ptarmigan.

Designed and produced by Tom Prentice for Scottish Mountaineering Trust (Publications) Ltd
Mountain artwork: John Mitchell
Typesetting: Ken Crocket

Printed & bound in India at Replika Press Pvt Ltd

Distributed by Cordee Ltd.
(t) 01455 611185, (w) www.cordee.co.uk

Contents

Preface to the Second Edition

Fifteen years have elapsed since the first edition of this book, which has proved itself very popular with walkers and climbers all over Scotland.

Although the first edition was reprinted, it has now been decided to offer a completely revised and expanded second edition. The recent greater availability of the oldest comprehensive maps of Scotland – those of Timothy Pont and Joan Blaeu, dating from the late 16th and mid-17th centuries – on the website of the National Library of Scotland (see Bibliography), has made life much easier for place name study.

Many hill names in this book have benefited from this availability, and some of the maps are reproduced in colour. Many of the thematic chapters in the first edition have been restructured, into regional chapters paralleling the Scottish Mountaineering Club's district and hillwalker's guidebook series: and the sizeable new chapter entitled Hill Name Generics is in effect a dictionary of the Gaelic, Scots, Norse, and Cumbric words for hills of various shapes and sizes.

Coverage of the Southern Uplands and Central Lowlands hills has been expanded, the former benefiting from the author's 2006 M.Sc. dissertation at Edinburgh University, on *The Hill Names of Southern Scotland*.

Acknowledgements

I would like to thank in particular many helpful observations on the first edition from Dr Adam Watson and Ian R.Mitchell, and the continued support of Dr Domhnall Uilleam Stiùbhart (of Edinburgh University and Sabhal Mòr Ostaig Gaelic College) whose assistance regarding Gaelic spelling, pronunciation and orthography has been invaluable. I also wish to express gratitude to the editorial team of Tom Prentice and Ken Crocket, for their patience and many helpful comments.

Peter Drummond
Spring 2007

Reader's Guide

Most of the hill and mountain names in this book are typeset in bold, to help you locate them when using the index. If the correct Gaelic spelling is substantially different from the usual map version, I have placed the common version first, and then bracketed the correct spelling with the words ('properly...').

Pronunciation guides appear after each of the Gaelic elements in the Hill Name Generics chapter (i.e. the main family names of hills like beinn, sgùrr, meall, etc), and after all Gaelic hill names with a paragraph of their own in the regional chapters. They give a phonetic guide to the pronunciation, by English-speakers, of Gaelic names. The phonetic script used is based on English spelling and it is therefore impossible to give more than a very rough approximation of the Gaelic sounds, which are quite different from those of English. But it should enable users to pronounce the names in such a way that they would at least be understood by a Gaelic speaker.

Gaelic pronunciation differs from area to area and it is not possible to cover regional variations here. Therefore you may hear quite different pronunciations in some places as well as anglicised versions, hence the book's occasional use of the bracketed phrase '(locally pronounced...)'.

Note that the key is based on standard Scottish pronunciation and not on standard Southern English. For example, 'day' and 'road' have simple vowels and not diphthongs. Note also that 'r' is always pronounced.

An accent on a vowel in a Gaelic name in this book, for example in the generics *càrn* or *sgùrr* or the frequently-occurring adjective *mòr* (big), indicates that it is a long vowel when spoken. Thus *càrn* would be pronounced *kaarn* (not *curn*), while Sgùrr Mòr would be pronounced *skoor more* (not *skuhr mawr*).

Although both grave and acute accents [ie à and á] can be found in other, usually older, Gaelic texts, modern Gaelic orthography uses only the former. Readers interested are referred to *Gaelic Orthographic Conventions* published by the SQA (Scottish Qualifications Authority) in 2005. Among Gaelic dictionaries, Dwelly's (see Bibliography) is the most detailed and reliable, and is scrupulous about the use of accents.

In the list opposite and throughout the pronounciations cited in the text, bold type indicates the stressed syllable. Where there might be confusion a hyphen has been used to separate syllables, while a colon indicates the lengthening of a preceding vowel.

Vowels

a	as in lesser
a	as in tap
aa	as in father
ay	as in day
e	as in red
ee	as in deed, weak
i	as in tip
Y	as in by
o	as in top
u	as in but
oa	as in road
aw	as in bawl
oo	as in pool
ow	as in owl
oi	as in boil
oe	approximately the sound in French **oeuf** or German **Ö**sterreich.

Consonants

Most of the consonants represent *approximately* the same sounds in English. Note the following:

g	as in **g**et
s	as in **s**it
y	as in **y**et
ch	as in lo**ch**; this is pronounced by putting the tip of your tongue on the back of your lower teeth, narrowing the gap at the back of your throat using your tongue and exhaling through this gap to make a sound without using your vocal chords.
gh	has no equivalent in English; it is a voiced ch (i.e. it is pronounced like a 'ch', but using the vocal chords).
d & t	are pronounced with the tip of the tongue touching the back of the lower teeth (and not the teeth ridge as in English).
b	is often transcribed as p, although the sound is actually somewhere between these two sounds in English, but somewhat closer to p: similarly d is often transcribed as t and g as k.
y	a superscript y (e.g. – neet^y) indicates a nasal y as in the word million.

INTRODUCTION

Scotland's hill names are more than just names. They are part of our heritage. For they allow us to see how Gaelic and Scots cultures in particular 'saw' the hills – their colours, their shape, their legends and their practical functions – through eyes that have been blinded now for most of us by our urban industrial culture.

In most European nations the names of the hills present no difficulty for they are in the living language of the local people. In Scotland, however, most of the hill names are in one of four languages other than the English which most of us speak. Of these four, two (Cumbric and Norse) are dead, one (Scots) is in a critical condition, and the other (Gaelic) is a daily language for only a relatively small number of people, mainly in the Western Isles.

Languages of the past and present

Of these four languages, Cumbric (sometimes called Brittonic or Old Welsh) is the oldest, and was used in the Scottish Lowlands and Southern Uplands by 'the Britons' until south-east Scotland was taken over by the Angles, and the south-west absorbed into the Gaelic-speaking Kingdom of the Scots (from Ireland), although the language lived on in pockets until the 12th century. Dumbarton Rock remains named as it was the 'fort of the Britons' (*Dùn Breatann*), and they left behind a few ancient hill names like the Ochils.

Old Norse, the language of the Viking invaders, was widely spoken in the islands – Orkney and Shetland, and the Hebrides – from the 9th to the 13th centuries, and its impact on names is largely confined to these islands and to a few northern coastal areas. On the Scottish mainland, only amongst the hills of Caithness and Sutherland are there many direct traces of their tongue, although later Gaelic hill words like *sgùrr* may well have a Norse origin. In northern England the Lake District hills contain a lot of Norse names reflecting their settlement there, and some of their hill words like *rigg*, *dodd* and *fell* migrated north of the Border where they were adopted by Scots speakers.

Scots is related to English, and is spoken over most of the Borders and the north-east and Central Lowlands. It has many distinctive hill-words like *law*, *fell* and *bin*, derived from Anglo-Saxon, from Norse, and from Gaelic. This language was at its peak in the 15th and 16th centuries, and since then has been on the decline among the Scottish people, especially under an anglicised education system and media.

Gaelic is by far the most important language in hill-words: virtually every hill in the Highlands has a Gaelic name, and many in the Lowlands too; only the south-eastern Borders are untouched by it. Some of these Gaelic names were, however, changed or corrupted by the passage of time, which makes it difficult to pin down the original meanings. Gaelic topographical place names were passed on by word of mouth, not in writing. And although this oral link may have been perfectly accurate while Gaelic was strong, and the local dialect unchanged, many centuries may have elapsed between the names being given by the local people and their being written down (often inaccurately) by the mainly English-speaking Ordnance Survey

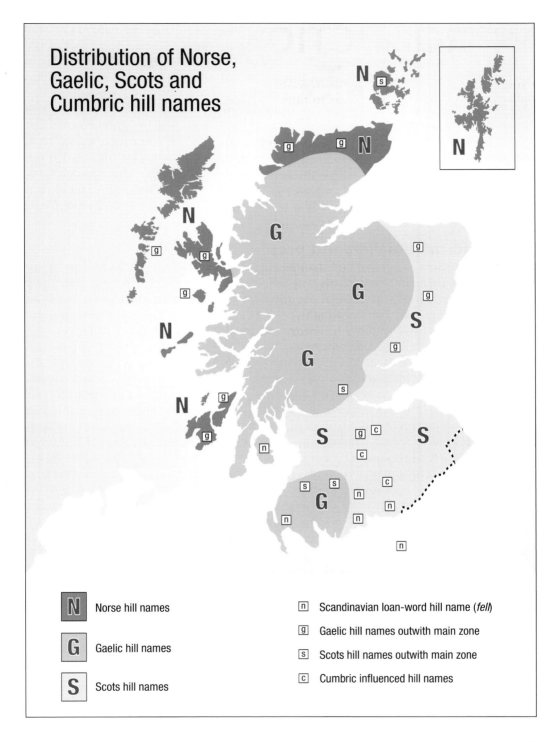

Distribution of Norse, Gaelic, Scots and Cumbric hill names

N Norse hill names

G Gaelic hill names

S Scots hill names

n̄ Scandinavian loan-word hill name (*fell*)

ḡ Gaelic hill names outwith main zone

s̄ Scots hill names outwith main zone

c̄ Cumbric influenced hill names

mapmakers in the mid-19th century, so that the original form of the name may have changed. This is especially true in the east and south of the Highlands, as well in the south-west of Scotland, where the dying out of Gaelic by the time of the Ordnance Survey mapping added further difficulty to correct transcription. This whole process is illustrated by the several possible interpretations of the names of higher peaks like Ben Nevis, Ben Alder and Ben Macdui: probably they, being highest, were named earliest and the long time exposure since then has blurred the picture we now have of their meanings. By contrast lower and less significant peaks, which would have been named later (in a process of 'filling in the gaps' between bigger hills), are often easy to decipher from a Gaelic dictionary, provided the Ordnance Survey maps have recorded the correct spelling. In some cases they recorded the approximate pronunciation rather than the correct spelling, as with Ben Attow rather than Beinn Fhada (the *fh* being silent).

Maps and map-makers

The Ordnance Survey carried out their first mapping in the mid-19th century. They were therefore in time to record many of the local Gaelic names of the hills, but sadly many of the memories and tales behind the names left the glens during the late 18th and early 19th century. For the cruel winds of the Highland Clearances and poverty-driven emigration swept many of the people out like so many autumn leaves, and their memories of hill names, passed on through generations in the glens, would moulder and die with them in city tenements or New World plains. In spite of this loss, much of this book is able to state or suggest why hills were given certain names.

Fortunately there are earlier maps than the Ordnance Survey's. One that I'll refer to frequently in this book is the one compiled in the 1590s by Timothy Pont, and still existing in fragments covering many parts of Scotland. He was a Scots speaker, but endeavoured to record the mainly Gaelic hill names that local people informed him about: since Gaelic and English dictionaries were not around, he wrote down what we'd now term a phonetic representation of the name, and these are surprisingly accurate even to a modern Gaelic speaker – for instance Bin Nevesh for Ben Nevis. Fortunately for us he thus captured the names of several hundreds of the most important hills and mountains over a century and a half before the Ordnance Survey – the reader wishing to read more about this is directed to Ian Mitchell's relevant chapter noted in the Bibliography at the end of the book.

Although many of Pont's maps were lost in a fire, fortunately many of them had by then been used by Dutch map-maker Joan Blaeu to produce a beautiful map of Scotland in 1654, aided by the work of Gordon of Straloch who also had access to Pont's maps. Some of Blaeu's maps are featured in this book's illustrations: and the reader who wishes to view more of them, as well as Pont's and many other older maps, is recommended to go on-line at the National Library of Scotland's website listed in the Bibliography.

The naming of hills

Names evolve from simple geographical descriptions to established place names:

Sgùrr na Cìche, literally peak of the breast, a Knoydart landmark. See p27, [Generics, cìoch]

people in an area might refer to a hill as *the black hill* or, in Gaelic, as *a' chruach raineach* (the brackeny heap). Over time, once this usage was of long-standing, the definite article (ie *the* in English, or *a'*, *am* or *an* in Gaelic), would be redundant and the name of Black Hill or Cruach Raineach would then be used locally on the understanding that it referred to a particular place, and this place name would be relayed to visiting map-makers. Sometimes the definite article still remains in the offical place name, as in A' Bheinn Ghlas, An Socach or The Buck.

It is difficult to be precise about when exactly hills were given their names. In southern Scotland the existence of Cumbric names like the Ochils (from *uchel*, high) or hills like Penvalla and probably Caerketton, indicate they were named by the 11th century, after which Gaelic or a form of Scots became dominant. The Norse hegemony in the islands and facing west coast was on the wane by the 13th century, so the *-val* and *-fell* names there (from *fjall*) probably date from before then. The Scots names of southern and eastern hills (like *law* or *kip*) were probably given after the 14th century when this language became dominant, and arguably were given between then and the 19th century, by which time some of the terms had begun to fall out of use in favour of English.

Many lesser hills appear to have been given their present name fairly late in the historical process. They usually had earlier names, but because they were unimportant hills, known to only a few people, then if a farmer moved away from a valley, and a new tenant took over, a new name may have been given. Also, hills have usually valleys on several sides, and the possibility of alternative names in different

The Cuillin (here Skye, but also Rum) from Norse kiolen, high rocky ridge

valleys arises, one of them being successful in catching the Ordnance Survey's attention for posterity. In the Borders, 45 per cent of all the hills mapped by Blaeu (1654) or Roy's Military Survey (1755), had changed their name by the time they were mapped by the Ordnance Survey: sometimes the generic (e.g. *law*, *fell*, *hill*) had been changed, sometimes the specific (e.g. Black, Culter, Mid), sometimes both (e.g. Corshope Hill to Mount Main). In the Highlands, similar changes took place but on a lesser scale

Some hills of course we can date very precisely – Sgùrr nan Spàinteach in Glen Shiel was where in 1719 the Spanish soldiers supporting the Jacobites were scattered by the Redcoats – but such precision is unusual. Indeed some hills have changed their names over the years – Suidhe Artair (literally Arthur's Seat) became Ben Arthur, and is now universally described as The Cobbler. The process of naming continues. As recently as the 1990s the Scottish Mountaineering Club had to establish names for four Corbetts listed in their Tables but un- or ill-recorded by the Ordnance Survey. They were christened Stob Coire Creagach (above Glen Kinglass), Maol Creag an Loch (above the Gaick Pass), Stob Fearthomais (south of Loch Voil) and Stob a' Bhealaich an Sgriodain (Ardgour): they were thus born great, thrust at birth straight into the honoured ranks of Corbetts! Stob Fearthomais was subsequently re-named Beinn Stacath after Bealach Stacath to the south, named by the Ordnance Survey on a subsequent 1:25,000 scale map.

The study of place names

The study of place names (including hill names) is called toponymics, a division of onomastics which covers all names including personal names. The bibliography of

this book lists a number of books and publications by scholars working in this field. It will be useful to mention at this point one or two who often crop up in the text: W.J.Watson was Professor of Celtic at Edinburgh University from 1915, and his book *The History of the Celtic Place-Names of Scotland*, still in print, remains the 'Old Testament' of Scottish place name scholars, packed with information and insight, rarely proved wrong by subsequent investigations.

The equivalent 'New Testament' is W.F.H.Nicolaisen's *Scottish Place-Names*, also still in print, and although he has few hill names, it remains the best theoretical work on the subject. The works by Adam Watson (and Elizabeth Allan), Angus Watson, Ian Fraser, mentioned in the Bibliography, and the Scottish Place-Name Society's website and newsletter, all carry reliable material for various areas.

Books sold in tourist outlets on Scottish place names are often unreliable, repeating errors made by earlier writers like J.B.Johnston. The Scottish Mountaineering Club Journal, by its very nature has carried useful information over the century, and two of the club's early Munroists in particular, the Reverends A.E.Robertson and Ronald Burn noted many pronunciations and explanations – the latter in particular, being a Gaelic speaker.

Alternative explanations of meaning

The reader might object that for some hill names with several possible meanings I have too often used words like 'perhaps', 'possibly' or 'probably' to indicate that we cannot be absolutely sure. It is axiomatic in place name study that one should always start from the oldest recorded form of a name, since this will be closest to the original meaning. However, hill names were generally recorded for the first time much later than farms or settlements which paid rent to landlords, and the names first recorded by map-makers (1590 onwards) are often our earliest sources. In consequence we are often at some remove from the original, which is why there are competing explanations for the meaning.

I have tried to lay out these various alternatives, seeing how well they fit the evidence, and as far as possible I have gone for the alternative that fits best in the context – the context of neighbouring hills, or of the normal distribution of the names (e.g. – that Norse names are confined to the northern and western isles and the north-west), or of similar instances elsewhere. For instance I reject one suggestion for the Cuillin mountains, namely that it is from the Gaelic *cuilionn* meaning holly (because of their jagged shape), and prefer instead the alternative of the Norse *kiolen* meaning high rocky mountain: this is because most of the names of Skye's high peaks are Norse, not Gaelic; because Gaelic tree hill names are not named from the hill's *shape*; and because there are Norwegian mountains with the name Kiolen, overlooking the fiords from where the Vikings sailed to conquer Skye.

Many Gaelic names are, however, quite clear in their meaning. They reveal an astonishing variety, without European parallel. In addition to a very large selection of names for the different shapes and sizes of hills, Gaelic hill names contain scores of different colours, of body parts, of people and creatures and plants of nature. It is exploring this huge and fascinating variety that makes up the bulk of this book.

CHAPTER ONE

HILL NAME GENERICS

Most hill names include a hill name generic, a 'family name'. Most place names (and hill names) have a generic and a specific (a 'first' or 'given' name) to distinguish them within the family generic. For instance Ben Nevis, Sgùrr na Cìche, Goatfell, North Berwick Law and West Kip respectively contain the generics *ben* (or *beinn*), *sgùrr*, *fell*, *law* and *kip*, which they share with many other hills: and again respectively, their specifics are Nevis (from *neimheas*), *cìche*, goat, North Berwick and West. In Gaelic (and Cumbric) names, the generic normally precedes the specific, while in Scots and English (and Norse) the specific is first.

Hill name generics are not a Scottish peculiarity, for most languages have several. French gives us for instance *Mont* Blanc, the *Aiguille* Verte and the *Dent* Blanche, and Spanish offers *Monte* Perdido and the *Picos* d'Europa. German has mountain-words including *Berg* (mountain), *Hugel* (hill), and *Kopf* (head) and the most expressive *Horn* as in the Matterhorn. Where Scotland differs from most small nations is that while they have basically one language to pick their generics from, Scotland draws from two main languages, Gaelic and Scots, but also has some from Old Norse and from Cumbric (also known as Brittonic or Old Welsh). This chapter is essentially a dictionary of these hill name generics.

Kips and Laws: Scots hill name generics

Most of Scotland's hills have Gaelic names, either in original or corrupted form. But in the Borders and in many lowland areas of east and central Scotland, their names are from the Scots language.

The Scots language is a close relative of English, but nevertheless a distinct entity. It is derived partly from Old English, the Germanic language of Britain's invaders from the east, and partly from a Scandinavianised dialect of immigrants from northern England. It was the dominant language of the lowlands and southern Scotland in medieval times, reaching its zenith in the 16th century, and subsequently being submerged, certainly in official writing and speech, by English, although it remains an established vernacular particularly in rural areas. Many of its words for hills and other relief features it shares with northern England, but it is in Scotland's south that these words really develop: *law* for instance is also found in northern England, but there are four times as many *law* hills in Scotland, and they are substantially higher hills than in their Northumberland patch.

In 1775 Captain M.J.Armstrong listed many Scots generics when he wrote of the shire of Peebles in the Borders:

> Hills are variously named according to their magnitude, as Law, Pen, Kip, Coom, Dod, Craig, Fell, Top, Drum, Tor, Watch, Rig, Edge, Know, Knock, Mount, Kaim, Bank, Hope-head, Cleugh-head, Gare, Scarr, Height, Shank, Brae, Kneis, Muir, Green,...

This book merely follows the captain's footsteps! He missed out several generics – like *pike*, *seat* or *side* – but got many of them.

Many Scots hill names have Northern Old English connections, but this does not mean that the poor, dependant Scots had to import English words to describe the hills for them. Many of the Scots hill names are original developments of Old English words (for instance *hlāw* became *law*) and Scots has also drawn upon its northern Gaelic reservoirs (for instance *cnoc* became *knock*) to brew its distinctive mix.

There are also Scots words fashioned from Old Norse or Gaelic material – like *fell* and *cairn* – and we inherited, neat, some Cumbric names, from the centuries when the Britons spoke the language that is the ancestor of modern Welsh. Names like *din* (hill-fort), *pen* (head, summit) and *bar* (top) all still exist in modern Welsh. In the Border hills they remain like a tidemark of history in names like Din Law and Skelfhill Pen near Hawick, and Carter Bar on the actual border.

This does not exhaust the Scots collection of hill names. Among others you will find, in different localities, a *boorachie* (small hill), a *scaup* (small bare hill, scalp-like), the expressive *snib* (a short steep hill), a *steel* (steep bank), a *tummock* (a hillock – probably from the Gaelic *tolm*) and a *type* (a low conical hill in Dumfriesshire). Not such a muckle as the Highland Gaels, yet the Scots have a fine hairst of hill names.

Beinns and Sgùrrs: Gaelic hill name generics

For most Lowland Scots a Highland mountain is simply a 'ben'. For a Gaelic speaker in the Highlands the word would be *beinn*, and he would be spoiled for choice among the many other words in the language for mountain, with *sgùrr* and *càrn* and *meall* outstanding among a collection of over 70. As an 1897 poem in the *Scottish Mountaineering Club Journal*, by L.W.H., put it:

> A mountain's a mountain in England, but when
> The climber's in Scotland, it may be a Beinn
> A Creag or a Meall, a Spidean, a Sgor,
> A Carn or a Monadh, a Stac, or a Torr.

Perhaps L.W.H. (probably Lamond Howie) was a little unfair on England, looking through tartan-tinted glasses. Northern England has *fell*, *pike* and *knott* as well as several generics that are also found in southern Scotland like *dod* and *rigg*, whilst southern England – which Scots often imagine to be flat – has its *downs*, its beacons and indeed the archetypal generic *hill*, which we are not above employing!

The Gaels developed their own mountain-words, partly from their parent language of Irish Gaelic, partly from Norse, to create a choice that seems to be unique in Europe for variety and descriptiveness. Further, by adding the diminutive suffix '-an' to many of the mountain-words small versions can be created, as in *meallan* and *cruachan* (little lump and little heap), and the grand total of Gaelic hill-generics approaches nearly a hundred. Turning to statistics for a moment, we find that nearly 30 per cent of the mountains in the Munro's Tables (those over 3000 feet, 914m) are either *beinn* or *sgùrr*, as are nearly 50 per cent of the Corbetts (mountains

between 2500 and 3000 feet, 762m – 914m). A further 30 per cent plus of the former and 25 per cent of the latter are made up by four other common mountain-words – *càrn*, *meall*, *creag* and *stob*.

Scottish hill name generics

aodann, aghaidh

Gaelic. (Pronounced **oe**:tan and **oe**-ee respectively). These, the Gaelic for face (so commonly used in English descriptions of rocky hills or cliffs), make relatively few appearances. The best-known is probably **Ben Aden**, *beinn aodainn*, above Loch Quoich, and nearby are **Aodann Chlèirig**, minister's face, and **Aodann an t-Sìdh Mhòir**, face of the big fairy hill. Elsewhere a corrie wall on Aonach Beag called **An Aghaidh Garbh** is the rough face, from *aghaidh*. And while English uses the term 'beauty spot' for both a scenic tourist attraction and for a focal mole on the female complexion, the nearest Gaelic equivalent is the unflattering **An Guirean** near Fort William, a little hill translating as the pimple or pustule.

aonach

Gaelic. (Pronounced **oe**:noch). An *aonach* is a mountain whose summit has the form of a fairly level ridge, generally with steepish sides. For example the long narrow plateau ridge which forms the central spine of the Black Mount (considered a classic traverse by ski-mountaineers) is **Aonach Mòr**, the big ridge. Another better-known Aonach Mòr is now the site of a major skiing and mountain bike development near Ben Nevis: its summit is the fulcrum of a three-kilometre long north-south mountain axis running from **Aonach an Nid** to **Aonach Beag**, slinging the high contours between them like a trapeze wire.

Glen Coe's north wall is formed by the **Aonach Eagach**, the notched ridge, a classic scramble along airy rock spires; from the north, against the light, it has the appearance of a fence of palings, like a Dolomite ridge. Beyond it, on the Glen's south side, Bidean nam Bian throws out three flat-topped spurs, the famous **Three Sisters of Glencoe** (so-named and painted by the Romantic Scottish artist Horatio MacCulloch). Two of the 'sisters' are **Aonach Dubh**, dark ridge, and its stunted sibling **Geàrr Aonach**, short ridge.

As these examples indicate, many of the 40 or so *aonach* hills are high peaks located in Lochaber, but there are some in the Glen Cluanie area (**Aonach air Chrith**, ridge of trembling, is one of the South Glen Shiel seven Munros). In the Strath Carron area, they are generally subsidiary ridges to greater peaks, and there are very few east of Speyside, but then there are few long narrow ridges among their broad plateaux. (The similar-looking word in **Meall an Aonaich** in the far north-west is in fact the hill of the gathering, not a 'ridged' *aonach* – in Irish Gaelic, *aonach* means a gathering or fair).

àrd, àirde

Gaelic. (Pronounced **aard**). Meaning simply a height, this is a very common generic

in village names from Ardentinny to Ardvourlie, but curiously it is rarely found in hill names. It might best be translated as a block of higher ground or promontory jutting out into the sea, or above a settlement, like **The Aird** by Inverness or **Ard Mòr** (49m) beside Waternish on Skye. Overlooking Kylesku is **Àird dà Loch**, height of the two lochs, a block of rugged land splitting the sea-loch: the hill above it is Beinn Aird dà Loch, indicating that *aird* is not itself a hill word. The word is often found in adjectival form as *àird*, as in **Cruach Àrdrain** near Crianlarich, Sutherland's **Meall Àrd** and **Fireach Àrd** on Loch Duich, high hill – an exaggeration of its 110m stature.

bac

Gaelic. Gaelic dictionaries define *bac* as a hollow, pit or bend: but whilst some of the fifty occurrences of the generic are hollows or gaps, some are definite hills, often quite high like **Bac nam Fuaran** (springs) at 833m in the Monadh Liath, or **Bac an Eich** (horse) at 869m above Strath Conon, and **Baca Ruadh** (red) on the Trotternish ridge. The high points of the uninhabited Treshnish islands off Mull are Bac Mòr (also known as The Dutchman's Cap) and Bac Beag. Perhaps, like the hollow in **Fuar Tholl** (cold hollow), the name was applied to tops *above* declivities.

bad

Gaelic. (Pronounced bad). Although in most place names this means a thicket or simply a spot, and usually applies to trees, it can also mean a tuft and is sometimes applied by analogy to granite tors like the **Bads of Ben Avon** on that mountain.

bank

Scots. More often associated with river borders, this word can also mean a hill-ridge in the eastern and central Borders hills – such as **Duddy Bank** in the Lammermuir Hills, **Cadon Bank** above Traquair, and **Scawd Bank**, a substantial summit of 547m right on the border.

bàrr

Gaelic. (Pronounced baar). It means a top, crest or summit (and can imply in modern Gaelic the cream of the milk) rather than the whole body of a hill. One author on Argyll place names wrote that it had more the nuance of an arable upland rather than a geographic feature, but nowadays most of them are smothered in conifers. One of the few high ones is 1004m **Meall a' Bhàrr**, apparently hill of the top or summit, in Perthshire – but it may be hill of the cream in the sense of the best grazing. The word however usually applies to low hills and, as a result, it has often been swallowed up in village names, like Barrhead.

The *bàrr* are thickest on the ground in Knapdale where there are over two dozen hills called **Bàrr Mòr** (big ridge) packed into a small area, but they are so low and the terrain so broken up, that they probably can't see each other and so each thinks it is the only big summit around. And in fact Knapdale and the adjacent parts of the Kintyre peninsula contain virtually all hills (or rather hillocks) using *bàrr* as a Gaelic

generic, as in **Bàrr a' Chapuill** (horse) or **Bàrr an Damh** (deer): there are quite a few in the south-west in Galloway, but here *bàrr* is more of an English language place name generic, with numerous **Barr Hill** locations. There are three hills with the name **Barskeoch** (from *sgitheach*, thorn tree) in the south-west, relics from the days when it was a Gaelic place name generic, but none of them are particularly high.

bell

Scots. In Scots a bell is a bubble or blister, and it seems to have entered hill names possibly on account of its shape. There are several shoulders of hills (for instance on the side of Mendick hill), and one isolated hill called by the apparently generic name **The Bell** , in southern Scotland and just over the border with England, as well as one or two in the English Lakes. The Lakes' connection (for instance Cat Bells and Ill Bell) may provide a clue pointing to a Norse ancestry in *bjalli*, or *ballar-fjell*, rounded hill, as in Orcadian expert Hugh Marwick's suggestion for Birsay's Belyafiold. **Yeavering Bell**, **Bell Craig** and **Bell Hill**, all in the southern Borders, belong to this family.

beinn, ben

Gaelic. (Pronounced bYn). The commonest Scottish Gaelic hill-word, with nearly a thousand specimens on Ordnance Survey maps, this means a mountain of any shape or size, although away from coastal areas it tends to indicate a higher, bulkier mountain than others. It is no coincidence that the highest mountain, Nevis, is a *beinn*, as are nine in the highest 30, and almost 30 in the top 100.

It is of Old Irish origin as *benn*, and in Scottish Gaelic is correctly *beinn*, although on maps it has often been anglicised (or scotticised!) back to *ben*. There are of course *ben* mountains (and cliff-tops) in Ireland, but it was in the Scottish Highlands that the word came into its own, like a child prospering once free of the bounds of home, perhaps rejoicing in the extensive rugged country it found here. Its ancestry perhaps goes even further back: Welsh had *bann* – Bannau Brycheiniog are the Brecon Beacons – Breton had *ban*, and all derive from Indo-European *bnd-no*, jutting out point: in all these languages, the generic had the double meaning as horn and peak. The Serbo-Croat word for a hill, *brdo*, is probably a distant cousin.

Although it is found almost all over the Highlands, *beinn* is especially common in the Inner Hebrides and the western seaboard (especially on and within sight of Mull), and in the south-west Highlands between Clyde and Rannoch, where there is the greatest concentration: in the hills round Arrochar, for instance, almost every mountain in view is a *beinn*. Further east and north-east of these areas, the name *beinn* is confined mainly to the *highest* hills within an area (like **Ben Alder**, **Ben Macdui** or **Ben Avon**), and thus it is significant that **Ben Nevis** is neighboured by hills with names with *càrn*, *mullach*, *binnein*, *aonach* and *stob*, but not *beinn*. In the far north-east they are little known (though **Bennachie** is one), while in the north-west Highlands, *sgùrr* tends to predominate in the highest hills, leaving *beinn* with lower peaks.

W.F.H.Nicolaisen argues in *The Distribution of Certain Gaelic Mountain-Names* that the fact that their specifics are usually easily-understood adjectives (for size or

colour, *mòr* or *buidhe*, for instance) or after their landscape surrounds, suggests recency in naming, as does the fact that some like Ben Nevis and Ben Lawers are named after nearby features. However their heavy concentration in the south-west Highlands, area of the earliest Gaelic settlement, might point to its early use compared, say, to *sgùrr* or *càrn* in the west and north.

The number of mountain-names in the west and on the islands where *beinn* is the second generic (Aonach-Bheinn, Creach Bheinn, Ladhar Bheinn, etc) suggests to some scholars either a translation from an earlier Norse name since they, unlike the Gaels, normally put the adjective before the noun, or at least Norse linguistic influence. Thus Skye's **Blà Bheinn** (Blaven) could be a Gaelic part-translation of an original Norse *Blá Fjall* (blue mountain), and **Suilven** was probably Norse *sulur* (pillar) or *Sulur-fjall*, to which the Gaelic speakers added *bheinn* (pronounced *ven*) to make it comprehensible in their language.

Beinn or *ben* however is a truly Scottish word, whose dominance in the whole country is shown by the fact that the anglicised version *ben* does not need translation. Indeed Scottish emigrants have taken it overseas to English-speaking places where it needs no explanation – a **Ben Lomond** mountain in Australia and a whole range in Tasmania, **Ben Nevises** in New Zealand and Hong Kong, and a **Ben Macdui** in South Africa's Drakensbergs. Ironically for a word that has fathered these emigrants, there are few *bens* in south-eastern Scotland. This reflects the vitality of the Scots language's own hill words like *law* and *knowe*.

The diminutive *beannan* is found in names like Eigg's **Beannan Breaca**, speckled, which can muster barely 300m, or **Am Beannan** above Loch Rannoch, a 386m shoulder. However in Galloway there are a large number of hills called simply **Bennan**, and they are often of substantial height. No *beannan* is as small however as **Beinn a' Bhaile** (hill of the farm) that rises to all of 20m in North Uist.

Ben is the anglicised version of the main Gaelic hill-word *beinn*. On maps nearly a quarter of the 1000 Highland peaks properly called Beinn are shown as Ben, especially those more popular with tourists like Ben Nevis, Ben Lomond, and Ben More.

The word was apparently first used in Scots-English in the mid-19th century, but only in the way we often use foreign words to refer to foreign things. Thus a Professor Shairp wrote a poem in 1864, attacking the advent of railways into the Highlands:

> Land of Bens and Glens and Corries,
> Headlong Rivers, Clean Floods,
> Have we lived to see this outrage,
> On your haughty solitudes?

The use of the word as a properly adopted Scots word appears to be barely a century old, the first recorded reference being in 1898, from a book called, paradoxically, *In Glasgow Streets:*

> An' the white snawdrifts sunlicht-kissed on the great bens.

So the word *ben* that is now seen as quintessentially Scots is in fact a relative newcomer in common usage. This recency is confirmed by the fact that very few hills outside the Gaelic Highlands carry the generic. There are a few bens in the south-west where they are corruptions of original Gaelic, such as **Benyellary**, from *beinn na h-iolaire*, mountain of the eagle.

bidean, bidein

Gaelic. (Pronounced beedyan). The suffix -*an* is normally the Gaelic diminutive, in the way that *lochan* is a small *loch*: and *bidean* is the diminutive of *biod* (see below). Yet there are *bideans* amongst the highest Munros, among them the mighty **Bidean nam Bian** (properly, Bidean nam Beann), 1150m above the sea at the mouth of Glen Coe. The Gaelic dictionary gives the meaning of *bidean* as a sharp point, pinnacle or top, so perhaps the implied smallness (the suffix –*an*) relates to the actual summit rather than to the whole bulk of the hill. As W.H.Murray wrote of Bidean nam Bian;

> ...(it) is the highest peak in Argyll and dominates Glencoe and Appin. But how small a summit for so large a mountain!...

Indeed many of the *bidean* names refer to a corrie or hollow beneath them – like **Bidean a' Ghlas Thuill**, top of the grey hollow – this confirming the idea of a small point above some more striking feature. Glen Dessary's **Bidean a' Chabhair** (hawk) is another lovely sharp-pointed example of the summit word.

The other spelling *bidein*, with the same meaning of a small point, is found on the islands of Lunga, Skye and Eigg, with **Bidein Bòidheach**, beautiful, and **Bidein an Tighearna**, of the landlord. In the Monar area, sharply-pointed peaks like **Bidein a' Choire Sheasgaich**, barren corrie – pronounced by philistines as corrie cheesecake – and **Bidean an Eòin Dearg**, red bird, show that there too the word suggests a definite shape.

bin, binn

Scots. Almost as common as *ben* in Central Lowlands is the other Scots corruption of *beinn* in the form of *bin*. In the north-east we find the **Bin of Cullen** and its side-kick the **Little Bin**, and plain **The Bin** near Huntly. In the Ochils lies **Binn Hill** (a Scots-English tautology) and nearby is the politically-famous **The Binns**, mansion house and estate on the low hills near Linlithgow, ancestral home of M.P. Tam Dalyell, asker of the celebrated parliamentary West Lothian Question. Immediately behind his house there rises a small sharp hill, the answer to at least the name question.

Byne Hill by Girvan, first ascent for many young holidaymakers, probably comes from this word too or possibly from the Scots *bine* meaning a wash-tub, to which upturned it has a resemblance. But the best-known of all the 'bins' is surely the Campsie Fells' **Meikle Bin**, Scots for the big hill. Seen from the grey guddle of urban Clydeside and the southern edge of the Highlands, it tapers to a sharp cone peeping above the flat plateau of its hill-range, a Mount Fuji of weekend promise. Certainly it's one of the few tops in the Campsies sufficiently *meikle* or peak-shaped enough to deserve the accolade of *bin*, this very Scots word for mountain. Interestingly,

there's an ancient name Mons Bannauc, which W.J.Watson located at the head-waters of the River Carron (here in the Campsies): based as it is on the root-word *banna* meaning peaked, it is probably this same Meikle Bin.

binnein, binnean

Gaelic. (Pronounced beenyan). *Binnein*, sometimes spelt *binnean*, like *bidean* ends apparently in the diminutive suffix -*an*, and is derived from *beinn* which originally meant simply the top of the hill; while *beinn* mountains are often round-topped – like Nevis – W.J.Watson asserts in *Scottish Place Name Papers* that *binnein* itself,

> ... always denotes a peaked hill, sometimes by no means diminutive in size.

He illustrates with Am Binnean in Glen Dochart at 1165m, the hill more usually known as **Stob Binnein**. Certainly the best-known *binnein* hills are not small hills: **Binnein Mòr** and **Binnein Beag** dominate the eastern end of the Mamores: Mòr has a roof-ridged outline when approaching from the west, but as the Scottish Mountaineering Club guide *The Munros* points out, it appears from north or south as a sharp peak – as does the Beag – thus confirming Watson's assertion.

Most of the thirty *binnein* hills are rather smaller than these famous ones, and are clustered in the southern Hebrides, Kintyre and Cowal, with a spin-off up Loch Linnhe and up Laggan-side. In West Lothian is **Binny Craig**, a delightful sharp point with a steep western cliff; Timothy Pont's 16th century map fragment records it as Bynnin Law, so the Craig is a later name, whilst the Bynnin is phonetically close to the source in *binnein*.

biod, bioda

Gaelic. (Pronounced beed). Meaning a pointed top, *biod* is found mainly in the far west. There are a dozen of this endangered species on Skye, like **Biod Mòr** and **Biod Buidhe** (big and yellow) but few on the mainland. Many of the *biod* tops are summits above cliffs, especially on the west coast of Skye: only a few hills outside the island bear the generic, one in the far north, and a small group championed by the shapely Graham **Biod an Fhithich** (raven) beside The Saddle in Glen Shiel. These hills appear to have in common at least one very steep side. The similar-sounding but unconnected word in **Am Bioran** above St. Fillans means simply, the stick, and there are other bioran, often rugged, in Perthshire's hills.

brae

Scots. The brow of a hill. Although this may appear to derive from the Gaelic *bràigh*, similar in pronunciation, it more probably comes via Old English from an Old Norse root *brā* meaning eyelash, later developing to mean eyebrow then simply brow, and applied by analogy to hills. There are about a dozen hills in southern Scotland containing this generic, the highest being **Whitelaw Brae** and **Struther's Brae** above the Ettrick; **Birnie Brae** also includes the word *birn*, meaning short heather. In the north-east the word has a slightly poetic nuance, as in the literary Braes o' Balwearie, or the Braes o' Mar.

bràigh

Gaelic. (Pronounced brY:). It means the upper part, or the height above, as in **Braeriach** or *Am Bràigh Riabhach*, the speckled high part. **Seana Bràigh** (old upland) in Ross-shire is one of the remotest Munros, while Breadalbane in north Perthshire is Bràghaid Alban, the upper part of Scotland. Brae is very much an eastern Highlands anglicisation, and *bràigh* names in the original are mainly to be found on the islands of the west, although there are some in the Cairngorms. The **Braes of Carse** above Perth are literally the heights above the flood plain (of the Tay).

In the west there are several hills called **Braebeg**, **Breabeg** and **Briobaig** – these may well be *bràigh beag*, little height, for the best-known Breabag is a hill lying in the shadow of Ben More Assynt. W.J.Watson speculated however that it could be from *breab beag*, little kick, signifying that the hill was split from its neighbours as if by a little kick. Further south, the deep glen between Ben Alder and Beinn Bheòil is the Bealach Breabag, the pass splitting the two hills apart.

bruach

Gaelic. (Pronounced broo-uch). *Bruach* is a bank or a slope, and most places with this generic are not hills. One of the few exceptions is **Bruach na Frìthe** in the Cuillin (one of the few there not to be a *sgùrr*), the slope of the deer forest or wilderness, and there's a shoulder top called The Bruach above Glen Avon in the Cairngorms.

burrach

Gaelic. (Pronounced booruch). **Burrach Mòr** is one of several gentle rises within the plateau of the Monadh Liath, at 828m: the map shows two cairns on its flat top, which may connect the name to the Gaelic word *bùrach* meaning, normally, a swelling or a heaping up. The hill **Borrach** on Arran is from the same word, as is the Scots word boorachie.

caer

Cumbric. This means a fort, often a hill-fort. **Caerlee Hill** and **Caerlan Rig**, both in the Tweed basin, are low hills but both have prehistoric forts on their summits, while **Caerketton** in the Pentland Hills has a recognised fort on top of its eastern subsidiary, as well as a Bronze Age burial cairn on the summit. *Caer* might be the generic in a nearby hill also with a huge prehistoric cairn on top, Carnethy Hill – Caer Nechtan (after the Pictish king) was suggested by one writer – but its Welsh cognate, the mountain-name element *carnedd* (pronounced almost identically ending in *thy*) and meaning cairn, is more apposite. Further south in the Pentlands, **Keir Hill** is from the Scots reflex of *caer*, viz. *keir*, a fort – which it has on top – but may have been named directly from a simplex form of *caer*. Interestingly **Quothquan Law** just south of the Pentlands was mapped by Blaeu as Kaerkuren Law and may also have this root, as may **Carlochan Hill** in Galloway which has a prehistoric fort on top. **Caresman Hill** near Peebles has prehistoric forts and settlements on two of its shoulders.

caisteal

Gaelic. (Pronounced kashtyal). Literally castle, this word has been poetically rather than historically applied to several tops of squat, fortified appearance, while genuine historic hill-forts are normally identified by the word *dùn* rather than *caisteal*. **Creag Chaisteal**, crag of the castle, near Loch Pityoulish is one exception, being the site of an old Pictish fort. In Glen Lyon, an old Gaelic saying tells:

> The Feinne (Fingalians) have twelve castles in the dark crooked glen of the rough stones...

Beinn Chaisteal at the head of this glen allegedly marks the spot where the westernmost of these castles stood. There are some 50 or so *caisteal* hills, mainly in the central and south-west Highlands. On Arran **Caisteal Abhail** is one of several castellated granite tors, although the Munro **An Caisteal** above Crianlarich is probably better-known if less clearly-shaped.

cairn

Scots. The Gaelic word *càrn* for a rocky hill has been appropriated by Scots as *cairn* for a hill, and indeed has passed into English as the term for the summit pile of stones. Quite a few of the Cairngorm mountains, including the flagship **Cairn Gorm** (blue hill) itself and its neighbour **Cairn Lochan** (hill of the lochan), have been scot-ticised in this way. Some way south-east, **Broad Cairn**, **The Cairnwell** of Glen Shee, and **Cairn o' Mount**, are almost as well known; the second name-generic of the last two has been scotticised too, from the Gaelic respectively *bhalg* and *monadh*: and in the 1928 Scottish Mountaineering Club guide to the Cairngorms, Henry Alexander suggested that Broad Cairn was an anglicisation of *bràghad càrn*, the upper part's cairn, as in the origin of Breadalbane, although this is unlikely. Most *cairn* hills are in the north-east or in the south-west, both areas where the original Gaelic names were often corrupted by Scots or English speakers before the Ordnance Survey came. There are over 60 hills called simply **Cairn Hill**, many in the south-west, some with prehistoric cairns: these are not a translation from the Gaelic but a Scots name indicating a hill with shepherds' cairns on it – often the older version of the name was Cairnie Hill, the adjective being clearer. See also p170.

càrn

Gaelic. (Pronounced kaarn). Most hillwalkers probably have a mental picture of a *càrn* (or its scotticised version *cairn*) in which the hill resembles a larger version of the conical pile of stones that marks most summits. Curiously, the leading Gaelic dictionary by Dwelly does not give hill or mountain as a possible meaning, only the pile of stones. Another dictionary, MacLennan's, does define it as 'a heap of stones, or a rocky hill or mountain'. But nature does not imitate the rocky pile idea, for just as real summit cairns are often weather-flattened assortments of rubble – or indeed (for many years) the remains of a crashed aircraft's nose cone on **Càrn an t-Sagairt Mòr** – similarly the *càrn* mountains' shape often belies the image of a rocky cone.

Although some of the western *càrn* hills like **Càrn Mòr Dearg** *are* conical, the majority of the higher *càrn* hills are in the Monadh Liath and in the eastern Grampians, which means that they are often rounded grassy hills of little distinction, on which the summit cairn itself may be the only eye-catching feature in a landscape swelling gently with monotony. Doric poet Charles Murray, praising the virtues of his local hill Bennachie, rather dismissed them:

> ... an' mony a Carn I trow,
> That's smored in mist ayont Braemar...

A hillwalker who has climbed one of the rounded grassy **Geal Chàrn** hills, around the upper Spey will realise that the Gaelic dictionary got it wrong on the rocky bit. In fact there are a score of hills with this particular name (white cairn), most within sight of each other in upper Speyside. Just over the watershed into Glen Roy there are three **Càrn Dearg** (red) cousins, Corbett triplets that belong to a family of 50 of that name. This area of the central Highlands is the ancestral home of over one thousand *càrn* hills, and certainly of the highest of them. The *càrn* hills found in the islands and south-west are generally low hills, reflecting the Irish original which meant simply a cairn, usually a burial cairn: the low *càrn* hills in Islay, for instance, may have been burial sites, or have been named Càrn Mòr for being figuratively like burial mounds – they rarely exceed 100m in height. The pattern of *càrn* names therefore suggests that they came into their own as a mountain name well away from the sea and Irish influence, while their absence in the Outer Hebrides rules out a Norse source.

Roman geographers – based on the maps of the Greek Ptolemy – described a tribe the Carnonacae in the north-west Highlands: their name can translate either as the trumpet people (literally 'people of the horns') – for which there's no historical evidence – or as 'the people of the rocky hills', an apparent reference to *càrn* hills. However these Latin names were given centuries before Gaelic had arrived here.

So there are two possibilities. One, that there is a mere coincidence between the name the Romans themselves chose to give the northern tribe, and the later Gaelic word *càrn* (that is certainly commoner in the Monadh Liath and Cairngorms areas than it is in the north-west). The other, that the Roman name was derived from the tribe's own name, perhaps based on the hills, in which case the later Gaelic speakers may have adopted this much older Pictish word. *Carn*, after all, is also found in old Welsh, in hills like Carnedd Llewelyn. The possibility is strengthened by the rarity of the word in the traditional Gaelic source areas of south-western Scotland. Also there are several chambered cairns in Ross and Inverness called **Càrn Glas** or **Càrn Liath** (both grey cairns) and this may indicate the 'Carnonacae' tribe's burial practices. (See panel in Central Lowlands chapter on Man-made Cairns.)

ceann

Gaelic. (Pronounced kyown). The whole head itself, in Gaelic *ceann*, is most often found in its anglicised form 'kin' applied to low-lying villages such as Kingussie and Kinlochleven. Indeed the only clear example in *Munro's Tables* is **Ceann Garbh**,

rough head, a top in the north-west. **Ceann na Beinne**, literally the end of the mountain, is a mere foothill rounding off the Cuillin. **Tom nan Ceann** near Glentromie, the knoll of the heads, has a more sinister significance, for here were heaped the heads of the decapitated Donalds after a bloody battle.

There are two separate mountains called **Maol Cheann-Dearg** and **Maol Chinn-Dearg**, literally the bald red head, which is especially apt in Torridon where sparse tufts of grass cling desperately to the steep sandstone sides but give up on its bare windswept pate. 'Bald' is at any rate a more flattering description than those summits sniffed at by Englishman Edward Burt in 1754, as having,

> ...the disagreeable Appearance of a Scabbed head.

Ganu Mòr, the summit of Foinaven in the north, is a corruption of *ceann mòr*, big head. The Norse *skalli* for skull is found in island hill names like **Scalla Field**, while near Elgin is a hill called **The Scalp**.

ceap

Gaelic. (Pronounced kehp). This means a lump, cap or a top of a hill, and appears in **Meall nan Ceapraichean**, hill of the stubby hillocks.

cìoch

Gaelic. (Pronounced **kee**:och). A nipple or breast. Gaelic society, at the time when most hills were given names, was not inhibited by the prudishness in body matters that was later imported into the Highlands by the English language and Presbyterian church. Sexual parts of the body, taboo to the incoming 'culture', are referred to quite openly in names. The words for nipple and breast, *cìoch* (or *cìche*, 'of a breast') and *màm*, are widely used in the mountains. *Uchd,* another word for bosom or breast, is rarer, but **Creag Uchdag** on the south side of Loch Tay is from a derived word meaning hillocky, or steep.

Màm has come to have the alternative meaning of a rounded hill, while *cìoch* mountains generally come to a point, either in the apex of a cone, or in the nipple-like summit tors. Thus **Sgùrr na Cìche** in Knoydart has a conical shape (although a little rounded just at the top) while **Màm Sodhail** above Glen Affric has a more rounded appearance overall. In granite hill areas like the Cairngorms the summit tors, granite rocks that protrude sharply out of the flat plateaux, bear names like the **A' Chìoch** on **Beinn a' Bhùird**, and Beinn nan Cìochan (the mountain of the nipples – the original Gaelic name of Lochnagar), suggesting the shape. Arran too is a granite island, and its **Cìoch na h-Oighe**, the maiden's breast, clearly outlines the combined breast and nipple shape when seen from North Glen Sannox – as does the **A' Chìoch** on Mull's **Ben More**.

Ironically one of the best known, and certainly the most aptly-named of the *cìochs* was discovered by an English speaker, Professor Norman Collie. He explored much of Skye's Cuillin range at the turn of the century, and one evening in Coire Lagan noticed a giant shadow swelling across the slabs as the sun declined in the west. On investigation next day he discovered and climbed **The Cìoch**, a rock breast

A' Chìoch, The Breast, above the Coire Lagan slabs, Skye.
See p85, and also 27, [Generics, cìoch]

protruding from the steep slabs and tipped by a stone nipple. Its existence had not previously been suspected, for the glen-living native Skyemen would have little use for such high rock gymnasiums in this bare corrie. It was however a Skyeman, John MacKenzie (Collie's guide) who christened it in his native tongue the following day in 1906. Since that day this dramatic rock has become like the great Black Stone of Mecca for rock-climbers in Skye, an object of pilgrimage and devotion. However while Skye thus gained a *cìoch*, Glen Coe has effectively lost one: for **Sgòrr na Cìche** at the west end of the glen is now more often known by the equivalent Scots name **Pap of Glencoe**.

Not every *cìoch* is on the high tops, for the **Cìochan** of **Ben Lui** (Beinn Laoigh, calf mountain) are well down its northern slopes, while the **Cìoch Beinn an Eòin** is on a easterly spur of the Coigach mountains.

claigionn

Gaelic. (Pronounced **klagin**ᵞ). **An Claigionn** on Deeside is literally the skull and is, as you would expect, a rounded hillock, of which there are several on upper Deeside. Cnoc nan Claigean on Berneray is reputedly man-made, heaping over a pile of skulls of those executed at the nearby chair stone.

cnagan

Gaelic. (Pronounced **kra**gan). An Cnagan Cruinn, the round little knob, is a stony hillock near Braemar, while in Ross-shire **Cnaigean na Leathrach** is the leather knoll where, when the river level was high and the knoll became an island, it came into use in the leather-tanning process.

cnap

Gaelic. (Pronounced **krahp**). *Cnap* means literally a lump or knob and is usually applied to hillocks, as in **Crappich** above Comrie. Knapdale in Argyll is a landscape of rugged little hills. It can also indicate hillocks on a big mountain's ridge, as in **Cnap a' Chlèirich**, cleric's knob, of **Beinn a' Bhùird** (most of the *cnap* are here in the Cairngorms) or the **Cnap Coire na Spreidhe** (knob above the cattle corrie). The word may be distantly related to the Old Norse word *gnipa*, a peak, found in the Northern Isles and in names like **Kneep** on Lewis: or more likely to the Norse *knappr*, a knob, as in Orkney's **Knap of Trowieglen** (hillock of the troll's glen). In turn the Gaelic word *creapall*, a lump, as in the **Knowe of Crippley** in Angus and Creap a' Choire Dhuibh near Kylesku, is possibly related.

cnoc

Gaelic. (Pronounced **krochk**). This indicates a knoll or eminence (of no great height) and applies to rounded hillocks. Due to this height limitation it is confined to the peripheral hills all around the central Highland mass, where there are nearly three thousand mapped hill names with *cnoc*. To use a faintly ludicrous metaphor, these are only the tip of the iceberg: Iona's people in the 1930s were able to identify 106 named hills of which 60 were *cnoc*, but only one of these, **Cnoc Druidean**, made it

to the Ordnance Survey 1:50,000 map today. *Cnoc* is especially thick on the ground in the far north, the Inner Hebrides and in Kintyre.

Of Irish origin, where *cnoc* is a very common hill name, it also has roots in the Welsh *cnwch* and Breton *cnoch*. In procreational turn it's the father of the scotticised version *knock* (see below) – there are for instance over 200 knocks in Galloway alone. The diminutive *cnocain*, little knolls, were said to conceal fairy pleasure-domes where baccanalian enjoyment was continuous, perhaps in confusion with *sìthean* night-clubs. The intriguing Coire Cheud Cnoc (corrie of a hundred knolls) near Loch Maree, is peppered with glacially-dumped hummocks, in what geomorphologists call basket-of-eggs topography.

cock

Scots. In southern Scotland, from Deeside to the English border, there are many hills called **Cock Law** (or Hill or Rig) or Cockplay Hill, or Cockup. There are nearly 50 such names for hills, and they probably refer to the cock birds of the black grouse: there are also **Hen Hills**, Knowes and Laws, from the female of the species. These names would indicate areas where they were common, or where they displayed.

In Scots the word *cock* can also mean a cap or headwear, sitting on one's topmost part, and the two hills called **Cocket Hill** refer to that style of hat, pointed fore and aft. As such it may have links with the Old English *coc* or *coce* meaning a hillock, or with the Gaelic *cochull* meaning a hood or cowl, as used in **Cockleroy** (*cochull ruadh*, red hood) above Linlithgow.

comb, coomb

Scots. *Camb* or *cam* in England can mean crest, from Old Norse *kambr*, and in the Lakes we find Catstye Cam and Hen Comb: in the Border hills we have two **Comb Heads** and a **Comb Hill**. The similar word *coomb* means, in Scots place names, 'a bosom in the hill' (probably from Cumbric and modern Welsh *cwm*), and so we have hills like **Coomb Dod**, **Coomb Fell** and **Law**, and **White Coomb** (named for the late-lying snow wraith in its south-east corrie). This latter was known in the late 18th century as White-coom-edge, a more appropriate name since it includes mention of the topmost part. Captain Armstrong wrote that it,

> ... is a pointed hill, almost perpendicular on east and south sides.

corr

Gaelic. (Pronounced korr). *Corr* means pointed or peaked, and the Gaelic dictionary says that a *corra-bheinn* is a pointed or steep hill; although thus a *beinn*, it is not necessarily very high, for the **Corra-bheinn** and **An Corrach** on Eigg are jagged fragments of the broken moorland overshadowed by **An Sgùrr**, and are barely above 300m. On the other hand **Corra Bheinn** on Jura, at 575m, stands well beside the famous Paps. *Corrag* is 'the pointed one', literally the forefinger, as **Corrag Bhuidhe** of **An Teallach** indicates. The **Core Hills** in the south-east, **Meall Corranaich** of **Ben Lawers**, and **Little** and **Meikle Corum** in the Ochils, are all of this family. In the

south-west the lovely hill name **Curleywee** possibly begins *cor* whilst in Angus, **Corwharn Hill** is probably *corr fhuaran*, point of springs.

craig

Scots. This is caught between Gaelic *creag* and English *crag* – in the Lake District, *crag* is the second commonest hill name generic after *fell*. In the south-west border hills, names like **Craiglee** and **Craigenreoch** are scotticisations from *creag liath* (grey) and *creagan riabhach* (speckled) in what was once a Gaelic-speaking area. In the eastern Border hills, the word order suggests that *craig* did not come from Gaelic, but from Scots, as in the Pentlands' **Green Craig**, White Craig and Cloven Craig.

creachann

Gaelic. (Pronounced krechan). A *creachann* is a bare wind-swept summit. Munro **Beinn a' Chreachain** with its 'stony dome-shaped summit' stands at 1077m above Glen Lyon and is sometimes translated as shell or scallop-shaped mountain. The word *creachan* or *creachann* originally did mean a clam or scallop shell, and by analogy with a bare exposed rocky-ribbed top led to the word being used for hills too, and Gaelic dictionaries define *creachann* as a rock, summit, mountain or bare rocky surface without foliage, as well as a scallop shell.

Duncan Bàn MacIntyre, in his poem in praise of **Ben Dorain** (very close to Beinn a' Chreachainn) says of a deer:

> Gasganach, speireach,
> Feadh **chreachann na beinne**...

> (Pert and slender-limbed,
> keeps to the **stony mountain summits** ...) (my emphases)

The hill and seaside meanings are curiously combined in **Creachainn nan Sgadan**, near Alness, hill of the herring, for it is said that a cloudburst over the summit one day rained not manna but herring from heaven – a meteorologically plausible fishy story.

creag

Gaelic. (Pronounced krayk). A cliff or precipice, *creag* has given us the Scots word *craig*. More unusually it is one of the few Celtic words that Old English (as spoken by the invading Anglo-Saxons) consented to adopt – as crag – Britain after all, was far more mountainous than the German plains of *Heimat*. The word has a common root with other Celtic tongues in the Welsh word *craig* and the Irish *croag*. *Creag* is not always a name for a hill top because clearly it might apply to cliffs breaking out on a slope, although for instance, about half of the mapped *creag* names in upper Deeside are in fact summits, with the connotation of being rocky.

There are nearly 3000 instances of *creag* on the Ordnance Survey maps of Scotland. Nine of the Munros, including the rocky amphitheatre of **Creag Meagaidh**, bear the word, and it is commoner among the lower tops, especially

where rounded hill-shoulders break off to fall steeply down in cliffs, like classical statues without their shorn marble arms. Often these hills are named from features beneath them, as in **Creag an Dubh Loch** – a severe test for cragsmen in the Mounth – the 70-plus hills called **Creag Dubh** (dark cliff) and the several instances of **Creag a' Chaoruinn** named after the hardy rowan-trees that sprout defiantly from the steepest and smoothest-shaven faces.

cruach

Gaelic. (Pronounced kroo*a*ch). Not a flattering name for a hill, for it means heap or stack, applied to anything from hills to peatstacks. Indeed there is a **Tom na Cruaich** hill above Blair Atholl, said to have been the cutting-ground for the local peat supply. Its Irish sibling *cruach*, often anglicised as *croagh*, was also initially applied to ricks, of turf, before being used for hill names. Not that this lowly start held it back – the famous Macgillycuddy's Reeks range is known in Gaelic as Cruacha Dubha, dark ricks, and there's an annual mass barefoot pilgrimage up Croagh Patrick in the west on the last Sunday in July. Health and safety considerations have covered up most of the bare feet, but the climb up this hill – locally known as 'The Reek' – is still popular.

Cruach as a generic name in Scotland is found mainly in the south-west High-lands, most famously in Munro **Cruach Àrdrain**, the high-stacked heap, and the Corbett **Cruach Innse**, the heap of the meadow. There are other lesser examples, including at least four hills called **A' Chruach** in Argyll alone. A hill near Sanquhar called **Cruereach** might be a clumsy version of *cruach riabhach*, or may derive from *crue*, Scots for a sheep-pen.

In Ireland, many of the *cruach* peaks have a distinctive symmetrical and triangular profile: and here in Scotland, **Ben Cruachan** which was formerly known as Cruachan Beinn, has just such a shape for its twin summits.

crùlaist

Gaelic. (Pronounced kroolasht). A rare name meaning a rocky hill. **Beinn a' Chrùlaiste** above Kingshouse on the edge of Rannoch Moor is the best-known, if overshadowed by much rockier hills to the west. (I have a good friend who, on being dragged up this hill on a misty day, grumpily decided its name must derive from the English word it sounds like.)

cùl

Gaelic. (Pronounced kool).This means the back of anything – *cùlag*, for instance, is a back tooth. **Cùl Mòr** and **Cùl Beag**, big and little back, are a fine and famous pair of Corbetts near Stac Pollaidh, and there's another pair on the east coast near Contin.

curr

This rare Scots hill name is found near Kirk Yetholm in **The Curr** and **Blackdean Curr** hills, and the nearby lost name of Corburn Corr. It probably comes from the

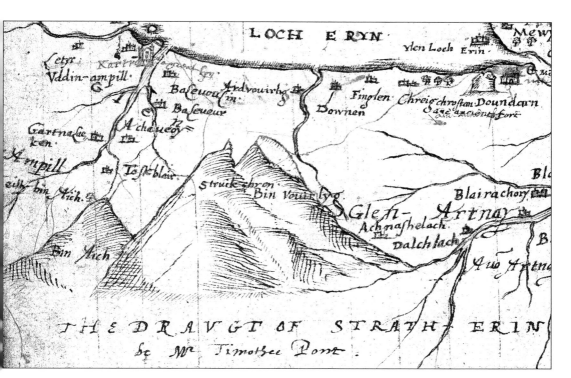

Above: Pont, c. 1590s. Southern edge of Highlands, Stuc a' Chroin and Ben Vorlich, with Beinn Each to the west. An example of Pont's accurate sketches of mountain shapes.
See p12, [Introduction, Maps and map-makers]

Below: Pont, c. 1590s. Glen Turret. Clockwise from the mouth of the glen, Pont mapped Kaishyvackan Hill, Luargin Hill, Hill of Turret, Strongabbyr Hill and Corybuy Hill. Modern maps identify Càrn Chois, Ben Chonzie, Sròn Challaid, Auchnafree Hill and Choinneachain Hill. Either the names of most of these hills have changed, or Pont's local informants identified heights that were significantly different to the Ordnance Survey's, 250 years later

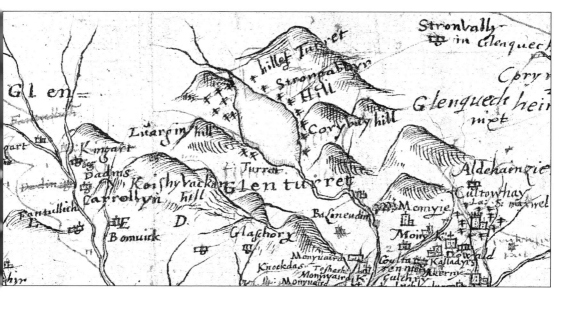

Above: West Kip, in the Pentland Hills, showing the 'pointed' aspect of a kip. See p40, [Generics, kip]

Below: Pont, c.1590s. Lochaber and Mamore Forest. Ben Nevis (profile of North Face cliffs to the right). Other named hills are round the coastal margins: Bin Vain above Inchree is probably current Beinn Bhàn, a shoulder of Beinn na Gucaig; while Bin-Glenselach appears to be current Creag Bhreac / Tom Meadhoin / Doire Bàn ridge on south edge of Glen Seileach. Maim-cheules above Ballachulish was possibly màm a' chaolais, the màm above the narrows, perhaps the current Màm na Gualainn

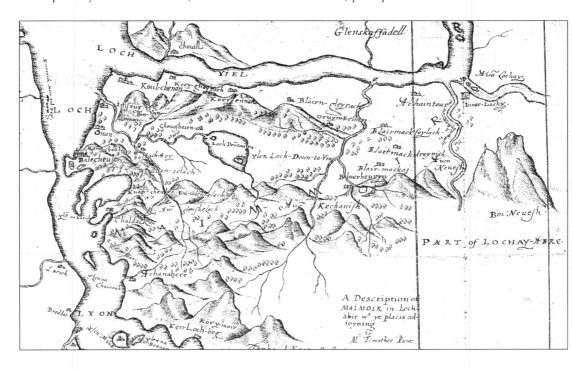

Scots word *currough*, meaning a cairn. The 18th century Peeblesshire mapmaker, Mostyn Armstrong, wrote:

> These piles of stones are often termed Cairn, Pike, Currough, Cross...

Currick, a hill just over the border and looking down on Kielder Water, may come from this too.

Cùl Beag, little back, with its big twin Cùl Mòr.
See p102, [North-West Highlands, Cùl Beag & Mòr]

din

Cumbric *din* means the same as Gaelic *dùn*, a hill-fort. It is still found in modern Welsh as *din* or *dinas*, and Welsh of course is the descendant of the Cumbric language of southern Scotland. Naturally, *din* and *dùn* have become confused, and it is believed for example that Dunpelder (the old name for **Traprain Law**) was originally *din peleder* (fort of spears). Nevertheless, some *din* have survived, in the form of **Din Fell**, **Din Hill** and **Din Law**, but also with the *d* sounded as a *t*, as in **Tinnis Hill** and **Tinlaw**: these often have ancient forts or remains on them.

dod, dodd

Scots. A *dod* or *dodd* is 'a bare round hill'. *Dod* is found in sizeable numbers in the English Lakes, such as Great Dodd or Starling Dodd. In Scotland there are *dods* in

the eastern Borders – such as **Deuchrie Dod** and **Wester Dod** in the Lammermuirs – as well as in the central and western Southern Uplands such as **Molls Cleuch Dod** and **Garelet Dod** near Moffat. There's a **Dodd Hill** in the Sidlaw Hills, and the generic is even found in the Shetlands, as in Dodd o' Flamaster. There are over a dozen plain Dod Hills in the Borders as well as several **The Dod**. The still-used Scots phrase 'a dawd o' tatties' for your plate conjures up nicely the shape of these lumpy hills.

dronnag

Gaelic. (Pronounced **dron**ak). **Beinn Dronaig** near Strathcarron is an example of this species. Meaning humped, or (the mountain of) the little height, it's a modest name for this Corbett of nearly 800m; whereas the 'hump' name is just right for **Dron Hill** in Berwickshire.

druim, drum, drim

Gaelic. (Pronounced **droe**-eem). A back. This is a very common Gaelic place name word, with over 1000 instances, referring in the hills to a long ridge shape. The spine in Gaelic is *cnaimh an droma*, literally the bone of the back, *droma* being the genitive case of *druim*. (Apparently the English word ridge underwent the same shift of meaning from human to hill.) Indeed there is a hill rising gently above Loch Cluanie called **Druim nan Cnàmh**, ridge of the bone or spine, with gentle rumples on its ridge reminiscent of the spinal vertebrae.

There are many Lowland ridges bearing the scotticised prefix *drum* as in Drumchapel, Drumbryden and Drumclog, to name but three which are now covered over by human settlement. In the Highlands two of many hill examples are found in Glen Shiel's **Druim Shionnach** and Perthshire's **Drummond Hill**, from the plural *dromannan*, also the origin of the common Scottish surname. Although this latter hill is not too far from the estates of the clan chief of that name, it more likely is named for its geographic peculiarity, as a gentle ridge sitting like an island surrounded by the flat expanses of Straths Tay and Lyon, and with much higher rougher mountains on all horizons. It appears on Pont's map as Drummyn Hill, with no last 'd', thus indicating the root form *dromannan*.

The ancient Gaelic name Druim Alban, the ridge of Alba (Scotland), referred to the whole dorsal ridge which separated the Scots from the Picts – although it is not clear from old texts whether this refers to the mountains running up the west coast from, say, Lochaber, or the ridge now known as the Grampians or Mounth. Drumochter, the famous rail and road pass where the snow gates are often shut in winter blizzards, is Druim Uachdair, high ridge. The only parts of Scotland without this generic are the Norse islands to the north, and the English-settled south-east. The Scots word *drum*, obviously from this same route, is frequent in Kirkcudbrightshire where it is used for small low hills, drumlins in effect.

dùc

Gaelic. (Pronounced doo:hk). This, a local word for hillock, occurs in **Beinn Dùcteach** in the Trossachs, a low hill between Munros and Corbetts.

dùn, dunan

Gaelic. (Pronounced doo:n). *Dùn* means a fortress or castle. The word used on a hill signifies the site of an old hill-fort of prehistoric times. It is believed there may have been nearly 1500 such forts scattered up and down the southern and western coasts (the east coast plains didn't offer such good defensive positions.) So the apparently singular **An Dùn** near Oban (*the* fort) was hardly unique, except in the sense that almost all of them were, to the locals, An Dùn (as English speakers might say 'the hill-fort' without using a specific). There's another **An Dùn** in the Grampians, with no record of a hill-fort on it, but which must rank as one of the finest natural defensive positions in the country. It's a 825m top, dropping steeply on all sides by at least 300m, and stands apparently astride one of the wide north-south Mounth passes, the land having been etched away on all sides by three streams and a loch. On Pont's map, it appears to be named **Doun Macwhillich**, perhaps after a local clan chief. Perhaps all traces of a fort have gone, bar the name. But on many others the builders' rocks remain.

*Dùn Caan, also known as Raasay's Cap when clouds collect on this island hill. See p78,
[Islands, Raasay]*

Often the *dùns* were vitrified forts where, it is believed, the rock rubble was fused together by great licking bonfires. A hill is a good point for both defence and observation, but you don't need to go all the way up to the highest contours to get these advantages. For instance, although the highest *dùn* is **Dùn dà Gaoithe** on Mull, the summit lies some distance above the recognised site of its fort; and most *dùns* are

lower, like nearby Iona's **Dùn Ì** at 101m.

Curiously the highest-known definite hill-fort site is not a *dùn*, but a hill in Sutherland called **Ben Griam Beg**, 580m, little mountain of Grimm, a Norseman; perhaps the local folk-memory had let *dùn* slip through to be caught only by later archaeologists. Also in Sutherland **Druim Chuibhe**, site of an ancient defensive broch, is not a *dùn* but a *druim* (ridge, of the stronghold): perhaps it was once the former but became corrupted to *druim*.

Dùn is found all over Scotland, in Norse areas like Raasay's **Dùn Cana** (**Dùn Caan** on the Ordnance Survey map), and throughout the Gaelic west, as well as the Pictish east where are found Dunedin (Dùn Èideann, now Edinburgh's Castle Rock) and Dundee. In the south the word *dùn* often became *dum* before the letters *b*, *m* or *p* (because the *m* made it easier to say), as in Dumbarton Rock (fort of the Britons) and **Dumyat** above Stirling (*dùn miathi*, fort of the Miathi tribe, old enemies of the Romans). At the western edge of the Campsies are **Dumgoyne** (*gainne*, arrow fort) and **Dumgoyach**. Dumgoyne is a superb steep site, and so precipitous that there has been a fatal hillwalking accident on its slopes. Even at the very south-east limits of Gaelic we find the word appearing in the Lammermuir Hills in **Doon Hill**, for on top are the faint remains of a 7th century palisaded palace of Angle kings. In the south-west, a former Gaelic-speaking area, there are over two dozen mapped Doon Hills, and well over half have identified remains of forts or other prehistoric remains. Unlike *dùn*, *dùnan* are not forts but little hummocks or hillocks.

Some of the *dùn* names hark back to distant legends. Near Loch Ness are **Dùnchea Hill**, from Cè, a legendary Pictish figure, and **Dùn Dearduill** maybe from Deirdre, whose love affair with Naoise led to them being chased across the Highlands – there's another Dùn Deardail fort near Ben Nevis. Kintyre is an area rich in legended ridges, like **Dùn a' Chaisteil**, fortress castle and **Dùn a' Bhuilg** quiver fort; **Dùn a' Choin Dhuibhe**, fort of the black dog, is where a chief's huge black wolfhound gamely held attackers at bay while help was sent for.

The Old English word *dun*, often used in English place names, does not mean fort, but usually a hill, often a flat-topped hill suitable for a village to be built on it: the word *down*, as in The South Downs comes from that word, too. In Angus, the hills **Brown** and **White Cathertun**, twin hill-forts, appear to be named from *caer* (a fort in Cumbric) transmuting to Gaelic *cathair* (normally a seat) and *dùn*.

edge

Scots. Of Northern English origin – as in the celebrated Striding Edge of Helvellyn, the word *edge* is used to describe the tilted slope of a hill, as in **Spartleton Edge** and **Blythe Edge** near Abbey St. Bathans in the Borders. Indeed in an 18th century map by Jenner, the Lammermuir Hills were mapped simply as The Edge hills. In the Pentland Hills, the names Bavelaw Edge and Cairn Edge were mapped in the 19th century, but seem to have fallen out of use, even though it perfectly describes the hills' contours there. The word's roots probably go back to the Old Norse *eggi*, which is a common Norwegian place name generic.

fell

Scots, English. This is a name that straddles the border with England, and in Scotland is found particularly in the south-west within view of the Lakeland Fells. The name originated in the English Lakes, to where the Viking settlers had brought *fjall*, a mountain, which their descendants made into *fell* – as in Scafell, Cross Fell and fifty others – it is the commonest hill name generic there. It spread to Galloway and Dumfriesshire, where there are many Norse place names, with Crif*fel* a landmark hill near the sea. In the south-west the higher hills in this area have Gaelic names, with the *fells* generally being lower, as poet Robert Burns observed:

> The Partridge loves the fruitful fells,
> The Plover loves the mountains.

... thus indicating the relatively lower height of the *fells*.

In the Dumfries and Galloway area the word was first used as a naming generic in the mid-15th century, quite late in the naming process, and therefore within a Scots-speaking context: thus there are four specimens of **Fell Hill**, and several hills called Fell of... (as in **Fell of Fleet**, after the river), as well as a simple **The Fell**. **Criffel** near Dumfries of course contains *fell* as suffix, and was possibly an original Norse name Krakkaval, raven fell. The word never caught on in the eastern Borders, where *law* ruled the hills; **Hart Fell** near Moffat and **Culter Fell** mark out the northern boundaries.

Curiously, it was a famous man from just outside that boundary who used the term to describe Highland hills, on his travels. When Borderer James Hogg, the famous Ettrick Shepherd and poet (1772-1835), saw the supposedly haunted Ben Macdui during a Highland journey, he wrote of a man he'd met who had,

> beheld the fahm [the 'Grey Man'] o'er the fell

...but the generic did not take in the Highlands, either. Jamieson's early 19th century dictionary of Scots says a *fell* was a hill, especially a rocky or precipitous one, perhaps reflecting the rougher topography of the Galloway area.

fiacail

Gaelic. (Pronounced **fee-a**chkil). A tooth. (Plural *fiaclan*). Many mountains around the world bear a resemblance to and the name of a tooth, as in Switzerland's Dent Blanche or North America's Moose's Tooth, and so it's not surprising to find them in Scotland. There are several **Càrn nam Fiaclach** hills in upper Deeside, and a **Fiaclach** on **Ben Wyvis**. On the granite Skye peak of **Marsco** is **Fiaclan Dearg**, red teeth, from the rock's colour.

The subtlety of the dental description can be seen, for instance, from the Mallaig train, passing beneath the long **Druim Fiaclach** ridge west of Loch Shiel: looking up at the ridge against a blue sky, you can see the delicate and compacted serrations that typify human teeth. Walkers on the ridge – the author speaks from the experience – might grate their own teeth at the jarring progress made high-stepping over

this myriad of vertical rocks that break the ridge's progress. A similar rock pattern jars the smooth swing of the boot on Càrn nam Fiaclan, a shoulder of the otherwise rounded **Maoile Lunndaidh**. In the east, **Cairn Gorm**'s Coire an t-Sneachda (the snowy corrie) has a toothed ridge leading up on either side of its steep headwalls – **Fiacaill a' Choire Chais**, steep corrie, and **Fiacaill Coire an t-Sneachda** snowy corrie. Just when you thought it was safe to go back on the rock... jaws!

There are jaws in the Borders hills too, for that appears to be the meaning of the generic in the hill-name **Carrifran Gans** near Moffat, from Scots *gansh*. The hill name's specific is from the Carrifran Burn and farm below, old forms of which include Corryffane, which might suggest Gaelic *coire* – there are other apparently Gaelic names nearby such as Loch Skene and Polmoody. It has almost certainly nothing to do with the suggestion by Johnston that it is from the Cumbric *caer y fran*, hill-fort of the crow, since there is no trace of a hill-fort here.

fireach

Gaelic. (Pronounced feeroch). This uncommon word for hill is few but far-scattered, from the Trossachs to Sutherland (both called **Am Fireach**), and from Skye to the edge of the Cairngorms. The term is usually applied to a small top on a ridge (like **Fireach Dubh**, 450m, above Loch Shiel) or shoulder (like **Fireach Beag**, 425m above Strath Avon), and sometimes to the whole steep slope of a hill leading to a minor top (like Fireach Garbh in Applecross).

gail-bheinn

Gaelic. (Pronounced **ga**l*a*vee*ny*). A great or rocky hill. It can also mean a huge billow or wave, poetically derived from the similar word *gaillionn*, whose meanings include a storm, or snow-whitened ground. This word may be the root of the western Munro **Gulvain** which certainly fits the description better than the alternative suggestion of *gaor bheinn*, filth mountain or *gaoir*, noisy. However, a report of the 1901 Scottish Mountaineering Club meet at Fort William mentions an excursion – probably using the Mallaig train – to 'Gulbheinn', and it is not impossible that it is one of the several Gulben hills in the Highlands, linked to the legend of Diarmaid. (See Ben Gulabin in The Cairngorms chapter).

glùn

Gaelic. (Pronounced gloo:n). **Glùn Liath**, a top on the northern spur of **Bodach Mòr** (big old man) in the Freevater Forest, is the old man's 'grey knee' or 'grey joint'. There are several *glùn* hill names in this same area.

grianan

Gaelic. (Pronounced **gree**anan). This comes from *grian*, the sun, and means a sunny spot or mountain top, a name found in several Highland spots. One example, **An Grianan** high above Glen Lyon, sits on a sunny south-facing shoulder of **Stuchd an Lochain**, providing the perfect belvedere for a cattleherd.

Stob Grianan in Glen Etive was supposedly the bower of the legendary Deirdre,

lover of Naoise. It was the spot where she dwelt in happiness before being tricked away to her fate in Ireland. In her farewell lament she speaks wistfully of,

> ...flocks of sunbeams crowd thy fold.

Indeed *grianan* is a common Irish place name generic, meaning sunny but also implying a view, most famously in Greenan Hill in Donegal, a huge hill-fort and headquarters of the Ui Neill kingdom.

gualann, gualainn, guala

Gaelic. (Pronounced **goo***a*lun). A shoulder. There are about four dozen instances of this body-name in the Scottish mountains, mainly in the south-west and the islands. The mountain called **Màm na Gualainn** above Loch Leven, really a southern outlier of the Mamores, means hill of the shoulder, referring to its shape and its lower height than the main range. More mysterious is **Gualainn nan Osna** in the far west, translating as the shoulder of sighing or blubbering. Does it refer to the wind moaning through the gap in the hills, to a long-forgotten tragedy... or was this 'a shoulder to cry on'?

head

Scots. This is a logical word for a hill top, but like its Gaelic equivalent *ceann*, it rarely features on the main summits. There are some distinct summits, such as **Yearngill Head** and **Cauldcleuch Head**, the latter a Donald: but most *heads* are tops or shoulders of higher hills. What many of them have in common is that their name – like the two just named – contains the name of the watercourse or gully (*gill* or *cleuch* in Scots) it stands above. Their distribution is very compact, with almost all of the 60 Head hills in southern Scotland occurring in the central Borders hills between the Tweed and Ettrick rivers.

heugh, height

Scots. A *heugh* is a cliff or 'rugged steep', and in the southern Borders are **Hart Heugh** and **Peniel Heugh**. They are perhaps derived from the Old English *hoh* and Middle English *hogh*, a hill. The similar-sounding but unrelated names of **Broughton Heights** (above the village of that name) and **Tamond Heights** come from *heich* or *heicht*, Scots for a height.

hill

English. What's this word doing here? – it's part of the book's title. Yes, but while we refer to mountains (as objects), the word *mountain* itself never occurs in a Scottish hill name (unlike Ireland, with its Brandon Mountain and others), whilst hill is a very common name-generic especially in the lowland and Borders areas. Certainly, it is sometimes an English tautology tacked on to a perfectly good Scots or Gaelic hill name generic, as in Dod Hill or Binn Hill or Cairn Hill: and yes, too, it sometimes replaced a perfectly good predecessor, as Cathadh became **Corryhabbie Hill**, and Inner Cairn in the Ochils became **King's Seat Hill**.

Professor Geoffrey Barrow of Edinburgh University has argued that the word *hill* is often used to refer simply to the summer grazing ground of sheep or cattle for a particular farm, and that many *hill* names thus contain the farm's name as the specific – as in **Turnhouse Hill**, the popular hill in the Pentlands. Approximately one third of all *hills* which are called X Hill are named thus, from their hill-foot farms. But the **Black Hills** (and other colours), **Gathersnow Hill**, **Common Hill**, **Hill of Stake**, are clearly bona fide *hill* names.

Southern and eastern England was the word *hill's* ancestral home, to which it came from the language's Germanic roots – Middle Dutch *hille*, Lower German *hull*, Old Frisian *hel*, to Old English *hyll*. And whether we like it or not, in Scotland it has replaced *law* and *knock* and *ben* in everyday conversation, although not in place names.

kaim

Scots. *Kame* or *kaim* probably comes from the Norse *kambr*, crooked – it occurs in Orkney and Shetland frequently – and refers to sinuous low hills snaking across valley bottoms, such as **Dun Kaim** near Carlops, and **Long Kaim** near Greenlaw. *Kame* is also used to denote mounds of glacial deposit, as in kame and kettle-hole topography.

kip

Scots. *Kip* means a sharp-pointed hill, as in the distinctive clean-cut lines of the **West Kip** in the Pentland Hills, or a jutting-out point on a hill, sometimes found in the Borders. Thus an early 19th century Borders writer states:

> I saw the bit crookit moon come stealing o'er the kips o' Boweshope Law.

Near Peebles the **Makeness Kips** are the only pointed set of peaks amongst the forested rounded hills of the area, their tips peeping above the gentle green swell. Near Dolphinton is the splendidly-named **Keppat Hill**, a small sharp-pointed hill of sand and gravel, from the adjectival form *kippit*. Just as fine, if not so descriptive, is its alternative local name as 'The Deil's Riddlins', where the legend is that the Devil himself sieved out the soil of a nearby hill, dumping the rocks in Biggar Moss and the sand here!

There are only a few *kips*, including five called simply **The Kip** or **Kipps**, but they have a wide family network abroad. Its distant language relatives include the Old English *copp* – there's a **Cop Law** near Ettrick – the German *Kopf*, the Dutch and Afrikaans *kop* and indeed the Gaelic *ceap*, all meaning 'head'. One of the loveliest *kips* (in the author's opinion) in West Kip in the Pentlands; seen from north or south, it has a striking conical shape, and from east or west its trademark nick juts out just beneath the short flat summit, thus encapsulating both nuances of the *kip* definition.

knees, kneis

Scots. This might appear to be knees, for hills with a knobbly knee profile –

especially as *shin* and *shank* are also used as generics. But in fact it is a corruption of *naze*, a nose or headland, and close study of maps will show that the term usually applies to hills with such a steep promontory. In the Borders there are nine hills with this generic, such as **Snickert Knees** near Crawford (perhaps from *sneck*, a notch or cut), **Law Kneis** near Ettrick, and **Muckle Knees**.

knock, nock

Scots. *Cnoc* is a Gaelic word for a lower hill, a knoll rather than a mountain, and the Scots form is *knock* (or more rarely *nock*). It was often used to described an isolated hill, and the word *knock* was used in everyday Scots until the late 19th century. There are enough Knocks in Scotland to fill a 'Who's There?' page, and one Galloway writer counted 200 in his native county alone.

It is widespread in areas where Gaelic was spoken but had died out relatively early, especially in the north-east lowlands and the south-west Borders, with very few in the south-east. The form of the name **Knock of Crieff**, on the fringes of a Gaelic-speaking area, shows that it was given by English speakers. Among the many others are **Knock Hill** near Huntly (locally, simply The Knock) – with its splendidly-named hill-foot farm Yondertown of Knock – and elsewhere **Big Knock**, **Meikle Knock**, and **Knock More** (all meaning the same thing in English, Scots and Gaelic!), whilst **Great Knock** in the Manor Hills tries to outdo them all. There are a dozen examples of Knock Hill – including one in Fife best known for the racing circuit at its foot – four simple hills called **The Knock**, and a **Knock Hills** range near Carter Bar on the border.

knowe

Scots. A *knowe* is the Scots version of the English *knoll* – the soft ending 'll' having frozen off in our cooler air. Sometimes it has been spelt without the final 'e' as in Fergusson's 17th century poem:

Nae sooner did the day begin to dawn,
Than I beyont the know fu' speedy ran.

However, while south of the Border the *knoll* betokens a small hillock suitable for fairies to dance around, here in Scotland a *knowe* can be of sterner stuff, rising to as high as 809m in **Fifescar Knowe** in the Manor Hills. Generally however, most *knowes* are subsidiary tops – the massif of **Dollar Law** alone has seven *knowe* tops within it – or the ends of spurs above a valley, rather than separate peaks. As one of Robert Burns' songs suggests, a *knowe* was big enough to be a sheep-farm and complete eco-system all rolled into one:

Ca' the yowes [ewes] tae the knowes,
Ca' them where the heather growes,
Ca' them where the burnie rowes,
My bonnie Dearie

Knowes are found especially in south-eastern Scotland and in the Borders near

the border, spilling over into Northumberland – but they are more numerous on this side. They are also a prominent feature in Orkney and Shetland where they take the name-form Knowe of... (as in **Knowe of Setter**). One traveller in Orkney says that in the 17th century they were often linked to fairies, and in much of Scotland they were known as trysting spots for lovers. Other specimens include the alliterative **Nickies' Knowe** near Moffat, and Edinburgh's Silverknowes and Kingsknowe, named after a 17th century tenant farmer, William King.

law

Scots. This is surely the archetypal Scots hill-word, its answer to Gaelic's *beinn*. This fine word is found in some small measure in the western hills (in the **Renfrew Heights** and Campsie Fells) but it is mainly a word of the east and south where Gaelic was not an alternative. It is particularly thick on the ground from the English border to the Lothians and Fife, with a scatter west into the Ochils, and northwards into the **Sidlaw Hills**, and even a sprinkling on the coastal fringes of Buchan.

The Sid*law* range in Tayside is a backdrop to **Dundee Law**, which in turn is one of a kenspeckle group including **Largo Law**, **Traprain Law** and **North Berwick Law**. This quartet owe their fame to their situation as steep-sided isolated hills rising like shark's fins above the surrounding sea of farmland or (in Dundee's case) housing. These confirm to the shape and situation suggested by the Scottish National Dictionary's definition of *law* as 'a rounded hill generally of a somewhat conical shape, and frequently isolated or conspicuous among others'.

Some of them are by geological origin volcanic plugs, stoppering up the neck of a dead volcano, and left standing by the erosion of surrounding crumbly rock. As such they were ideal defence sites in the pre-nuclear age; **Dundee Law** has an ancient hill-fort on top – *dùn* is a Gaelic word meaning fort and the town therefore takes its name from this hill – while **Traprain Law**'s earlier name was Dunpelder, fort of spears. Both Dundee and **North Berwick Laws** have giant arches of whale jawbone on top, in the former's case because the town was the home port of many whaling ships.

Although some of the Borders' *laws* fit the definition of isolated – like **Yetholm Law** above the village of that name – many other *laws* are less distinctively-shaped. Such 'bye'-laws were well described by Borderer James Hogg who wrote over 150 years ago:

> The common green dumpling-looking hills commonly called law.

Maybe Hogg had in mind Pudding Law, near Town Yetholm. Among the many others will be found the Pentlands' **Twin Law** and **Castlelaw Hill** (below which lies another defence site, with a Stone Age earthwork), the Manor Hills' **Broad** and **Dollar Law**, the simple **Law** near Elvanfoot, and five plain names **The Law**.

Largo Law on the Fife coast was the site of one intriguing speculation: in the late 18th century's Statistical Account, the minister of the parish speculated that the name *law* came from the Swedish *loa* or Danish *lue* meaning flame, referring to the

warning beacons that were lit there if enemy ships appeared. Other ministers, in parishes such as Stewarton and Carluke, opined that a hill called *law* indicated that they'd been used in the past as sites where feudal lords dispensed justice, gallows included. These ministers lived too far from the south-east where its plain hill-meaning would have been obvious.

North Berwick Law, visible from much of the Lothians, Fife and the Firth of Forth

In fact, the word *law* is Anglo-Saxon in origin: there was an old southern English word *hlāw* meaning burial mound, which came to mean hill (sometimes shaped like a burial mound) as it spread to north England. When it crossed the border into the Tweed basin called The Merse, almost every low rise was named a *law*, and even today the farmhouses standing on them bear the name. But as it moved onto the higher ground round about, it began to apply to serious hills, reaching 840m in Broad Law.

The only part of south Scotland where *law* failed to penetrate is Galloway and Dumfriesshire. One striking feature of *law's* distribution is its almost complete mutual exclusivity with *fell* hill names: the watersheds between the Teviot, Tweed and Clyde to the north, and the Esk and Annan to the south, form a weaving line from east to west, north of which lie *laws*, south of which lie *fells*, generally with nary an intruder. This suggests that the process of naming the hills was given from the inhabited valley bottoms on either side, spreading upstream (with the settlement process) rather than east-west along the hill tops. While *fell* in Galloway and Dumfriesshire probably spread from north-west England then up the Annan and Esk, *law* seems to have spread up the Tweed and its tributaries rather than directly

over the hills from north-east England. The very few *law* hills south of the watershed, and the fewer *fell* hills north of it, are all insignificant hills, and may reflect a farmer moving from one area to the other.

leac, leacann

Gaelic. (Pronounced lyehk). *Leac* means a large flat stone, from a bare rock on a hillside to a bare hill top. Stonehaven's **Leachie Hill** is from this word, and **Creag Leacach** above Glen Shee – not far away **Craig Leek** is its anglicised form – while **An Leacainn** by Inverness is from the related *leacann*, the broad (slabby) side of a hill. In the Campsie Fells, **Lecket Hill** is a classic example of the Gaelic eye for detail; a gentle green hill with a flat boggy top, only after a long squelchy approach do you reach the summit, and there you find the only outcrop of rock in the area, exposed like a grave slab, peeping from the moss.

leitir

Gaelic. (Pronounced lyaytyeer). A slope – often running down to the water's edge (hence *leth-tìr*, half-land) – this often appears in settlement names like Letterewe, as well as in hill names like **An Leitir** near Sligachan in Skye where the hill takes the form of an evenly-rising slope tapering to a broad ridge; the slope on this one is the hill. The similar-looking but unrelated word *leathad* also means a slope, as in the well-known peak above Rannoch Moor, **Clach Leathad**, the stone slope, sometimes known as Clachlet. (See also Ben Ledi in the Southern Highlands chapter.)

lurg, lurgann

Gaelic. (Pronounced **loo**roogan). *Lurgann* is a shin, and the derivative *lurg* is a hill ridge descending gradually down to low ground. **Lurg Mhòr** near Loch Monar is thus the Gaelic for 'big shin' or 'long shank', an apt name for a mountain so far from the nearest road end! This mountain's form is of an extensive ridge throwing a long sinewy spur east towards Loch Monar. There are about 20 *lurg* hills, all over the Highlands, and in those areas where Gaelic largely died out before the 19th century, they are mapped as **Lurg Hill** or **Lorg Hill**, both in the north-east and in Galloway.

màm

Gaelic. (Pronounced maam). This, the word for a breast, has moved from anatomy to topography to describe a round hill of breast-like form. Found all over the Highlands, it lies especially down the western seaboard area between Mull and Skye. *Màm* can also apply to a pass in the hills, as in Màm Ratagan on the road to Glenelg, probably from the shape of the saddle between two breasts. (See the inset on *màm* in the Islands chapter, and The Mamores in the Central Highlands chapter).

maol

Gaelic. (Pronounced moe:l). Like *màm*, *maol* has moved from body to hill. It means bald head, or a promontory, headland or great bare rounded hill. Peaks like **Maol Cheann-Dearg**, bald red head, in Torridon are very well-named steep-sided

flat-topped lumps where the vegetation straggles to survive on top. **A' Mhaoile** in Sleat is simply the bald one, or blunt one. A related word *maoilean* means either a bald person or the bleak brow of a hill, as in **Na Maoilean** near Oban and the Munro called **Maoile Lunndaidh**. These high northern examples obscure the fact that most of the *maol* names are in Islay, Jura and Mull, with a few on the mainland nearby, which suggests an generic brought from Ireland which failed to catch on in the wider Highlands. **Glas Maol** in the east was earlier known as A' Ghlas-Meall, suggesting that the current name is a corruption of the older generic. Its Welsh cousin *moel* had better success with many high hills in North Wales, such as Moel Ysgyfarnogod.

meall

Gaelic. (Pronounced myowl). *Mealls* have a bad press. One Gaelic dictionary defines them as 'lumps, or knobs', another source as 'heaps, hills, eminences or mounds'. The word can apply indeed not just to hills but also to banks of clouds, swellings in general and even to buttocks! Skye author Alexander Forbes goes so far as to refer to *meall* hills as 'heaps, or almost shapeless lumps'.

Certainly, half of the Munro Mealls are in Perthshire where the hills often have the lumpy bumpiness of middle age – these and the uninspiring but ski-famous **Meall Odhar** at Glen Shee are enough to give a *meall* a dull name. In Portree, the low hill Am Meall is also known locally as The Lump: near Gairloch the hill **Meall nam Meallan** (which fathered hamlet names Mellon Charles and Mellon Udrigil) is literally the lump of the little lumps.

But what about the **Meall Garbh** on **Ben Lawers** plunging down hundreds of cliff-metres into the depths of Lochan nan Cat, or **Aonach Eagach**'s rocky ridge which ends on the craggy **Meall Dearg**? And whilst Glen Lyon's **Meall Buidhe**, yellow hill, is truly a grassy lump, Knoydart's **Meall Buidhe** is on its north side a bare rocky mass with grass struggling in crevices to survive like late spring snow. Indeed it is higher than its neighbour Beinn Bhuidhe. So the charge against *meall* that it is a 'lump' that lowers the tone of Scotland's mountains must, on the evidence, be found 'not proven'.

What is true is that a *meall* alongside a *beinn* is normally a hill amongst mountains, lower in height. There are more *meall* in Scotland than there are *beinn* – approximately 1,600 to 1,200 – yet *beinn* outnumbers it nearly three to one among the higher peaks as listed in the Munro and Corbett tables. In the 100 highest mountains there are only four *mealls*, and of these the highest (**Meall Garbh** of **Ben Lawers**) is 33rd in the rankings, against nearly 30 *beinns* and their top two spots.

Outside of its Perthshire heartland most *mealls* are lowly hills, but common enough except in the old Viking areas of the north and in the islands of the west: here it seems to be substituted by the similar word *maol*, a 'great, bare, rounded hill', and *mol* in Lewis. In Galloway, hill names such as **Meaul**, **Millbawn** and **Mulldonoch** almost certainly come from *meall*, as older forms in Blaeu maps show – the last-named for instance as Mealdonach: there are some 70 hills starting Mill- or Mull- or similar, such as **Milldown** (*donn*, brown) or **Millfore** (*fuar* cold).

monadh

Gaelic. (Pronounced mon*a*gh, or mon*a* in the east). This is a very old word meaning mountain. It comes from the same linguistic root as Welsh *mynydd*, Breton *menez*, Latin *mons* and *mountain* itself. Significantly it does not exist in Irish Gaelic and this led W.J.Watson to suggest that it was a British word (the language now referred to as Cumbric, the pre-Gaelic language of the Highlands) which the Gaels took over because it was useful. ('Survivals' was the noun he used for such language transfers.)

Sadly in Scotland it has since fallen from grace for it is used in modern Gaelic to indicate simply dry upland moor (contrasting with wet boggy *mòinteach*). At one point in the past, about 13 centuries ago, Monadh referred to the entire Highland area. A ruler who died in 560 AD was described as the King of Monadh, and there are references in literature to Sliabh Monadh and Monadh Druim-uachdair, mountain of the high ridge (now Drumochter). Gradually the word's application was focussed down on more specific locations, often plateaux or mountain blocks. In the south-west we find **Monadh Leacach** (slabby) near Inveraray, once described as:

> ... verie dangerous to travel in time of evil stormy weather, in winter especiallie, for it is ane high Mountaine

Other 'high mountaines' include **Am Monadh Dubh** above Rannoch Moor, now literally translated as The Black Mount. Other hues show up in **Monadh Bàn**, white, and **Monadh Gorm**, blue, west of Loch Lochy, and the **Monadh Liath**, **Monadh Mòr**, and **Monadh Ruadh**, the grey, big and red *monadh* on either side of Strath Spey. Interestingly there is no mass duplication of the colours in the way that there are many examples of Càrn Gorm or Meall Buidhe, for instance. This might suggest that the *monadh* blocks were originally named to distinguish different masses within the whole Highland chain, whereas later 'coloured' peaks picked out local variations, and underlines the fact that *monadh* referred to sizeable blocks of hill country – the word might best be translated, in its original form, as massif.

Later the word seems to have been diluted, applying either to mere shoulders of a hill like **Monadh Odhar**, dun-coloured, in Glen Artney. In the Loch Arkaig region there are four *monadhs* all referring to the shoulders of hills, **Monadh Gorm**, **Beag**, **Ceann-arcaig** and **Uisge Mhuilinn** – respectively blue, small, end of Arkaig, and mill-stream (properly Uisg' a' Mhuilinn).

To the east and south the word *monadh* became scotticised, into *mounth*, *mont*, *mond* or *mon*. The plateau south of Lochnagar is the **White Mounth**, and there's another area of this name north of Inverness. Scotland's most easterly Munro is **Mount Keen** (probably from *caoin*, gentle) and out on the eastern Buchan lowlands are fishermen's landmark **Mormond Hill** (*mòr-mhonadh*, big *monadh*), and **Fourman Hill** near Huntly, from *fuar mhonadh*, cold *monadh* – where the snow lies late. **Monameanach** hill near Glen Shee is *monadh meadhonach*, the middle mountain. And there are many other Mounts, Monds, and Monts, like **Dechmont** hill (*deagh mhonadh*, fine *monadh*), all from this root.

mount, mounth, mon, munt

Scots. The Gaelic word *monadh* (and its Welsh cognate *mynydd*) meaning a mountain or high moorland has ancestral links with the Scots *mounth* and *mount*. **The Mounth**, formerly the name for all the high ground now referred to as the Grampians, now refers only to the east-west ridge south of Deeside; it contains **Mount Keen** (probably from the Gaelic *caoin*, meaning gentle or pleasant), **Mount Battock**, and the **White Mounth** (Lochnagar's broad shoulders). It is locally pronounced as in the English word 'month'.

In the Pentland Hills there's a group of *mounts*: **Black Mount**, **Faw Mount** (speckled), **Mount Maw** and plain **The Mount**, which at only 537m is a dwarf of the genus mountain. They are all within a short distance of the striking **Mendick Hill**, which is probably derived from Cumbric *monith*, (root of modern Welsh *mynydd* which is pronounced ending in *th*): hence the earliest recording of neighbouring Black Mount by Pont in 1590s is as Black Munth, and this suggests that the generic *mount* in this area derived indeed from *monith*. Minch Moor near Innerleithen may also derive from *mynydd*.

Mount Skep near Galashiels is from the Scots word for a basket, or beehive, from its shape. **Mons Hill**, near Dalmeny, from where you look over the Forth and its mighty rail bridge, is probably from this source. In parts of Scotland, a *munt* refers to a low tree-covered hill: in Fife, for instance, **Mount Hill** near Cupar is locally known as The Munt.

mullach

Gaelic. (Pronounced **moo**loch). *Mullach* means a height or summit, usually indicating a rather undistinguished top at the highest part above some more interesting feature. Most of the high *mullachs* are Munro tops rather than separate mountains – **Mullach nan Coirean** (summit of the corries) being an exception – their full names often referring to a corrie or slope at whose head they stand. **Mullach Coire Mhic Fhearchair**, Farquhar's son's corrie and **Mullach an Rathain**, pulleys, in Torridon, **Mullach Fraoch-choire**, heathery corrie, and **Mullach Lochan nan Gabhar**, goats' lochan, are examples of this. The mass of *mullachs* are spread down the western seaboard of the Highlands, and this mainland pattern is mirrored in others on the islands from Arran to Harris, and as far out as St. Kilda's Mullach Bi. For some reason the colour yellow – **Mullach Buidhe** – is common, but no other shades, whereas the *mullach* hills in Ireland come in all colours. In the far south-west is **Three Mullach Hill**, a partial translation of an older Gaelic name.

And whilst *mullach* may not have any great mountains named after it, it features in the lovely Gaelic saying;

Anail a' Ghàidheil air a' mhullach
(The breathing space of the Gael, it is on the summit)

muir

Scots. Although *muir* is the Scots for moor, and we don't think of moors as hills, it occurs often enough in hill names to make us reconsider. **Allermuir** in the

Pentlands, Minch Muir in the Borders, and other names like **Cademuir** and **Cairns-muir** – and indeed Grasmoor in the English lakes – are all definite hills rather than slight rises in a moor. The generic would have begun its life as a simple description of its agricultural function, but progressed to mean the hill on which the function (grazing) took place. **Cairnsmore of Fleet** in the south-west was once Cairnsmuir, and indeed it is in effect a large grazing *muir* identified by its several large cairns.

naze

Scots. This means a promontory, according to the Scots dictionary. There are a couple of hills a few kilometres apart in upper Nithsdale in the western Borders, called **Rough Naze** and **Herd Naze**. Both are slightly rising tops in the middle of long plateau-like ridges, so the dictionary's meaning seems appropriate, and parallels the shape of a headland of the type commonly called *ness*, of which there are several in the English Lakeland. According to the accomplished Victorian climber Cecil Slingsby, in *Norway – the Northern Playground*, the 'flattish-topped round-ended snow-sprinkled' buttresses high above valleys in the Horungtinder are known as *naasi* – this is a possible ancestor. (See also *knees* above.)

òrd

Gaelic. (Pronounced awrsht). An *òrd* (genitive form *ùird*) is, in the Gaelic dictionary, a hammer, and *òrdag* is a thumb or big toe, by analogy with its shape. It is also used for a steep-sided hill, although not in the dictionary as such, usually not very high. Examination of Ordnance Survey maps suggests that in plan they are of elongated oval shape, and often run north-south. **Òrd Bàn** on Speyside, and the **Ord of Kessock** at 191m overlooking the A9 road bridge have this shape and orientation; the latter is also the site of a large Stone Age fort, as are some others.

There are several examples of **The Ord** and **Ord Hill** in the north-east and around to the Moray Firth. Sometimes it is applied to an area of ground with morainic hummocks, rather than to individual hills – **The Ords** in Shetland and Muir of Ord near Inverness suggest this. Further up the A9 the road cuts round The Ord of Caithness, a headland rather than a hill, which was described in MacFarlane's Manuscripts as;

> … almost the highest mountain in this area and nearly impassable, separating Sutherland from Caithness.

In the late 19th century a man coming north over it into Caithness was known locally as an ord-louper! There are *òrd* further south: **Beinn Ùird** near Loch Lomond has the elongated oval shape and the north-south alignment. Angus' **Ordies Hill** looks like *òrd deas*, southern hill, but Adam Watson says it is the Buchan diminutive ending applied, as in *mannie*. In the Borders the word *urd*, as in **Ladyurd Hill**, **Lochurd Hill** and others, may well be related: for while these hills, near Blyth Bridge, may be named after farms at their feet, the farms in turn may well have been named after the knobbly hills near them. Ladyurd Hill in particular is of the elongated oval plan shape. Their connection with Gaelic *òrd* is suggested by the fact that there are a couple of

hills within a kilometre or two whose names appear to be translations of its other meaning, such as **Hammer Head** above Broughton. (There is a Norse word *urd*, which in Shetland names usually occurs as ord, meaning talus or stonefall or sometimes an individual stone, but it does not seem directly connected to the hill-generic.)

pap

Scots. Pap is another Scots word with Northern English connections – the **Maiden Paps** near Hawick are but a few kilometres from the Border – but it is from a Norse root, perhaps via the Lake District. Indeed another Maiden Pap in Caithness in the north is in old Viking territory. ('Maiden' in Northern England can signify a hill-fort). Pap means a breast, or nipple, and unusually for Scots words it has penetrated into Gaelic territory, which has its own perfectly good word *cìoch*. Several Gaelic mountains have kept their original *cìoch* (genitive, *cìche*) but others have been ousted by this incomer. The distinctive **Sgòrr na Cìche** at the mouth of Glen Coe is now widely known in English as the **Pap of Glencoe**, probably due to the linguistic influence of the tourists who visit this area.

The famous **Paps of Jura**, a landmark in any hill-view in the south-west Highlands, were also named by Scots or English speakers, for according to Martin Martin's 1703 book *A Description of the Western Isles*:

> ... the two highest (hills) are well known to seafaring men by the name of the Paps of Jurah.

The native Gaels had quite different individual names for Jura's peaks (see The Islands chapter), and while the Scots mariners' phrase is felicitous as regards their well-rounded shapes it rather overlooks the fact that there are a *trio* of peaks of roughly equal size, just as Glen Coe's Pap is a singular example of the species! At least **Lochnagar**'s **Meikle** and **Little Pap** summits achieve the desired number: these Scots names are the translation of the old Gaelic name Beinn nan Cìochan, the mountain of the little nipples, for like other Cairngorm tops the granite rocks have weathered to produce tors which stand proud of the swelling plateaux like nipples. One of the few examples of *pap* in southern Scotland is the **Pap Craig** on the southern slope of **Tinto**; distinctly mammary when seen in profile.

pen, pin

From the Cumbric (or Old Welsh) language that was spoken in southern Scotland in pre-Gaelic and pre-English times, there remain words like *pen* meaning a head or hill top. In present-day Welsh *pen* is still in use, as in Pen-y-Fan (the head of the slope) in the Brecon Beacons. In the Scottish Borders **Pennygant Hill** south of Hawick is clearly Welsh in sound, possibly *pen y ghant*, head of the boundary (cognate with northern England's Penyghent hill). **Penvalla** and **Penveny** hills (and the lost name Penairs, now Wether Law) are above Stobo, Penveny perhaps *pen faen*, head of the stone; **Penbane** near Durisdeer is from Welsh *ban*, a peak. The generic *pen* became a Scots loan-word, applied to steep striking hills, as in **Ettrick Pen** and **Skelfhill Pen** near Hawick. What many of the *pen* hills have in common is

49

prehistoric forts or other remains on or near their summits, which reflects the peoples who named them – Cumbric speakers driven into the hills by the Anglian farmers' invasion of the Tweed lowlands.

The apparently similar prefix *pin-* is not related. **Pinbreck Hill** and **Penderry Hill** near Loch Ryan, and several others in south Ayrshire, are memorial names for farms that stood at their feet, whose name began *peighinn*, Gaelic for pennyland, a unit of land measurement; most have a Gaelic specific (in these two examples *breac*, speckled, or *doire*, oakwood). The three **Pin Stane** hills near Elvanfoot appear to be idiomatic references to the stone that was used to 'pin' a dry-stane dyke successfully.

pike

Scots. This word is usually associated with the English Lake District, with its Langdale Pikes, and another thirty peaks to its credit – its roots lie in the Old Norse *pik*, a peak. This in Scots can mean a sharp pointed hill – which the two Pentland Hills called **The Pike** certainly aren't – but more usually refers to the summit cairn. The 18th century Peeblesshire mapmaker, Mostyn Armstrong, wrote of them:

> These piles of stones are often termed Cairn, Pike, Currough, Cross...

There are about two dozen *pike* hills on the Scottish side of the border, with names like **Pike Fell**, Law and Hill, and a similar collection just over into England, quite separate from the Lakes grouping.

ploc

Gaelic. (Pronounced plochk). A *ploc* (or *pluc* – pronounced ploochk) means a small lump, or plug – and every schoolboy knows what a 'plook' is. Best known is **Am Ploc** (the lump) above the calendar standard village of Plockton. Originally *ploc* was a lump of earth, or clod. There are several *ploc* in this corner of the west coast. Equally expressive is **Am Bulg** in Angus from *bulg*, a bulge or belly.

rig, rigg

Scots. A very common generic found the length and breadth of the Borders hills (although there are fewer in the Gaelic areas of Galloway), a pattern mirrored south of the border. The word has both Old English and Old Norse (*hyrgg*) connections. It means a ridge, usually a straight, steep-sided one. In the English Lakes there are instances such as Blea Rigg and High Rigg, while southern Scotland has a large number of examples such as **Rig of the Shalloch** in Ayrshire, **Mid Rig** and **Firthhope Rig**. Near Glen Trool **Rig of the Jarkness** is another splendid name, of obscure meaning – possibly from *dearg*, red. Further north, in the Pentland Hills, most of the *rig* names are shoulders rather than important tops, like Millstone Rig and Cock Rig; while in the Lammermuirs and Moorfoots, one in six of all hill names contains *rig*.

In central Scotland the word has got mixed up with an old Scots term referring to the run-rig system of farming, practised communally with a series of long parallel ridges or furrows. Lanarkshire hamlets like Limerigg and Stanrigg, standing at nearly 240m above sea level, could derive their name either from their farm history

or from their airy situation on the edge of the Slamannan plateau. In the north-east, the skyline between Mount Battock and the Braid Cairn is locally known as **The Riggin**. When the Reverend Ronald Burn traversed the far north-west in the early 20th century, he was shown a hill with the Gaelic name Druim na Saobhaidhe, but also known as Mid Rig by the shepherds who had been imported from the Borders the previous century.

ruigh

Gaelic. (Pronounced ree) The Gaelic word *ruigh* for forearm has passed into the description of topography, referring to the outstretched base of a hill or the sheiling ground for summer pasturage. By definition, it does not usually apply to summits of hills, but **Druim Righeannach** in the west is the ridge of the outstretched bases, from *ruigh*. **Meall Ghaordie** (sometimes Meall Ghaordaidh) may possibly come from *gàirdean*, the upper part of a shoulder or arm, and a similar limbed comparison may exist in **Beinn Udlamain** near Loch Ericht, possibly from *udalan* (pronounced ootalan), a ball-and-socket joint.

sàil

Gaelic. (Pronounced saal). Gaelic for a heel, *sàil* is found in examples such as **Sàil Mhòr**, big heel, of Beinn Eighe and in **Sàil Liath**, grey heel of An Teallach. Both are long slopes running down from tops which themselves round off a chain of peaks, like the heel at the end of a loaf. **Sàileag**, little heel, is a steep grassy hill linking its more rugged neighbours in Glen Shiel, and not far away **Sàil Chaoruinn**, heel of the rowan-tree, rounds off a northern spur. **Quinag** in plan is shaped like a giant Y, and the two north-pointing forks are, appropriately, **Sàil Gharbh** and **Sàil Gorm**, rough and blue heels. *Sàil* is a word favoured by the Gaels of the north-western Highlands, there being two main clusters – one in the far north within sight of Quinag, the other in sight of An Teallach. The actual summits may bear the name, but the *sàil* is probably the long slope that falls away from them, for it is that which makes them distinctive among hills – walkers approaching one are in for a long slog, and perhaps indeed sore heels.

seat, side

Scots. Seat, as found in Edinburgh's **Arthur's Seat** and the Campsie Fells' **Earl's Seat** expresses the idea of a high throne for the powerful in the land. That's why the other common name using this term is **King's Seat** (there are 20 occurences of this name) also referring to the mighty in the land – there are hills of this name in the Ochils, the Sidlaw Hills, and near Dunkeld. Its language root is the Old English *soeti*, and the hill-word *side* – as in the Borders hills of **Faw Side** (*faw* or *faugh* meaning mottled) and **Hummel Side** (*hummel*, low-lying). In the English Lakes, there are hills called White Side and Slight Side, probably from this same root.

sgàirneach

Gaelic. (Pronounced skaarnoch). The Gaelic dictionary says *sgàirneach* means a

quarry, a scree, or stony hillside, or even the sound of falling stones, and is applied to hills by way of comparison, as in **Sgàirneach Mhòr** above Drumochter. The Reverand Ronald Burn was told locally, in 1917, that this hill's name really meant 'rough nasty big brae'! There are ten occurrences of the name, usually applied to steep rocky slopes: two of them, Sgàirneach a' Chait and Sgàirneach nam Broc, the wildcat and the badger, above Loch Lubnaig and Glen Lochay respectively, suggest these rocky screes were home to animals.

sgiath

Gaelic. (Pronounced skee*a*). Gaelic for wing and by analogy for the shelter of its crook – in west Perthshire it commonly means shelter, as in **Sgiath Mhic Griogair** above Brig o' Turk, the hiding-place of (Rob Roy) MacGregor the bandit. Facing each other across Glen Lochay, **Sgiath Chiùl** (corner) and **Sgiath Bhuidhe** (yellow) hint at the wing's protective crook, for they are long narrow ridges, running at right angles to the westerly gales. The trio of hills on Skye's Sleat peninsula called *sgiath-bheinn* – **Sgiath-bheinn an Ùird**, **Chrossavaig** and **Tokavaig** – are wing-hills that also form a longitudinal barrier to the ocean gales.

sgòr, sgòrr

Gaelic. (Pronounced sko:r). There's a confusion in Gaelic dictionaries about *sgòr* and *sgòrr*, which is not surprising given the similar spelling: Dwelly's says that *sgòrr* equals *sgòr* (with a long *o*), meaning sharp steep hill, whereas *sgor* (with a short *o*) is a mark or notch. MacLennan's agrees that a *sgor* is a cleft in a rock but he has no *sgòr*, and says that *sgòrr* is a peak or cliff or sharp point. Added to this, Sgor has often been mapped without the accent – e.g. the Cairngorms' Sgor an Lochan Uaine, while in the reliable *Place-names of Upper Deeside* it is Sgòr.

In all probability *sgòr* and *sgòrr* are varieties of *sgùrr*, and the difference in spelling and pronunciation appears to be one of Gaelic dialect rather than type of hill. *Sgòr* is found mainly in the Cairngorms, such as **Sgòr Gaoith**, wind hill, with a scattering in Lochaber and the Monadh Liath, where the hills are certainly not sharp. No *sgòrr* name enters this area – its territory is farther west into Benderloch, in Jura, the Small Isles (where it seems to apply to steep cliffy headlands), and patchily up the north-west coast. Curiously, it doesn't really get tangled up with *sgùrr* except briefly near Loch Shiel, and is distributed on the fringes of the mainland heartland of *sgùrr*. But the differences in dialect, evidenced by the difference in spelling and pronunciation, parallel differences in the topography they refer to. For whilst *sgùrr* and *sgòrr* are rocky, conical shapes in the west (as most peaks there are), in the east where plateaux predominate, they can be – like Sgor Gaòith itself, and **Sgoran Dubh Mòr** nearby – minor rises on a massif.

sgoran

Gaelic. (Pronounced skoran). A 1988 issue of *High* magazine carried a fine story of a winter expedition above Loch Einich under the intriguing sub-title "What is a Sgoran?"... but furnished no answers to the question! The answer is that it is the

diminutive form of *sgòr*, suggesting a little rock or tor, and is found mainly in the eastern Highlands. **Sgoran Dubh Mòr** above Loch Einich is the big dark *sgoran* and has a summit granite tor, and there is an **An Sgoran** near Cromdale on the eastern flanks of the Cairngorms.

On **Ben Rinnes** above Dufftown three granite tors around the top are called the Scurran – the **Scurran of Wells**, of **Morinsh** and of **Lochterlandoch** – obviously a local dialect word for *sgoran* and signifying a tor or rock on a hill (the '*sg*' of Gaelic is pronounced '*sk*'). As one John Brown, shepherd, explained to the local Round Table in 1873:

> I had thocht mony a time about that mysel fin' I wis herdin sheep and lookin at the scurrans u' the hillheid. The top o' the mountain has been worn down by the weather leaving this scurran as a remnant.

There is also a related word *sgoraban*, small pointed rock, found mainly in Wester Ross, and the adjectival *sgorach* as in **Sgorach Mòr** and **Beag** in Cowal.

sgùrr

Gaelic. (Pronounced skoo:r). The Gaelic dictionary tells us that a *sgùrr* is a high sharp-pointed or conical hill. One description in a walkers' magazine, of a traverse of the switchbacking Mamores range, praises its peaks as 'real Sgurrs', implying a sterner test of mountaineering than is offered by mere *beinns*. And on Skye the Cuillin ridge, rockiest mountain range in Scotland, is dominated by *sgùrr* hills, with nine of the ridge's ten Munros. This might suggest that a *sgùrr* is a 'mountain's mountain' while a *beinn* is of more pedestrian character. And there is a general belief among walkers that *sgùrr* is a jagged rocky peak (like a German horn) while *beinn* is more rounded, if higher. The savage sharpness of any *sgùrr* in the Cuillin contrasted with the broad shoulders of Ben Nevis seen from the south provide the stereotypes by which others are judged.

Sgùrr hills are largely confined to Skye and to the mainland west of the Great Glen, while excluding the far north. A handful also lie just east of the Great Glen – in the Grey Corries, the Mamores and by Ballachulish – within a few kilometres of Ben Nevis. In the west, and in Lochaber, steep-sided narrow ridges run westwards to the Atlantic whose sea-lochs bite deep into the land. To the east where there are no *sgùrr* hills, the land is by contrast a great rolling plateau, most obvious in the Cairngorms. The overall pattern seems to confirm the idea of youthful thrusting *sgùrrs* compared with round-shouldered old *beinns*.

The case for *sgùrr* as a hard rocky peak is well presented by Gaelic poet Sorley Maclean in his paean to **Sgùrr nan Gillean** in the Cuillin:

> *... Ach Sgùrra nan Gillean sgùrr as fheàrr dhiubh,*
> *An sgùrra gorm-dhubh craosach làidir,*
> *An sgùrra gallanach caol cràcach,*
> *An sgùrr iargalta mòr gàbhaidh,*
> *An sgùrra Sgitheanach thar chàich dhiubh.*

... Sgùrr nan Gillean the best sgùrr of them,
The blue-blacked gape-mouthed strong sgùrr,
The sapling slender horned sgùrr,
The forbidding great sgùrr of danger,
The sgùrr of Skye above the rest of them.

Sgùrr appears to be a word deriving from the Norse word *skör* meaning an edge – there are cliff edges called Score in south-west Skye, which may be the taproot of the many *sgùrr* peaks in the Cuillin nearby. The densest cluster of *sgùrr* hills is on the mainland opposite Skye. It was probably a late generic, spreading into the hills after the *beinn* names had been given: for instance, the *sgùrr* peaks of the **Five Sisters** range are really tops in the massif called Beinn Mhòr, and naturally would have been given later than the main mountain mass' name.

Sgùrr nan Gillean, Skye, peak of gullies (or, less likely, young men).
See p88, [Islands, The Cuillin]

The aptness of the generic led to its adoption right across to the Lochaber area, but its spread further east and south was stymied by the generally rounder peaks there and the inertia of the established word *beinn*. There's a diminutive, **An Sgùrran** the little *sgùrr*, in Skye.

Sgùrr's failure to be adopted into Scots, unlike other Gaelic words like *beinn*, *gleann* and *càrn*, is probably due mainly to its failure to reach the southern Highlands, the contact zone with the Scots lowlands.

shank

Scots. Scots for a leg, the cousin of Gaelic *lurg* as in **Lurg Mhòr**, is found in half a dozen hill names, mainly of shoulders or minor tops, such as **Culter Cleuch Shank**, and **Meg's Shank**. It refers to a long ridge descending gradually to the low ground.

sìdhean, sìthean

Gaelic. (Pronounced **shee**:han). Usually spelt *sìdhean* (or *sìdh*) inland and in the south, and *sìthean* (or *sìth*) in the north and on Skye. It means a fairy hill, or one shaped that way. The air of Celtic folklore is thick with fairies good and bad – indeed fairies were often known simply as 'the people of the hollow hills' – and there are as a result numerous small hills throughout Gaeldom called *sìthean*.

For instance two knolls known simply as **Sìthean** lie by Loch Morlich, reputed to be the home of Domhnall Mòr, King of the Fairies, who once did the locals a good turn by driving away some unwelcome outsiders. Another **Sìthean** near Bernera in Lewis was reputedly a hill where lived fairies who borrowed the locals' pots and pans on a rather careless basis. One angry housewife, seeking her pans, walked into the hill by a door which appeared on as side, and was pursued home by a fairy dog for her pains. In Argyll **Cnocan Sìthean** is known as 'Crockiver's Fairy Hill', and its legend that an old chief was buried on top was confirmed by excavations last century – he was probably the 'Ivor' whose Gaelic name was in this Cnoc Iomhair.

Usually *sìthean* conform to the nursery image of little knolls – like the glacial sand hummocks that give Glen Shee its name – but **Sìthean Mòr** at 123m on Handa might suggest big fairies. Bigger still however are Strathyre's 570m **Beinn an t-Sìthein**, Loch Monar's **An Sìdhean** at 814m, the 873m **Ben Hee** in the north-west, and finally **Schiehallion** (fairy hill of the Caledonians), the Perthshire Munro. **Ben Tee** near Loch Ness is probably *beinn an t-sìth*, because it has a very sharp cone shape, especially from the west. In giving these names the shape or outline was of course more important than the occupants!

sliabh

Gaelic. (Pronounced **shleeuv**). As in the modern Irish hill-word *slieve*, this Old Irish Gaelic name meant mountain or extensive tract of moorland, but it never really caught on in Scotland. Like the ANZACs at the Dardanelles, the generic never really got off the beaches: most *sliabhs* in Scotland are found within view of the Emerald Isle, and failed to penetrate inland.

Thus Machrihanish, just across the sea from Ireland, is overlooked by **The Slate** hill, the islands of Islay, Jura and Arran have a few, and there are several in the western fringes of Galloway, usually anglicised to *slew*. The failure to get beyond their beachhead means they are low hills in Scotland, whereas Slieve Donard in the mountains of Mourne is the highest peak in north-east Ireland. And in the Isle of Man the second-highest hill is Slieau Freoagahane, over 300m high.

Interestingly, outwith the south-west most of the few *sliabh* names are on upper Speyside, a geographical leapfrog away; hills like **Sliabh Loraich** – from *lorgach*,

extensive – which refers to a hill slope rather than to a top, for nearby a low summit is called **Cnoc an t-Slèibh**. There may well be a connection with Irishman St. Columba who founded a chapel at Ruthven near Kingussie, and whose men may have brought hill-words as well as the new religion from the south-west to this locality. Slieve Donard after all was named in honour of a saint, Donart, who founded a monastery near the Mournes. The rare adjective *slèibhteach*, mountainous, may be the root of **Slèiteachal Mhòr** in Lewis, while Berneray's **A' Bheinn Shlèibh** returns to the original sense of a dry moorland.

Sliabh Ghaoil on the Argyll coast is literally the darling or beloved hill, locally translated as the Mount of Love. On its slopes, according to legend, the Fionn warriors caught up with the eloping lovers Diarmaid and the beautiful Grainne. Unfortunately for him, she was still the legally-wedded wife of Fionn MacCumhaill, a chief, who then devised a trap for his wife's lover in which he perished, poisoned by a boar's bristles. This legend is more usually signified by a mountain name like **Beinn a' Ghulbein** (see **Ben Gulabin**, in the Cairngorms chapter).

slinnean

Gaelic. (Pronounced **shlee**nyan). A shoulder-blade. Walkers often refer to the shoulders of a hill, the ridges leading out and down from its top, and the word has passed into some two dozen Scots hill names including two Cat Shoulders and a Hound Shoulder. There is only one Gaelic instance on Ordnance Survey maps, **Sneachdach Slinnean**, the snowy shoulder-blade of **Càrn Bàn** in the Monadh Liath – though this shoulder is 'back-to-front', since the adjective should follow the noun to give *slinnean sneachdach*. Gaelic prefers *sròn* (nose) to shoulder for ridges.

slugan

Gaelic. (Pronounced **sloo**gan). *Slugan* refers to the throat or more precisely the gullet, hinting expressively at narrow mountain defiles such as the Cairngorms' cleft of Gleann an t-Slugain, and the several hills called **Meall an t-Slugain**.

snib

Scots. A *snib* (sometimes snab) is a short steep hill. In Galloway are found Snabb, **Snab Hill** and **Snibe Hill**, while over in the Lammermuir Hills we find The Sneep, a short steep promontory jutting out into a valley near Spott.

socach

Gaelic. (Pronounced sochkoch). There are ten hills called **An Socach** – three of them are Munros – and a couple called **Socach Mòr**. This is literally the *socach* and big *socach*: the noun *socach* means a pert female, while the adjective means snout-like, or beaked: perhaps pertness implies having your snout stuck-up in the air? The usual translation is the snout, but this comparison with the front end of a pig is rather unfair to these fine hills, and perhaps we should consider the feminine interpretation.

spidean

Gaelic. (Pronounced speetyan). A word of the mainland opposite Skye – where it may be a dialect version of *bidein*: the Reverend A.E.Robertson, the first Munroist, noted that the sharp peak **Bidein an Eòin Dearg** was known locally as 'The Spidean'. It usually applies to points above distinctive features, like corries. There's an old Highland game 'spidean', similar to pitch and toss, in which a small stick called a *spid* is placed in the ground for the players to throw at: this 'spiky' image is the one used for the hill name.

Torridon's **Liathach** mountain has **Spidean a' Choire Lèith**, grey corrie, and neighbouring **Beinn Eighe** has **Spidean Coire nan Clach**, stony corrie. **Spidean Mialach** above Loch Quoich appears to translate as the lousy *spidean* (in the strictly biological sense), although originally in Gaelic it meant animals in general, here perhaps referring to deer. Edward Ellice in *Place names of Glengarry and Glenquoich* opines that it may be from *nialach (or neulach)*, cloudy... but then, he was the landowner and perhaps this ethereal meaning suited him better! Not far away, the highest point of **Fraoch Bheinn** is known as Spidean Mhic Iain Ghlas (peak of grey MacIain): the Gaelic-speaking Reverend Ronald Burn, the second Munroist, was told of how the thief MacIain was chased up this hill and killed on the summit, and for many years afterwards corn could be seen growing out of his boots on the spot.

sròn

Gaelic. (Pronounced strawn). Whereas English uses 'shoulder' for the ridges falling from a hill top, Gaelic generally goes for *sròn* meaning nose, and by extension a promontory; apt because, like a nose, such a ridge may be concave or convex, rough or smooth, broad or narrow, but always projects out from the hill face. Because it is a hill*side* rather than a hill *top*, there are few actual summits with this name, and those that there are taking their name from the slope they top, like *sàil*.

Sròn a' Choire Ghairbh, nose of the rough corrie, near Loch Lochy is the only Munro in *Munro's Tables*, while other *sròn*s in the Tables including two cases of **Sròn Garbh**, rough noses, are the subsidiary tops of bigger mountains. There are hundreds of *sròn* hill names, covering all the Highlands. Harris' **Sròn Ulladal** cliffs which plunge down for over 300m must be one of the most magnificent specimens. Older maps name it as Strone Ulladale.

Strone is one anglicised version of the word, with **The Strone** hill in Angus, and **Stronend** in the Fintry Hills as examples, while outwith Gaeldom in the Ochils, the splendid Scots-named hill **The Nebit** means the hook-nosed one. And an English name, or rather local soubriquet, in the Highlands is **Wellington's Nose**, the summit of **Fuar Tholl** when seen from Loch Carron, where it resembles a reposing face.

stac

Gaelic. (Pronounced stachk). A precipice or a steep high rock or hill. This is famed because of the spectacular hill **Stac Pollaidh** the stack at the pool, often horribly anglicised to Stack Polly. (The very shapely cone of **Beinn Stack** near Kylesku is another case of the word being anglicised on the map). To the Vikings *stakkr* meant

steep or precipitous, and was applied to sea 'stacks' like St Kilda's Stac Lee (*stakkr hlidh*, sloping steep rock) as well as to hills. To the Gaels it meant steep, columnar rock formations – such as compose Stac Pollaidh's stunning pinnacled ridge – or a steep conical hill like **An Stac** in the west.

Stac Pollaidh, steep rock at the pool, from the myriad of large and small lochs surrounding it

The name of the hill called the **Stack of Glencoul** is a mapmakers' anglicisation; local Gaelic, even in translation, had no such name, for them it was simply the local *an stac* without need of qualification. In the north there are several hills called **Ruadh Stac** (red steep hill), while **Ruadh Stac Mòr** (big red steep hill) in the Fisher-field Forest has recently been elevated to full Munro status.

Stac has a discontinuous distribution: in the Hebrides, they are usually sea stacks; one the north-west coast, in sight of the sea, are the well-known ones named above; but then, across the Great Glen, there are groups in the Monadh Liath and southern Cairngorms suggesting crags, like Stac na h-Iolaire (eagle). **Stac Gorm** and **Stac na Cathaig**, the blue and jackdaw stacks, are two fine craggy little Marilyn peaks above Strath Nairn.

steel

Scots. This is a steep bank or hill-spur, coming from an Old English word *stigel*, the predecessor of stile (i.e. something for climbing over), and occurs in the Lake District in Steel Knotts and Steel Fell, as well as High Stile. In the Borders we have **Ashiesteil Hill**, 401m above Peel Hospital, **Stiel End** and **Steele Knowe**. An 1885 account from Berwickshire states:

There are five ravines subsidiary to the main Stonecleugh running between it and the Lammermoor ridge... some of the intervening high slopes being elevated spurs called steels.

stob

Gaelic. (Pronounced stob). This mountain-word leads a double life east and west. Literally meaning a short stick or upright post (in Gaelic and in Scots), it rings with the English 'stub', and in the hills can aptly suggest a short stubby top. Thus in the east, in the Cairngorms, a *stob* often crowns the highest point above a corrie bowl like a skelf on a roughly-cut thumbnail, as in **Stob Coire an Lochain**.

In the west however a *stob* is a peak, not a mere point: Lochaber, home of many *sgùrrs*, also boasts a fine chain of *stobs* that make up the Grey Corries range, as well as those which blacken the setting sun from Rannoch Moor, like **Stob Ghabhar**, goat peak, **Stob Dearg** and **Stob Dubh**, the red and black peaks (now known as the Buachailles). Nearly two-thirds of the high *stobs* – and there are a very few lower ones – lie in Lochaber, and they usually have full Munro status, whereas their eastern cousins in the Cairngorms are normally mere subsidiary tops of larger mountains.

Above Balquhidder is a simple **The Stob**, part of a group clustered round **Stob Binnein** (or Stobinian). The *stob* hills are a close-knit family: there are 130 *stob* hills but the vast majority are in a tight cluster between Fort William and Killin in the south-western Highlands. **Stob Hill** and **Stob Law** in the south-east Borders are probably from the Scots word *stob* for a stake. Stob Law is a big hill, but appears to have a late name, for in 1775 Armstrong mapped it as Sandyknow Head.

streap

Gaelic. (Pronounced shtrehp). A verbal noun meaning the act of climbing or scaling – or simply a climb – this is a nicely expressive description of the steep **Streap** hill above Strathan in the far west. In the far north, **Beinn Dìreach** means the perpendicular, upright or just straight hill.

stùc

Gaelic. (Pronounced stoo:chk). *Stùc* means pinnacle or steep conical hill, or a hill projecting from a larger one, steep on one side and rounded on the other; it appears to be related to the Old Norse word *stac*. Unlike *stac* however *stùc* is found all over the Highlands, from **An Stùc** near Ledmore junction in the far north-west to another steep hill of the same name in the Ben Lawers chain in the south. Probably the best-known *stùc*, by sight, if not by name, is **Stùc a' Chroin**, hill of the little sheepfold, lying near the southern edge of the Highlands and thus visible over a wide area of the central belt of Scotland.

Similar words *stuaic* (a projecting rounded hillock), *stuic* (the anglicised form – as in **The Stuic** on **Lochnagar**) – and *stùcan* (the diminutive) are all related cousins. But while *stoc* differs by only one letter there is no connection: the hill **An Stoc-bheinn**

by Lairg could mean the tree-trunk hill, although it is probably from Norse *stakkr fjall*, the latter generic translated into Gaelic.

Stùchd is another form of *stùc*, according to a Gaelic dictionary, although its dozen examples are geographically confined to the southern edge of the Highlands, and tend to be distinctive in shape with flat-topped summits. The *stùchd* spelling may on the other hand simply reflect the spelling peccadilloes of the original Ordnance Survey. surveyor in this area.

The Perthshire mountain **Stùchd an Lochain** (affectionately known as the Stui) was described in a 1590 document as Stuic-an-Lochain. It has a flat summit ridge scooped around a splendid corrie lochan down to which it throws grassy gullies and rocky ribs. Further south **An Stùichd** is a flat-topped shoulder south of Loch Voil, and there's an **An Stùchd** in Kintyre. Dwelly's dictionary states that a *stùc* is 'a little hill jutting out from a greater one, steep on one side and rounded on the other...' but Stùchd an Lochain can hardly be described as that, since it is the highest in its chain.

suidhe

Gaelic. (Pronounced soo*y*a). A seat, or level shelf on a hill-side. The concept is well expressed in Arran's rocky bower **Suidhe Fhearghas**, Fergus' seat (an early ruler who climbed it with his court to survey his fiefdom). High above Applecross, **Càrn an t-Suidhe** is said to be where Saint Maelrubha's body lay, while his pall-bearers rested, on his last journey from Loch Maree to the sacred burial ground below; bed or bier rather than seat being the meaning here. This story, and the widely-scattered nature of the 25 *suidhe* hills, points us to a religious aspect of the name, because many of them are named after saints. **Suidhe Chatain** and **Bhlain** (Chatan and Blane) on Bute, **Suidhe Pàdraig** and **Columchille** (Patrick and Columba) on Arran, **Suidhe Ghuirmein** and **Chuimein** (Gorman and Cumine) near Fort Augustus. So not just anybody could have a *suidhe*. One *suidhe* was lost to us, when what is now **Ben Arthur** or more frequently **The Cobbler** was mapped in the 16th century as Suy Arthire by Timothy Pont, clearly Arthur's Seat.

There are **An Suidhe** hills above Inveraray and on Speyside, but the most photographed yet unrecognised must surely be **Meall an t-Suidhe** hill of the seat, the mere 700m flank of Ben Nevis above Fort William. It is sometimes spelt in anglicised form (roughly as it is pronounced) – Melantee Hill.

Suidh' Fhinn in Skye, a knoll on the shoulder of **Beinn na Grèine** (mountain of the sun) above Portree, is where Fingal sat to watch his Fionn warriors hunting in Glen Varragill below; and he had another vantage point near Slioch, **Suidheachan Fhinn**, a plural form suggesting almost a sofa on the hill! Above Tarbert, **Cnoc an Suidhe** (properly *Cnoc an t-Suidhe*) was the 'council hill' where justice was dispensed, and people even condemned to death – here the 'seat' was the seat of justice.

In the east the word has become *suie*, as in **Suie Hill** in the north-east. Whilst *suidhe* were generally not for ordinary mortals, the word *cathair* meaning seat was available to IKEA mortals: **Cathaireachan Dubha**, the black knolls near the keeper's house at Dundonnel was where shepherds could sit to watch their flocks. For some reason, such grassy benches are especially common in Caithness.

tap, top, tip

Scots. Obviously meaning a hill top, this is found in a few names in the farthest south-west and in the north-east, but not in between. In remote Galloway lies a hill called **Tops of Craigeazle** (*creag iosal*, low crag), the highest point of a branch of the **Rhinns of Kells**. While in Grampian Region above the village of Rhynie stands a summit, site of an old hill-fort, called **Tap o' Noth**. One writer derived its name from the Gaelic *taip a'nochd*, meaning (according to him) the top of searching or observation – in other words a lookout post for the old hill-forters, in line with the many instances of **Ward** or **Watch Hill** in northern Scotland. However Noth is simply a local farm district, above which it is the – very striking – top or tap. More romantically, legend has it that its 'house-giant' Jack o' Noth, having stolen the sweetheart of Jack o' Bennachie nearby, was flattened (together with his 'bidie-in'!) on his own hill top by a huge boulder hurled by his cuckolded neighbour. **Bennachie** itself has a summit called the **Mither Tap**.

Interestingly, neither the Tap o' Noth, the Tops of Craigeazle, nor the Mither Tap are actual main summits in their own right but merely the highest points of a long ridge which bears the name of the hill proper, respectively Hill of Noth, of Craigeazle, and the **Oxen Craig** of **Bennachie**. This suggests that the 'top' idea is similar to that of the later *Munro's Tables* in which the highest points are the summits or proper 'Munros', while other high points on shoulders are mere 'Tops' often by-passed by Munro-baggers.

In south-western Scotland the Scots hill names of **Tippet Hill** (several), **Tappetknowe** and **Tappet Hill** come from the adjective *tappit* (more usually applied to hens) meaning crested, and there's a local name **Tintock Tap** for Tinto's summit. **Welltrees Tappin** near Sanquhar contains the word *tappin*, a local Ayrshire word expressive for a top, but not as delightful as the alternative Scots word *tappietourie* (literally the 'tower' on top), meaning a cairn on a hill top. Back in the north-east are the **Tops of Fichell** (probably from Gaelic *fiacaill*, a tooth), the **Meikle Tap** (big top) on the **Hill of Fare**, and the expressive **Tips of the Clunymore** above Dufftown.

teanga

Gaelic. (Pronounced tyoegha). A tongue. The tongue-like ridges of **Teanga Mhòr** and **Teanga Bheag** in the **Red Cuillin** of Skye clearly protrude like rounded glacier snouts down to the valley. There are over a dozen hill names with *teanga*, mainly found in Mull and Morvern, and in Lochaber near the solitary Munro of the species, **Meall na Teanga** above Loch Lochy. Not far away is the intriguing **Teanga gun Urrain**, literally the tongue without a responsible person – a gossip, perhaps? – or more likely a tongue of land with disputed ownership. In the Renfrew Heights there is a broad ridge called simply **The Tongue**, a simple translation into English of an original Gaelic name. And another 'tongue', that of Old Norse, was at work in the Hebrides in hill names like Barra's **Ben Tangaval**. This points north to a probable origin in Old Norse, not just of the Gaelic word but also of the very idea of hill-spurs as tongues, for *tunga* is a very common hill-generic in Iceland (there are many Tungufjall hills there) and in Norway.

tiompan

Gaelic. (Pronounced tyowmpan). *Tiompan* is a rounded one-sided hillock: it is probably of Norse origin. The word also means a musical instrument. The Clach an Tiompain (stone of the lyre) near Strathpeffer was so-called because when struck it made a hollow sound. It featured in a prophecy of Coinneach Odhar, the Brahan Seer, that one day the sea would flood the land so that ships could ride anchored to the stone. There are others of this name in Islay and Glen Almond.

tolm, tolman

Gaelic. (Pronounced tool*a*m). A rounded hillock, or a knoll, deriving like *tulach* from the root *tul*, a hillock. **Sgùrr Thuilm** (the genitive form) near Glenfinnan is distinctive in outline, for it is far less rocky or pointed than its neighbours, and has the gentler shape of a lowland hill. On the other hand Skye's **Sgùrr Thuilm** is a more pointed peak, with scree slopes, but compared to its rugged Cuillin neighbours it offers, as one guidebook says, an 'easy walk back to the valley'.

There is a tradition that tulmen hills (from the Gaelic diminutive *tolman*, plural *tolmain*) were knolls concealing fairy palaces that resounded to continuous revelry, pre-modern disco palaces! There's a tale from Barra about a herdgirl who was hammering a stake into a tulmen to tether her calf, when up popped a fairy woman to ask her why she'd disturbed her in this her dwelling. She promised the milkmaid that if she moved to grass a little further on she'd get milk from her cattle for life. Needless to say...

tom

Gaelic. (Pronounced towm). Of Irish origin, it initially meant a copse of woodland, and this is the meaning it had in south-west Scotland, its original beachhead. But as it marched Birnam-style across the country it changed to mean a hillock or knoll – perhaps because it was often only on agriculturally-useless hillocks that trees were left standing. Mere knoll it may have been, but it has several Munros to its credit: the summit of **Tom Buidhe**, yellow knoll, at 940m above Glen Doll is a gentle hillock barely noticeable amidst the wide plateau of **The Mounth**. But by the time it reached the far north it took on still grander forms like **Tom na Gruagaich**, the first mighty summit of **Beinn Alligin** above Loch Torridon.

The intriguing **Naked Tam** hill near Forfar is probably a partial translation of *tom nocht*; and the several hills of the south-east called **Corum** are from *corr-thom*, pointed knoll (*th* not being pronounced). The word is found all over the Highlands except in the south-west where the original sylvan meaning was retained, although the low hill in Inverness city **Tomnahurich**, *Tom na h-Iùbhraich*, hill of the yew-tree, might suggest that the 'tree-roots' remained. This hill is also known as **Tom nan Sìthichean**, knoll of the fairies, and the Brahan Seer had prophesied that the day would come when the hill would be under lock and key to stop the fairies doing their mischief: and, indeed, long after his death, this hill became the city's cemetery, protected by a fence and a padlocked gate.

tòrr, tor

Gaelic. (Pronounced toar). In Gaelic, or in the Scots versions 'tor' or 'tore', this is a mound or a low conical hill, as **The Tor** above Loch Alvie clearly shows. In distant Cornwall, its virtually-extinct Celtic language had the word *tor* for the granite rocks that outcropped on the great moors, like Wild Tor on Dartmoor. Both languages may have taken their inspiration from the Latin *turris*, a tower, but it was the Cornish version which won its place in the English language to the extent that the granite outcrops of the Cairngorms are often referred to as the tors – of **Ben Avon**, etc – even though there is a Gaelic word *bad* for these features.

Among Gaelic speakers the word was used mainly for lower hills, such as **An Tòrr** at 187m above Loch Caolisport, or **Tore Hill** above Boat of Garten. The *tòrr* hills are thickest on the ground in the south-west islands and the west coast up to Skye, with a scattering on the Moray Firth lowlands and in southern Scotland. The top end of the Pentlands, scraping Edinburgh city, has **Torduff**, **Torphin** and **Torgeith** (respectively dark, white and windy), all little hills in the shadow of that range's big hills.

tulach

Gaelic. (Pronounced *too*loch). The word *tulach* means a hillock, a knoll, or a 'little green eminence'. Obviously it applies mainly to lower hills, but it is featured in **Glas Tulaichean**, and in **Beinn Tulaichean**, the Munro above Loch Voil which has a summit ringed by small crags and boulders. Because it is mainly a word of lower ground, particularly in the south, it has suffered the same fate as *bàrr* and *àirde* – swallowed up into settlement names (as in Tulliallan or Tillicoultry), corrupted by non-Gaelic speakers (as in the **Touch Hills** south-west of Stirling), and having to carry a tautological translation as in Brechin's **Tullo Hill**, Blair Atholl's **Tulach Hill** or Tayside's **Tulich Hill** (all meaning 'hill hill'). The odd-sounding **Mortlich** hill above Aboyne is probably *mòr thulaich*, big knoll. It is found almost entirely in the southern and eastern fringes of the Highlands on lower hills, apart from a few specimens in Easter Ross. W.J.Watson suggests that it is a substitute for the south-west's *bàrr*, for low hills, north of the Forth-Clyde area.

type

Scots. This stands for a low conical hill, in the dialect of Dumfriesshire. **Type Knowes** near Moffat is an example, but they are so smothered in conifers now you'd be hard pushed to see the *type* for the trees.

uchd

Gaelic. (Pronounced oochk). This means a bosom or breast, and by analogy a steep hill. **Uchd Mòr** in Skye is the big hill, while **Uchd a' Chlàrsair** is the harper's hill in Atholl. **Creag Uchdag** near Ben Chonzie may be from *uchdach* meaning steep, although *uchdag* literally means panting, which is what you might do on it... **Outh Hill** in Fife also comes from this word.

CHAPTER TWO

THE ISLANDS

Scotland has many islands. One book claims there are 787 islands, restricting the count to those of size big enough to

> ... afford sufficient vegetation to support one or more sheep or which is inhabited by man.

This count excludes sea-washed skerries, large or small, such as the all-rock Rockall. The superb *The Scottish Islands* by explorer and sailor Hamish Haswell-Smith counts 165 islands of 40 hectares (100 acres) or more; he counts the Uists and Benbecula as one, and excludes both Skye and Seil on account of their bridge links to the mainland. Alternatively, restricting the count to those with a Marilyn (a hill at least 150m above the sea, and with at least a similar drop on all sides) there are 53 islands in the frame, supporting 227 Marilyns, listed in Alan Dawson's *The Relative Hills of Britain*. There are other islands not so high above the waves but with distinctive hills, such as Coll and Tiree, Iona and Gigha, Colonsay and Benbecula – they may be Marilyn-deprived, but any hill rising out of the sea is worth its name! Many of these islands have mountains or hills of note and some, like the Cuillin of Skye or Arran's Goatfell, are famed far into the mainland. This chapter visits the higher hills of these and other sizeable islands.

Norse was the ruling language in many of these islands, especially in the north and north-west, from the 9th until at least the 12th century, longer in the Outer Hebrides. The suffix -ey or -ay in many of their names (eg, Islay, Scalpay) is from the Norse word for an island. As a seafaring people the Vikings used hills primarily as landmarks, and consequently most of their names are simple descriptions of their function (like Ward Hill, from the Old Norse *varð* or *varða* meaning watch place, from where a watch could be kept in case of attack, or a hill with a beacon or cairn), or their shape.

Adjectives meaning rough, stony, flat or high recur, and not for them are the human or animal associations of the later Gaels. The words *bjerg* (a precipice) and *klettr* (a rock or cliff) are quite common, but are overshadowed by the main Norse word for mountain, *fjall*. The word *fjall* became *field* in Shetland and Foula, *fiold* in Orkney, and as it sea-frogged round Cape Wrath and down through the Hebrides it became the suffix -*val* (as in Rum's Askival) or sometimes -*shal* (as in Lewis' Cleit-shal). By the time it reached the English mainland of Cumbria it had become *fell*, a word now thoroughly absorbed into the English language, as in the Lakeland Fells and fell-walkers.

Arran

The granite knot of Arran's higher hills is a landmark in the Firth of Clyde and from much of south-western Scotland, and on a clear day its profile can be seen from over 60 kilometres inland.

This knot of its northern peaks is largely Gaelic-named. Although the glens of

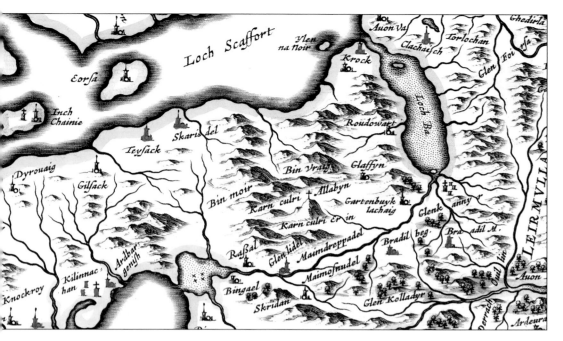

Above: Blaeu, 1654, Isle of Mull. Extract centred on Bin Moir (Ben More), with nearby the intriguing Karn culri Allabyn and Erin (hills of the back to Scotland and Ireland).
See p72 & 77, [Islands, Iona & Mull]

Below: An Teallach, a mountain mainly composed of red sandstone rock, has this grey quartzite rock spur, Glas Mheall Liath, the grey hill. See p104, [Grey Hills, liath]

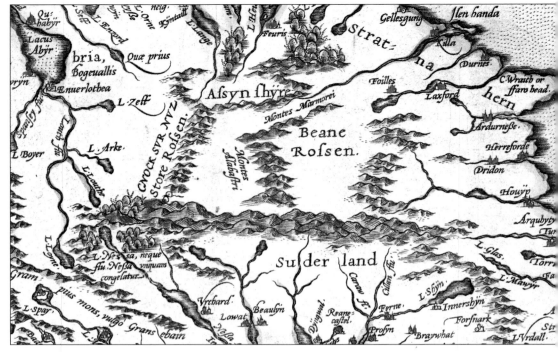

Above: Ortelius, 1573, Scotiae Tabula. Northern Scotland (north to the right). Centrally are the Montes Marmorei and Montes Alabastri (marble and alabaster mountains) – could this refer to Beinn Eighe and Liathach? See p144 [Central Highlands, White Hills] – and at the head of the Spey, bottom left, Grampius mons, vulgo Gransebain (Grampians). See p126, [Cairngorms, The Grampians]

Below: Sgòrr na Cìche, peak of the breast, popularly known as the Pap of Glencoe, dominates the view up Loch Leven. See p147 [Central Highlands]

Caisteal Abhail, Arran: the 'castle' refers to its rocky battlements. See p25, [Generics, caisteal]

north Arran have Norse names – Glen Rosa, Sannox and Iorsa – the heights are largely Celtic. **A' Chìr** (formerly Cìr Bheag) and **Cìr Mhòr** are the (cock's) comb and the big comb (with their rocky teeth), **Caisteal Abhail** is possibly castle of the fork (*caisteal a' ghabhail*), with its granite battlements: but a local form noted in 1772 by Thomas Pennant was Grianan Athol, *grianan* being a sunny spot (as in Greenock) or summit, and 19th century writer W.Lytteil suggested the second word *abhail* was *ha fjell* (high fell) corrupted. The mountain's profile has also been known as The Ptarmigan and as The Sleeping Warrior for it is said to resemble a warrior's effigy reposing full-length on his bier. **Am Binnein** is the pinnacle or high conical hill, and **Suidhe Fhearghas** above Glen Sannox is Fergus' seat: Fergus was a ruler of Arran, Bute and Kintyre as viceroy for the Irish conquerors, the first 'King of the Scots'. Sir A.Ramsay's 1841 book on the island's geology quotes a local tradition that he went up the hill with his attendants to get a view of his domains and, being fatigued by the ascent, they sat down to dine on top. While Fergus was a definite historical figure, circa 500 AD, the Fingalians or Fianna who are named in the hill-forts Caisteal an Fhinn and Dùn Fionn were legendary warriors.

The softer contours of the outlying hills enfold **Beinn Nuis** (probably Beinn an Ois, hill of the fawns – at its southern end is Creag nam Meann, crag of the young roe), **Beinn a' Chliabhain**, (hill of the little basket or creel), **Beinn Tarsuinn** (transverse or crosswise hill) – there are four hills of this name – and the shapely **Cìoch na h-Òighe** (the maiden's breast). West of Glen Iorsa a Graham dominates the hill mass.

Its topmost peak is known as **Mullach Buidhe**, yellow summit – one of three such on the island – distinguishing it from **Beinn Bhreac**, speckled hill, the subsidiary top to the north. Immediately south is the craggy top of **Beinn Bharrain** by which the whole peak has come to be known. In 1904 R.Currie suggested baron's hill, but Ian Fraser's *The Place-Names of Arran* a century later is certainly closer with a source in *barran*, a fence or mountain top. The highest peak in south Arran, **Tighvein**, looks like house mountain (from *tigh bheinn*), but is correctly Taobh Bheinn, side mountain.

But among all these Gaelic peaks the highest hill in Arran stands as the odd mountain out, for **Goatfell** 874m, might appear to be an English name. On the surface this name could be taken at face value, for goats and hills are associated in the popular mind. Indeed among the many novice walkers whose holiday itinerary includes this hill – in the patronising words of an earlier Scottish Mountaineering Club guidebook 'The ascent of Goat Fell is a popular amusement among summer visitors to Brodick …' – there must be many who feel that their achievement merits them mountain goat status. And there are other goat mountains elsewhere in the Gaelic Highlands, such as **Stob Ghabhar**.

But although Goatfell is *apparently* English, unlike any other important Arran place name, it is more probably of Old Norse origin. One of the earliest references we have to the mountain is in 1632 when 'Lugless' Willie Lithgow enthused:

> Goatfieldhill which with wide eyes overlooketh our Western Continent … a larger prospect no Mountaine in the world can show, poynting out three Kingdoms in one sight …

Totall Discourse of the Rare Adventures of Long 19 Years

This version of the name has the superfluous word 'hill', but more importantly it draws attention to the 'field' element of the name, from the original Norse *fjall* (a mountain). Many longship lengths away in the Shetlands, *field* is the standard derivation from *fjall*. The name Goatfieldhill has a close similarity to the first-recorded mapping of the hill as Keadefell Hill, on Blaeu's map of 1654. The Gaelic version of the name is Gaoda-bheinn, and Thomas Pennant in 1772 wrote that:

> … Goatfield or Gaoit-bheinn, or the mountain of the winds, of a height equal to most of the Scottish alps …

Voyage to the Hebrides

Local Gaels of that time, that Pennant spoke to, had perhaps taken the Norse original of *geitar-fjall* (meaning goat fell – or more precisely nanny-goat fell), Gaelicised it into the similar-looking *gaoth*, wind, and translated *fjall* into *beinn*, but it probably co-existed with the older Norse name. Since English-speakers are linguistically more comfortable with Norse than Gaelic name-elements, they easily translated *geitar* into the similar-sounding and identical-meaning word goat.

But why did the Norsemen name only this one hill on the island? Probably because, as seafarers, it was a mountain critical for their navigation in the Firth of Clyde which it dominates, and the other hills were inconsequential to them.

Doubtless too their early wanderings in the adjacent Norse-named island glens had alerted them to the numerous wild goats watching them from the hill's skylines.

The Vikings were not the only warriors around: on the north coast of Arran at **An Scriadan** meaning The Scree, huge blocks of sandstone crashed down nearly 300 years ago with a tumult that was heard in Bute. The Sleeping Warrior had stirred a little in his sleep.

Barra

Barra in the Outer Hebrides is scattered with Norse names. Among them is the highest point **Heaval**, now called **Sheabhal**, 384m. The suffix -*val* is from the old Norse *fjall*, while the prefix may come from *hav*, the sea, or more simply and likely *hei*, a mound, particularly as it is pronounced **hay**:uval. Intriguingly, on Blaeu's 1654 map, the hill is named Whytefealt: the suffix is clearly *fjall*, as used elsewhere on this map, but while *whyte* could be the English colour, it may also come from Norse *hvitr*, white, and may refer to the outcrops of whitish gneiss on its slopes and at the very summit. Just along the ridge to the north is **Hartaval**, (now called **Thartabhal**), one of a Hebridean pair, the other being in north Skye.

In the west is **Ben Tangaval**, (now called **Tangabhal**), peak of the tongue peak, the Ben being a superfluous addition. Highland mountains elsewhere, such as **Meall na Teanga** above Loch Lochy, take their name from a protruding tongue shape and significantly, in Norway, *tunga*, a tongue, is a common place name element, while Iceland has literally dozens of Tungufjalls. **Ben Cliad** in the north appears to come from the Gaelic *cleit*, a rocky ridge, a word probably derived from Norse *klettr*.

Just off Barra lies Mingulay. It has a **MacPhee's Hill**, (now called **Cnoc Mic a' Phì**) said to be named after a boy who went with the rent collector there to collect Chief MacNeill's dues and then was abandoned by his adult 'colleagues' when they realised that the plague had struck among the islanders. It was fully a year before they judged it safe to return to collect him, and no doubt he spent much of this time on this hill scanning the horizon for the boat's return, like a Hebridean Robinson Crusoe.

Benbecula

Like **Eaval**, on nearby on North Uist, Benbecula's highest point **Rueval**, (now called **Ruabhal**) 124m, is an island of a hill in an encompassing sea of lochs, all inside the coastline. *Ru* is a Norse word meaning stream, and it may refer figuratively to this watery environment. On Thomson's travelling map of Scotland of 1821, the hill is marked as Benbecula Knock, clearly an outsider's Scots appellative.

Bute

This is probably the only Scottish island of any size whose highest hill bears a completely English name – **Windy Hill**, 278m. Nearby **Tòrran Turach**, meaning the turreted hillock, indicates that Gaelic was the old language of the island, so Windy Hill's name is not deep-rooted – indeed it was unnamed on the one inch 1899 Ordnance Survey map, and cannot be a simple translation. The only high hill in this north part of the island to be shown on Blaeu's Atlas of 1654 is a Drumnachany Hill, perhaps

ridge of the bog cotton or bog myrtle, and now a lost name for the ground between Rothesay and Kames which is 100m lower than Windy Hill.

The only other hill shown on Blaeu was Suychattan in the south, now **Suidhe Chatain**, the seat of the 6th century Saint Cattan, uncle of Saint Blane whose own eponymous hill is nearby (St Blane's Hill) – they kept hill names in the family, then. The hill above Rothesay Bay where the golf course now runs was said to be known as Canada Hill, where people gathered to watch their destitute friends and family sail off into emigrant exile across the Atlantic.

Canna

Canna in the Small Isles peaks at 211m on **Càrn a' Ghaill**, cairn of the stranger from *gall*, the Gaelic word for Norsemen. It also has a **Compass Hill**, so-named in English because of the iron in its dolerite rock 'drawing a ship's compass several points' – thus Gavin Maxwell in *Harpoon at a Venture*. **Sliabh Meadhonach** (middle hill) whose first name-element *sliabh* (unusual in Scotland) indicates early settlement from Ireland, where *slieve* is a common name for a big hill, as in Slieve Donard, the highest of the Mountains of Mourne.

Coll

Coll's high point of **Beinn Hogh** 103m, resembles in name the Norse word for a burial mound, *haugr*, often corrupted to *heog* or *ho*. **The Hoe** hill on Barra's Pabbay island is from the same word, and in present-day Norway *haug* means simply a summit. Another burial hill on the island is **Cnoc a' Chrochaire** the hangman's knoll, and it marks the exact spot where four men were hanged in 1596 for betraying island chief Neil Mor to the invading Duarts. Their bones were found interred on the hill top three centuries later.

Colonsay

Càrn an Eòin at 143m is cairn of the bird. An old book on the place names of Argyll translates it as John (Eoin)'s little cairn, but while birds are common in Gaelic hill names, personal names are rare. Besides there is some interesting circumstantial evidence in naturalist Fraser-Darling's 1960s natural history book *The Highlands and Islands*, which tells us:

> In gazing on these woods now (which were planted by an improving landowner) and noting Colonsay's wealth of small birds, we should remember the effort entailed in establishing these conditions

So the 'hill of the bird' is most fitting. Just offshore, the islet of Oronsay has a **Càrn Cùl ri Èirinn**, hill of the back to Ireland, thus sharing with Iona and Mull a name and a piece of the legend of Columba.

Eigg

The conventional explanations of the island's name are a hollow, or a notch, both translating from Gaelic, *lag* and *eag* respectively. The latter is more likely, from the nick of low ground between the higher ground to the south and north, although the

farm and bay named Laig lie on the west of this pass.

Both are quite inadequate to describe her most outstanding feature, the single giant rock molar of the Sgurr of Eigg soaring up to 393m almost from the sea. The peak, known variously as **An Sgùrr** (the rocky peak), the Scuir and the Scurr (it was Scur' Eigg on an 1825 estate map), was fortified by the Picts about two millennia ago, with a stone wall barricading access to the very summit, and a crannog on the loch just below it. It is obviously linked by name to the many *sgùrr* mountains in Skye and on the mainland.

An Sgùrr, Eigg. Literally The Sgùrr. See p52, [Generics, sgùrr]

Apart from An Sgùrr, and a couple of low *beinn* hills, Eigg's hill names are dominated by diminutives – appropriately since they lie in the Small Isles – and signified by the suffix -*an*: packed into its small area are a *càrnan*, a *beannan*, a *bidean*, a *cruachan*, a *corragan*, and a *dùnan*.

Fair Isle

Fair Isle's highest hill is **Ward Hill** 217m. This is from the Old Norse *varð* or *varða* meaning watch place, from where a watch could be kept in case of attack, or a hill with a beacon or cairn. The highest hills of Orkney and Hoy are also Ward Hills, and there are others in the Shetlands and in Caithness. These former Viking islands' Ward Hills are very functional names compared to their Gaelic cousins on the mainland, for unlike them the hills of the Northern Isles don't have colours or creatures in their names.

Foula

On the jacket of Sheila Gear's book about Foula, *Island West of the Sun*, is a photo of the whole island taken from a boat approaching from Shetland, as the first Vikings probably saw it. In it the hills of Foula dominate the island, and reflect the very pattern of the ocean, with waves of high ground swelling up from the west to break steeply down on the trough before the next rise.

Not surprisingly the names of these hills are Norse, changed little from the long-ship days except that *fjall* (a hill) has become *field*, as in Shetland. Above the long-ships' former beaching place is **Hamnafield** (harbour hill). Other field names include **Bodlafield** and **Codlafield**, respectively from *bollotr* (rounded hill) and *koddi* (small rounded hill, literally pillow), and **Nebifield** and **Tounafield**, from *nebb* (nose) and *tuva* (mound). The highest hill is **The Sneug**, 418m, from the Old Norse *knjukr* – found in modern Iceland hill names such as the stunning Gleradalsnjùkur – a steep conical mountain. The Norse *gnupr*, a peak, is found in **The Noup**: while the hill **Soberlie** may be a compound of three words – *saudhr*, *bol* and *hlit* – respectively sheep, hill and resting place. The only hill without direct Norse ancestry has that fine northern Scots word for small, in the **Peerie Hill**, although it too comes originally from Norse.

Gigha

Gigha's 103m **Creag Bhàn** is simply the white cliff, from the pale epidiorite rock that is exposed on the hill's top. And **Dùn Chiofaich** was the hill where the Celtic chief of that name fought Diarmaid over his wife, and was hurled from it to his death.

Harris

Harris is the hilly end of the Long Isle, its mountains sharing the accommodation with Lewis' peat bogs. Although it was an important part of the Vikings' southern empires, Harris was also later a centre of the Gaelic-speaking Lordship of the Isles, remaining a relative bastion of the language even today. So in its lonely hills are names Norse, names Gaelic, and names with parts from both languages like the double-barreled children of the aristocracy. Names like Stulaval, Husival Mòr and Beinn Dubh stake out this tripod.

In a moment we will look at more examples, but first the question, why should some be Norse, others Gaelic, and still others hybrid? One theory put forward by Alexander MacBain in his *Placenames, Highlands and Islands of Scotland* is that the Gaels, while applying Gaelic names to the spots immediately surrounding their coastal settlements, kept the older Norse names inland for the landmarks encountered during the summer movement to the hill pastures. However, in Harris settlements like Rodel have Norse names, as do the high peaks.

A more likely explanation for the mixture is that when the Gaels took over they retained the Norse names for both villages and hills, using Gaelic for their own new hamlets and for 'filling in' the gaps in the hills left by the Norsemen: most of the Gaelic names in Harris proper refer to the corries, noses, passes and shoulders rather

than the peaks. Some of the Gaelic hill names incorporate the Norse word *-val* as a suffix, from *fjall*, a peak.

The 'pure' Norse names include **Ullaval**, now called **Ulabhal**, (Ulli's or Ulfr's peak – he being the landowner), **Husival Mòr**, now called **Huiseabhal Mòr**, (big house peak), **Stulaval**, now called **Stuabhal**, (probably from *stol*, a shieling hut), **Uisgnaval Mòr**, now called **Uisgneabhal Mòr**, (oxen peak) and **Gillaval** (gully peak). **Oreval**, now called **Oireabhal**, has been translated as moorfowl mountain from *orri* – the bird now commonly known as a grouse – but in Orkney many old Norse names beginning with *or* signify 'of water'. On the other hand Orri is a common Norse nickname – based on the bird name – and he, like Ulli, could have been a landowner. These names are all very spare of description. This fits with mountain names in Norway, home of the Norse, where summits are named

> ... in relation to nearby valleys, farms, etc ... locations which were more important ... than the uninviting peaks.

Roineval, now called **Roineabhal**, was at the centre of a 1990s planning application to have its rock quarried and shipped away. It is a difficult name: there's a Norse word *ron* meaning a stream between two bodies of water, and the hill does stand guard above the rip-tided Sound of Harris – as does another Roneval above the narrow Sound of Eriskay, a few kilometres south, both waters running from Minch to Atlantic seas. Or, given that there are several Roineval hills in the Hebrides, it may be from *hraun*, a rough place or wilderness.

Hybrid Norse-Gaelic names include **Mullach** (summit) **an Langa**, possibly from the long Langadale valley below – but much more likely the *mullach* (summit) of An Langa (the long peak) – indicates that the Gaelic speakers came later than the Norse and incorporated their names into their own, rather than trying to 'paint over' them. **Clett Àrd** (properly, Cleit Àrd) combines Norse *klettr* (rock) and Gaelic *àrd* (high) and **Gillaval Glas** is the grey gully peak. The Gaelic adjectives for big and small, *mòr* and *beag*, are found as appendages in the likes of Tirga Mòr and Husival Beag.

Pure Gaelic names are rare in Harris proper, though common just across the border in Park, Lewis. The long summit ridge of the island's highest hill running south from Mullach an Langa to Clisham includes **Mulla fo-thuath** and **Mulla fo-dheas** literally north and south summit: such geographic directions are very unusual in Gaelic names. Also unusual in Gaelic use are nearby **Sgaoth Ìosal** and **Sgaoth Àrd** – literally the low and high steep hills (from *sgoth*, steep rock or high hill) – **Mullach an Rùisg** (peeled summit, referring to the peat turfs that 'peel' easily off it), and **Màs Garbh** rocky bottom. Just over the border in Lewis is **Rapaire** dividing hill, from Norse *hreppa*, although it could conceivably be from the Norse *reip*, a rope (made from heather).

But what of **Clisham**, now called **An Clisham**, Harris' highest hill at 799m. Being the highest, it surely should be a Norse name in tune with its neighbours, and a possible explanation could involve a prefix *klif* meaning a cliff or rocky area, pronounced klee as in Sutherland's **Ben Klibreck**. The suffix could be from *hamarr*, a rocky outcrop or hillside, a common name in Norway's hills. Clisham could then simply be rocky cliff, which is a fairly accurate description of its geography. It may

have had an older name, because on Blaeu's 1654 map of Harris there's a summit named Bin Ostrafeald, clearly the Gaelic *beinn* preceding Norse *austur fjall*, eastern peak: no hill bears that name today, and although Blaeu's map is very distorted (in covering contorted topography!), it must have referred to a big hill among Harris' finest.

Hoy

Since 1966 when the BBC carried live coverage of the second ascent of the Old Man of Hoy, this famous sea-stack has become the instantly recognisable symbol of Hoy, indeed of Orkney itself. Yet overshadowing the Old Man rises St John's Head, a cliff over twice the Old Man's height at 335m. The endless lines of Atlantic breakers that thump ashore at its feet are paralleled in the lines of sandstone strata that climb skywards up the cliff, with tiny wheeling specks of white to give it perspective. So for the Vikings who discovered Hoy some time before the BBC, the island was simply *ha-ey* or high island. Among the shoals of the Orkney Islands, Hoy looms humped like a whale.

Its highest point is neither the Old Man – a common term for a Scottish sea-stack – nor the cliff, but **Ward Hill** further inland, at 479m. On Blaeu's map of 1654 it was Warth Hill, so its name comes from the Old Norse *varða* meaning a cairn, ward, guard or watch, where lookouts were probably posted in times of trouble. Standing where it does with a splendid view over the sheltered anchorage of Scapa Flow, sea-heart of the Orkneys, and with a clear view to the south over the Pentland Firth where lived their Pictish enemies, its situation fully merits its name.

Other Hoy heights include **Cuilags** (behind St John's Head), the **Knap of Trowieglen** (from the Norse *gnipa*, a peak) and **Withi Gill** (from Norse *hvitr*, white, and *gil*, a gully).

Iona

The many thousands of pilgrims who visit this lovely island, a splash of white sand and green grass in a turquoise sea, take away abiding memories of it. But it is unlikely that these would include the name of the island's highest hill, for it only rises to 101m. However, its name, simply **An Dùn** or sometimes **Dùn Ì**, (the fort of Iona) suggests a past importance, for *dùn* is a generic Gaelic name indicating the site of a prehistoric fort, on a hill top used as a defensive site. At one point in Scotland's history there were nearly 1500 such hill-forts in use.

The more usual association between Iona, home of St Columba, and peace, was made at a later date. Prior to Columba there was supposedly a colony of Druids here, and the Druidic sun circle symbol which they worshipped is incorporated into the Celtic cross in front of the Abbey. However, **Cnoc Druidean** is the knoll of starlings (not the Druids!), while Christianity is reflected in **Cnoc an Aingeil**, the Hill of the Angels, where Columba supposedly met the heavenly visitors, and the hill whose name **Càrn Cùl ri Èirinn**, hill of the back to Ireland, refers to the saint's determination to turn his back on his homeland until he'd converted the Scots to Christianity. Colonsay also has such a hill, as does Mull – and Blaeu's 1654 map shows the latter to be partnered by Karn culri Allabyn, hill of the back to Scotland, just east of Ben

More. **Tòrr an Aba** the small hillock beside the Abbey, is the knoll of the abbot, where Columba is said to have had his cell. The island's other named hill **Druim an Aoineidh** means the ridge of the steep rocky brae, a name of prosaic geography beside the romantic history of its neighbours.

Iona's hill names are instructive in what we have lost. The Ordnance Survey 1:25000 map shows ten hill names. A 1934 book *Iona Past and Present* by local authors A. and E.Ritchie, listed 106 hill names known to the Gaelic-speaking islanders, many of them *cnocan*. Similar disparities between mapped hill and landscape names and those known to local speakers, in areas such as Lewis, confirm that map records are a mere selection of the many given names.

Islay

Overshadowed in mountain terms by its neighbour Jura and her Paps, Islay is chiefly known for its whisky industry, and in recent years for its peat bogs, fought over by distillers and conservationists. Its rolling landscape does however rise to 491m in **Beinn Bheigier**. This name is rather obscure, the Gaelic dictionary giving no exact equivalent, and the nearest are three rather uncomplimentary words, *baghaire*, a fool, *bagaire*, a glutton or fat man, and *baigear*, a beggar. One modern dictionary has a rarely-used word, clearly based on English, meaning baker.

An explanation has been suggested from Blaeu's 17th century map on which there is a Bin Vicar, for Beinn Bheigier may be *Beinn a' Bhiocair*, the vicar's mountain - one Brian Vicar Mackay was granted land on Islay in the 15th century. However, Ballivicar is over a dozen kilometres away from the hill, and vicars are more usually known as ministers or priests in Gaeldom. Blaeu's map of Scotland is generally quite accurate in locations, when compared with modern maps, but Islay seems to be exceptional with big distortions. It also shows the apparently largest hill, indicated by the size of the line engraving, as Cor Bin, and two other hills Scor Creigach and Bin Leargy which do not appear on other modern or historical maps of Islay; on the other hand on modern maps there's a **Corra-Bheinn**, a **Crackaig Hill** and a An Leargan slope just across the sound, in *Jura*, indicating that Dutch map-maker Blaeu may have got confused by his main source Pont's hand-drawn manuscripts, the originals of which don't survive.

Glas Bheinn, grey hill, stands today where Cor Bin stood in Blaeu, and Beinn Bheigier is its slightly-higher southern neighbour, whereas Blaeu's Bin Vicar is to the north. Blaeu's other mystery hill Bin Rownidal is the modern **Beinn Bhreac**, its location confirmed by more accurate early 19th century maps by Langlands and Thomson as Ben Ronastill; and for both of them, **Beinn na Caillich** is the other significant hill in east Islay.

At the northern tip of Islay rises **Sgarbh Breac**, literally the speckled cormorant, a bird which appears in hill names as a very limited edition, only in Islay and in Harris. To the west is its pair, **Sgarbh Dubh** (dark), and at the very northernmost point, below a knoll is Sgarbh Beag (small). Clearly the names were given by fishermen off the coast. Another bird of the sea appears in **Sgòrr nam Faoileann** (common gull) on the east coast. The rather odd-sounding name of **Beinn Tart a' Mhill** (pronounced *vill*) in the west is possibly a *fjall* name, because Islay has a fair number of Norse place names.

Jura

Like a rock band's players the higher hills of this island are best-known by their group name, and only the keenest fan could name the individuals. The famous **Paps of Jura**, the three distinctive swellings above the horizontal sea-lines, are a landmark from many summits of the south and west Highlands. The name was originally given by sailors, for whom they were a clear landmark in the south-western coastal waters, likening them to *paps*, the old Scots word for breasts. The earthy mariners' name was perhaps too much for the author of *The Placenames of Scotland*, the Reverend J.B.Johnston, who could only bring himself to say of them that:

> They are so-called from their shape.

Blaeu's map of 1654 labels them as the The Papes of Ijura, while Martin Martin got the spelling closer to modern usage in his 1703 book *A Description of the Western Isles:*

> There are four hills of approximately equal height, of which the two high-est are well known to seafaring men by the name of the Paps of Jurah.

In fact there are only *three* sizeable hills of roughly equal height – the next highest being 240 metres lower – and *all* three of them are now collectively known as The Paps, in spite of the obvious anatomical absurdity of such a number. A 20th century poem by Andrew Young gives the correct count:

> Before I crossed the Sound,

Màm, Mull and Medicine

The Gaelic word *màm* normally means a breast. Naturally then, it is used in hill names, from their shape: *cìoch* (also meaning breast or nipple) is used for more pointed or nippled hills, while *màm* describes more rounded tops. (In French the hill-word *mamelon* has the same *double entendre*). But *màm* can also mean a pass or gap between hills, as it were the negative image of the rounded peak, probably from the cleavage-like position between two breasts. Whilst *bealach* is the usual Gaelic word for a pass, in some areas like Knoydart most passes are *màm* – Màm Barrisdale and Màm Meadail, for example, both called after the Norse-named glens (*dalr*) below them.

There are around 70 occurrences of *màm*, mainly in the south-western seaboard and Mull areas, and the vast majority are passes not peaks. Of the few that are peaks, Mull has **Fionna Mhàm** (fair or pale breast), Morvern has **Màm a' Chullaich** (boar) and Lochaber has **Sgùrr a' Mhàim** although both peaks' names may well refer to the pass just below the summit: **Càrn a' Mhàim** in the Cairngorms similarly comes from the famous pass it guards, the Làirig Ghru. Also in Lochaber is **Màm nan Gualainn**, *màm* of the shoulder, really a parallel outlier of the **Mamores**, whose range name, probably *màm mòr*, comes from their

Storm-shattered and sharp-edged,
These breasts rise soft and round,
Not two but three.

What of their individual names? The highest, and most central peak, is **Beinn an Òir**, hill of gold. In the absence of legends connecting this with some treasure trove, it most likely gets this name from the amount of the mineral iron pyrites, better known as Fool's Gold, found both here and on Islay. The name is old-established, for on Blaeu's 17th century map it appears as Bin na Noir, and Dean Monro, last Catholic bishop of the Isles, referred to it as Binannoyre a century earlier. A scar on the hill running from shoreline to skyline is **Sgrìob na Cailleach**, the witch's scrape, where she is said to have gashed the hill with her broomstick in an aerial hit-and-run: more prosaically, it is simply a volcanic dyke; Blaeu mapped the knoll atop this, **Cnoc na Sgrìoba**, as Bin na Kailly.

To its west, above the narrows of the Sound of Islay, lies **Beinn a' Chaolais**, peak at the narrows. To the east is **Beinn Shiantaidh**, consecrated or holy peak, locally A' Bheinn Sheunta: this after all is not far from Iona and the seaborne missionary invasions from Ireland. Jura was originally known in Gaelic as An t-Eilean Ban, the blessed or holy isle. There is another holy peak, **Ben Hiant** in Ardnamurchan.

There probably was an earlier Norse name for the Paps, now lost – how could they not have named such distinctive sailors' landmarks? In the island's north, Norse names like Rainberg Mòr (*bjerg*, a precipice or hill) and Scrinadle (perhaps *skrið dalr*, scree glen) have a Viking twang, while **Brat Bheinn**, **Corra Bheinn** (steep hill) and

skyline shape.

There is a nice tradition, related in Carmichael's *Carmina Gadelica*, that in Mull, Morar and district, a cure for swellings on the body involved passing iron blades over the victim then either pointing it at *màm* hills, or invoking them, so as to transfer the sickness from human to hill. The healer would intone 'This be on the Màm of Doire Dubhaig' and so on. In some areas the cure involved swinging an axe down to arrest it just above the patient's swellings, before invoking the hills – this must have involved a most plausible bedside manner on the part of the healer – don't try this at home, reader.

The tradition, described in *The Magnificent Charm of the Màm* by Raghnall MacilleDhuibh in an article in the West Highland Free Press, suggests there are 12 Mull hills called Màm, used in the therapy, which may have been true in the past but there are only a couple today: and of the 27 then said to lie in the Mull – Jura – Islay area, visible from Colonsay, only two are identifiable on maps today, and one is a pass. Knoydart is also an area with several *màm* spots, and nine were used in the 'cures' there, many of which are still recognisable, like Màm Uchd and Màm Barrisdale.

Staon Bheinn indicate perhaps the historical influence of Norse word order for place names with generic noun *beinn* following the specific, the reverse of the standard Gaelic pattern.

The west coast and the islands have nine hills called Corra or Cora Bheinn or Corrach Bheinn: Maclennan's Gaelic dictionary says the full name means steep or pointed mountain, which most of the examples indeed are, while W.J.Watson claims that in the Monadh Liath area *cor* means a rounded hill. The highest is **Corra-Bheinn** on Mull, the lowest being a steep-sided shoulder of **Easaval** or **Easabhal** in South Uist.

Lewis

Lewis' highest peak is not **Beinn Mhòr**, big mountain, at 571m but the slightly higher **Mealisval**, now called **Mealaisbhal**. The -*val* ending is the standard outer isles' form of *fjall*, the old Norse for hill or mountain. And while there is also a Norse word *meal* meaning a sandbank, or *melr*, grassy, the Gaelic *meall*, a hill, is the more likely candidate for the first part, producing the meaning 'lumpy hill hill'. Similarly the mountain **Kearnaval**, now called **Cearnabhal**, a few kilometres away is certainly Càrn-fjall, also a tautological 'rocky hill hill'.

In the Park district around Beinn Mhòr, Gaelic rules the tops. There is **Càrn Bàn** (white cairn), **Sìdhean an Airgid** (fairy hill of silver), **Monadh Mòr** (big mountain) and **Crionaig** (from *grionaig*, green grazing land). Also in southern Lewis, near the boundary with Harris (where Norse names dominate the hills), are **Tahaval**, now called Tahabhal, and **Cracaval**, now called **Cracabhal**, (perhaps from *kraku*, a stake), as well as Gaelic names like **Beinn a' Bhoth** (bothy mountain).

Although the rest of Lewis to the north was firmly under Norse control for many years they must have paid scant regard to the lowly hills that struggle like shapeless prehistoric animals from out of the blanket peat bogs that cover Lewis. It was left to the later Gaels to name them, chief among them being **Beinn Mholach**, rough or hairy hill. Interestingly, when Blaeu produced his Atlas in 1654, sea navigation was still the dominant transport in the isles, and hence hills as landmarks were vital, and his map picks out relatively low hills that nevertheless functioned as markers – Bin Mournaidgh, Bin Parvas, Bin Etisfeald, and Bin Rovafeald, all less than 300m, but important from the Minch. Respectively these peaks are nowadays known as **Mùirneag**, **Beinn Bharabhais**, **Eitseal** and **Ròineabahal**, all but the first certainly being Norse names. In Gaelic *mùirneag* is a woman, variously a cheerful, tender or beloved woman, though why this 248m hill should be the focus of Lewismen's desire is obscure – perhaps, being the only solid ground in a vast lochan-studded bog, it represented metaphorically the ideal woman in their life.

Mull

Ben More, in Gaelic Beinn Mhòr, 965m, is sometimes cursed by lazier Munro-baggers for it is now the only Munro requiring a ferry trip. Others hold it in more affection. An anonymous Gaelic poet wrote:

> ... Straths grass-tawny, stepping waterfalls,
> And mighty Ben More of the eagles, set high over all

Waterfalls do step over the staircased layers of lava that form the island's base; and eagles nesting on nearby Creag na h-Iolaire (crag of the eagle), have long soared above the hills.

The name Ben More simply means big mountain, from its relative size on the island, and in contrast to the neighbouring **Beinn Fhada**, long mountain. A subsidiary summit is called **A' Chìoch**, the breast, for it tapers smoothly to a point, without the main peak's shoulders.

The island is known in Gaelic as Muile nam Mòr-bheann, Mull of the big mountains, and there are many other sizeable hills on it – no other Munros, but one Corbett, **Dùn dà Gaoithe**, fort of two winds or maybe windy fort, seven Grahams and a further 18 Marilyns. Many have straightforward names – **Ben Buie** (yellow), **Creach Bheinn** (boundary), **Cruach Choireadail** (heap of the Coire Adail), and **Sgùrr Dearg** (red) – although it is but one of a couple of *sgùrr* on the island.

Beinn Talaidh however, which used to be a Corbett before demotion to Graham, is more difficult: it appears on Blaeu's 1654 map as Bin Tallow, and 19th century evidence in the Ordnance Gazetteer suggests it is Beinn an t-Seallaidh (pronounced in Gaelic with the *s* silent), mountain of the view or outlook, which it certainly has being central to the island's hilly north. The explanation is certainly sounder than one earlier translation as Valhalla hill – indeed the Norse seemed to have only left one hill name in Mull, **Gometra**, the high point of its eponymous island off the west coast. Beinn Talaidh was known to 19th century sailors as Sugarloaf, from its shape. Its neighbour **Beinn na Duatharach** is the hill of murkiness or mystery, probably referring to the weather on it – Blaeu's spelling of Bin Dountagek was perhaps the mystery, although probably that was his geographically displaced representation of Dùn da Gaoithe.

Blaeu's map has some other mysteries in Mull. On the long southern peninsula he has mapped Pin Binkorran and Pinnin Morie, and comparison with the present seems to indicate **Beinn Chreagach** 377m and Binnein Ghorrie (a cliff top height circa 300m): to an English-speaking ear (so to speak) the Gaelic *b* of *beinn* or *binnein* can sound like a *p*, as shown in west Ireland where the dozen *beinn* mountains above Galway Bay are known as The Twelve Pins of Connemara. For some reason Mull has nine Beinn Chreagachs (rocky hill) out of only 12 examples in Scotland.

Another pair of names difficult to tie down to present hills lie just south of Ben More (Bin Moir) on Blaeu's map. These are Karn culri Erin and Karn culri Allabyn, the cairns respectively of the back to Ireland (**Càrn Cùl ri Eirinn**) and the back to Scotland (Càrn Cùl ri Albainn). The former is shown as a hill with a large cross on top, the latter is less clear. The former name also exists in Iona, where it is linked to Saint Columba who, on climbing this hill and 'finding he could no longer see his beloved country, had the cairn erected'. Another version holds that he determined to turn his back on Ireland until he'd converted the Scots to Christianity. And another hill of this name is found on Colonsay's Oronsay.

Charles Maclean's *The Isle of Mull – Place-names* identifies the Càrn Cùl ri Albainn as the pass between Ben More and Tòrr na h-Uamha, at 332m, but not the Erin hill

which is clearly more significant on Blaeu's map: if the former is correctly positioned, then the Càrn Cùl ri Èirinn is probably the hill now known as **Cruachan Dearg** (red stack). At 704m it is apparently the same height as the adjacent **Corra-Bheinn** (steep hill), and one might speculate as to whether they were the pair involved. There *is* a hill of the cross, **Beinn na Croise**, on Mull, but it is eight kilometres south of this, and much lower.

Orkney

The mainland of Orkney offers little challenge in height to its offshore island Hoy, whose Ward Hill rises to 480m. Yet the main isle's highest hill at 268m is also **Ward Hill**, a name it shares with others on Shetland, Foula and the mainland. From the Norse *varða*, it means a guard or beacon hill, and like Hoy's Ward Hill it stands above Scapa Flow, the great sea anchorage between these two watchful island hills.

Most Orkney names of farms and villages are of Norse origin, which makes the relative absence of Norse names on the hills rather odd. Apart from Ward Hill itself and **Vestra Fiold** (from *vestr fjall*, west hill) in the north-west, the remaining eminences usually end in the English *hill*, as in **Starling Hill**, **Wideford Hill** and **Hill of Miffia** (mid-fell), indicating a later naming by Scots-speaking immigrants.

After Norway's mountains the Orkney hills were as molehills to the Vikings and they would barely have rated them, except for the highest as watchtowers. The modern use for Orkney's hills, for telecommunications masts and the prototype windpower generator on **Burgar Hill** (from *bjerg*, a precipice), make them distinctive to our eyes, while to the Norsemen one Ward Hill was enough for the whole island.

Raasay

Raasay the roe-deer island rises to 443m in **Dùn Caan** (properly Dùn Cana). A flat-topped hill, it had the doubtful distinction of being Highland-danced upon by Boswell in the course of his journey at the heels of the great Dr Johnson. Boswell recorded that the summit was a landmark to sailors who knew it as **Raasay's Cap** (probably because the clouds collected on it to form a bonnet).

While the word *dùn* signifies a hill-fort, the only history Boswell afforded us was his report of the local legend of the entrapment near the top of a maiden-eating sea-horse. Martin Martin, 16th century traveller, was told by locals that it was named after one Canne, cousin of a Danish king, a story backed by McFarlane's Geographical Manuscripts linking its name to Cannus 'whom they relate to be Denmark's son' – Denmark in this context meaning Norse or Viking. There was also a 7th century Celtic prince, Cana Mac Gartnain. His first name is close, too, to the proper Gaelic name for the hill, Dùn Cana, and it may well have been his fort, particularly as the whole name reflects Gaelic not Norse word order. Certainly it is the ideal site, its flat top ringed on three sides by short but steep cliffs.

Rum

Rum's highest range, like Skye's, is called the **Cuillin**, although it is not clear whether one name imitated the other or whether they were both named

independently. It is almost certainly from the Norse *kiolen*, a word still in use in Norway for a rocky mountain range, which Rum's group and Skye's clearly are. But unlike Skye's Cuillin the Rum Cuillin's *individual* peaks' names are apparently largely of Old Norse rather than Gaelic origin, probably because on Rum the individual peaks are quite distinct from each other, with large drops in between. Askival and Allival, Trollaval and Barkeval, Ainshval and Orval, trip off the tongue like characters entering Edvard Grieg's *Hall of the Mountain King*. What does each have to say for itself?

The -*val* suffix is the Hebridean form of the main Norse word for mountain, *fjall*. **Askival**, the foremost at 811m, is probably from *askr* meaning ashwood but used figuratively for a spear, a name apt both for its pointed form and for the minds of the warrior-namers. One writer has suggested the name is from *hoska*, dangerous, but to a seafaring race, daily facing a watery fate and who had no reason to venture up mountains, the characterisation would be quite inept. And in Sutherland the same word *askr* is the root of the hill name **Asc-na Grèine** (spear of the sun), from the same pointed shape.

Hallival (previously Allival) is probably from the Norse *hallr*, a slope or ledge. Other suggestions have included *hali*, a wild beast's den, and another writer goes for *all*, an eel, from the sinuous shape of the ridge, but this is fanciful, implying either an aerial vision or the use of maps. The prime candidate for the origin of Hallival must indeed be the ledge mountain, very accurate because, as the old Scottish Mountaineering Club guidebook puts it;

> ... The conspicuous **escarpments** [*my* emphasis – especially as this author nearly came to grief on them] which run nearly round the summit of Allival, except on the south, are of allivalite, a pale variety of gabbro

Hallival thus joins Skye's **Marsco** (home of marscoite granite) and **Cairn Gorm** as one of the few peaks to have rocks named after them. And over at the western tip of this diamond-shaped island, **Bloodstone Hill** also has a name connected with minerals. Standing poised above plunging screes and cliffs, it used to be quarried for the bloodstones or carnelians on its north side, and the beach far below is stained with them. Bloodstone is a green rock, spotted with the red mineral jasper, and was used to make jewellery. Blaeu's 1654 map shows just two peaks on the island, Bin Moir (big mountain – certainly the Cuillin massif) and Bin Oir, which in Gaelic would be gold hill, but is probably an error for **Orval**, the highest peak outwith the Cuillin.

Trollaval is sometimes shown on maps as Trallval, but the former is surely the happier sounding. The trolls, goblins or giants of Norse legend, were skilled metal workers living in the mountains, occasionally sallying forth to steal from humans. Dwarves in some legends, giants in others, craggy peaks like Trollaval could surely accommodate all sizes. Now, high on this mountain are the burrows of the shearwater, a bird whose night-time shrieks and mutterings may have suggested the subterranean sounds of trolls to the Vikings. The birds' habit of flying unseen in and out of its nesting area under cover of darkness would add to the mystery of the noises. Further north but still in Viking territory another shearwaters' breeding area on the Faroes bears the name Trollkarp. In Iceland trolls are common in hill names;

Trollfjall near Akureyri, for instance, is named from the line-up of weird rocky pinnacles above its eastern slopes; and the famous rock wall, the Trollveggen in Norway's Romsdal, is similarly decorated atop its cliffs.

Barkeval is from *bjarg*, a precipice, for its southern slopes are particularly broken up by cliffs. **Ainshval** is perhaps from *ass*, a rocky ridge, **Orval** is probably the water peak (or possibly Orri's peak, as on Harris' **Oreval**) and **Ruinisval** from *hruna*, a heap of rocks.

As on Harris and Skye the lower peaks and passes have become the crumbs picked up by Gaelic to name, as in **Meall Breac** and **Mullach Mòr** (respectively speckled hill and the big summit) to the north. One commercial map of these islands carries alternative 'Gaelic' names for the main peaks: for Hallival there is Ailbe Meall (from *ailbh*, rock, and *meall*, hill); for Askival there is Aisge Meall (*aisgeir*, rocky mountain hill); Ais Meall (hill hill) for Ainshval and Tràill Meall (drudge hill) for Trollaval, complete the list of optional names. But these place names just do not ring true. They are out of line with the dominant Norse pattern of the northern Hebrides, with the pronunciation of the names, and their Gaelic 'meanings' tenuous.

St Kilda

The highest point of these savage ocean-whipped rocks is **Conachair**. It has been interpreted as 'the coming together of the hills', but Gaelic dictionaries tells us that a conachair is 'a sick person who neither gets better nor worse'! Alternatively it means simply 'uproar', an apt description of the continual racket as ocean, winds and gannets wheel around this defiant rock. However, it is most likely to be the 'place of folds', from con- and cra. This explanation would fit with its land-locked cousin, **Creag Chonochair** in Glen Spean. The second biggest island is Boreray, and its high point is **Mullach an Eilein**. Literally this is just the summit of the island, and such a put-down name seems to be the fate of several small islands lying off larger ones – Arran's Holy Isle has **Mullach Mòr** (big), Skye's Scalpay has **Mullach na Càrn**, summit of the hill, and the largest of the Shiant Islands off Lewis, has **Mullach Buidhe** (yellow). Cruach, a heap, is another fate of these runts – off Jura's north tip, above the awesome Corrievreckan whirlpool, the island of Scarba is topped by **Cruach Scarba** – not much of a name for a hill over 400m high.

Scarp

Lying off Harris' west coast, its peak **Sròn Romul**, 308m, combines the Gaelic *sròn*, a nose or headland, with Romul, a Norse personal name, for the Vikings quite often left their own first names on a place.

Seil

Seil island is famed chiefly for the hump-backed bridge that leads onto it from the mainland, over a sea-channel as wide as a small river, and given away only by the tresses of seaweed: it is known as the Bridge over the Atlantic. This tendency to exaggeration is complemented by its hill **Meall a' Chaise** struggling to reach all of 146m and meaning hill of steepness.

Shetland

Shetland's hills are a tale of 'wards and all', for scattered across the island group are names like **Ward of Scousburgh** (one of its tops mapped by Blaeu 1654 as Russafealt Hill, *russa fjall*), **Ward of Bressay** and several plain **Ward Hills**. They derive from the Old Norse *varð* meaning watch place, from where a watch could be kept in case of attack, or *varða*, a watch hill with a beacon or cairn for travellers and seafarers. One pair of these hills, originally called Vordeld, with ruins of watchtowers on top, are commonly called the Vord Hills or – lamented Danish writer Jakobsen – as the 'Wart of … ' by 'the younger generation'. On these seafaring islands the need for a high vantage point to spy the fishing boats in time of storm, or the enemy in time of trouble, would have been essential, and hence the many Ward Hills here, as in Orkney and Fair Isle. In the Shetlands there are over 30 such hills, appearing in various guises such as Ward or Vord or Virda.

However, the highest point in these isles is not a ward hill but **Ronas Hill**, 449m, probably from *hraun* meaning rocky – in 1654, Blaeu mapped it as Renisfelt Hill, the suffix *-felt* being *fjall*. Although it also had watchtowers on top like the ward hills, what makes it distinctive is the collection of large pink granite boulders scattered all over the top, through which you pick your way. In its role as a landmark it can be seen from the fishing boats 50 kilometres out over the Bank Haaf, with Ronas Hill

> … sitting like a kishie (peat basket) upo da water.

In the 19th century they sometimes called it the Bloberg or Blaberg (*bla bjarg*, blue rocky hill), since hills seen from such a distance appear blue.

The use of the English word *hill* (in Ronas Hill and Ward Hill) in this Norse heartland may seem peculiar, and there are many other eminences called Hill of … as in **Hill of Deepdale** or **Hill of Fitch**. Evidence suggests that these generally lower hills were named later, in the 16th century, by Scots incomers, filling in the gaps left by the Norse names which focussed only on the highest ground. Another apparently English name, *field*, is not what it seems but in fact the Shetland version of the Norse *fjall*, a peak: **Scalla Field**, the skull or bald-headed fell, is a nice description of this wind-scoured pate, **Hoo Field** is high fell, and **Hamari Field** is from *hamarr*, a rocky outcrop.

Other Norse hill-words are found in the **Beorgs of Skelberry** (from *bjerg*, a precipice or hill), **Lamb Hoga** and **The Heog** (from *heog*, a hillock or burial mound), and **The Neap** on Unst (from *gnipa*, a peak). **The Compass** Hill near Sumburgh airport has nothing to do with air navigation, but is a corrupted form of *kambr*, a ridge or mound: **Hoo Kame** and **The Kames** are more faithful to the original.

On an island which lived by the sea and for whose seamen landmarks were vital, the southern headland **The Ords**, rising 283m, would be significant. Its name comes from Norse *urð*, a heap of stone, and it may be related to the Gaelic *òrd* meaning a steep rounded hill.

Skye

Skye is so important to Scottish mountaineering that in previous editions of their

district guidebook series, the Scottish Mountaineering Club had one volume titled *The Islands of Scotland*, and a separate one for Skye alone. This is mainly to do with the significance of the island's Cuillin for both rock-climbing and walking, but is also a reflection of the size and hilliness of the whole island. Skye is also fascinating for its place names, as a point where the powerful tides of Norse and Gaelic names come swirling together – more Gaelic than the Outer Hebrides, but more Norse than the mainland.

The Cuillin

The Cuillin is possibly the most famous mountain range in Scotland. This spectacular rocky horseshoe has almost as many spellings of its name as it has separate peaks. It can be properly singular or incorrectly plural (The Cuillins), and has been spelt Coolin, Cuillin, Culinn, Culen, Cullen, Cullin, Cuilfhionn, Cuidhean, Cuilian, Cuilluelun, Culluelun, Gulluin, Quillen, Quillin and Cuchullin; the first two are in most general English use today. In Gaelic the range is An Cuilfhionn or An Culthionn, the Cuillin.

There is a tradition that the range is named after Cùil Fhionn, the corner or hiding place of Fingal, Celtic hero and leader of the Fingalians, who pops up in several places in Scotland. Indeed, above Portree, stands Suidh' Fhinn, his seat, a knoll on the shoulder of **Beinn na Grèine**, mountain of the sun, where Fingal is said to have sat watching his warriors hunting in Glen Varragill below. Another stronger tradition attributes the range's name to Cuchullin, an Ossianic hero who is reputed to have built a fort at Dunscaith near Loch Eishort and kept the Norse at bay. In 1772 traveller Thomas Pennant wrote, of the view from **Beinn na Caillich**:

> Quillin, mountain of Cuchullin, like its hero stood like a hill that catches the clouds of heaven.

Note that he clearly regards the range as one mountain, a perception which we'll see is important to the name. A few decades later came Sir Walter Scott, for whom romantic legend was the very stuff of historical analysis. He wrote:

> Coolin the ridge, as bards proclaim,
> From old Cuchullin, chief of fame

Scott's influence almost single-handedly started the Scottish tourist industry, and in 1823 a publication entitled *Scottish Tourist and Traveller* proclaimed:

> ... the gloomy mountains of Cuthallia [sic] that rise in majestic grandeur ... being the ground over which the mighty hero of the Celtic bard, whose name they bear, often pursued the clan.

Scott's works were so influential in shaping public opinion that even a level-headed man of science, the geologist J.D.Forbes, could publish a paper in 1845 titled *On the Topography and Geology of the Cuchullin Hills*. If this Ossianic tradition were true (and many were later shown to have been invented), it would make the range unique in Scotland in being named after a historical character or legend, and would not accord well with island naming traditions.

Attempts at linking the name to the Gaelic have included Thomas Pennant's 'narrow dark hollow' (presumably from *caol*, narrows, as in Kyle of Lochalsh), and another writer who took the meaning to be 'fine corner' (from *cuil*, a corner). But the main Gaelic claim is for *cuilionn-mara*, the sea-holly whose blue flowers' outline the jagged peaks are said to resemble; or simply *cuilionn*, the prickly holly-tree itself. In 1897 Professor Norman Collie – not a native Gaelic speaker – wrote an article in the Scottish Mountaineering Club Journal on the range entitled *A' Chuilionn*, thus staking its claim ... but getting its gender wrong in the process (it should be An Cuilionn). There are a few holly-trees in the vicinity of Glen Brittle, and the Cuillin's jagged outline could spark off in the mind the image of a holly wreath: and there are parallels, for there is a **Meall a' Chuilinn** near Strontian on the west coast some 75 kilometres distant. In an earlier Scottish Mountaineering Club guidebook to the island, the holly's claim to the name is supported with the statement that

> ... the Highlanders nearly always name their places from their appearance or local peculiarity ...

While this is true in general, other Gaelic mountain names relating to trees or flora do not come from their *appearance*. The many hills with a tree name – usually birch, pine or rowan – refer to specimens growing there. Holly rarely gets a mention in hill names, because unlike the Scots pines and the rowans, it is rare to find an isolated and therefore distinctive specimen growing alone in a corrie. Also, when a mountain is named after a tree, it is invariably prefixed by one of the Gaelic hill-words like *beinn* or *meall*. So the case for holly is not very strong, although we can't rule out the Gaels calling it their holly-peak using *their* nearest word to the Old Norse name that we're about to meet.

Irish place name research has established that the word *cuilleann* means a steep or very steep slope, which might seem appropriate. However the element does not appear to be used for mountain names, but rather for settlements at the foot, like Kilcullen in County Kildare. The only instances I can find in Scotland are the hamlet of Gualachulain (*guala*, shoulder) at the foot of **Beinn Trilleachan**'s long steep slopes, and **Stronchullin Hill** near Ardentinny on Loch Long.

Colin Phillip, in a 1916 volume of the Scottish Mountaineering Club Journal, referred to two gentlemen with whom he discussed the name: the first a Welshman who said to him 'We have an old Celtic word *coolin* meaning worthless' – apt enough for its stony wastes, but not a word in my Welsh dictionary; the second, a Dane, suggested that the name might be Old Norse, since (he said) *kjolen* meant high rocks. The Dane is probably right, for there are several reasons why the Norse connection is the most likely.

Firstly, there is the fact that almost all the main hill names in Skye are Norse, sometimes with the Gaelic word *beinn* prefixed – from **Ben Volovaig** in the north to **Ben Cleat** in the south, from **Hartaval** and **The Storr** in the east to Healaval and **Ben Idrigill** in the west. For a seafaring people like the Vikings the hills' function as landmarks was all-important, which is why they identified and named all the high points on Skye, Rum and the Outer Hebrides. And since the range – or from the maritime

Mountains named by mountaineers

The vast majority of hills in Scotland were named by local people, Gaelic or Scots speakers, before the 19th century and prior to the arrival of the Ordnance Survey. This was true in most of Europe, a continent with long linguistic traditions, but contrasts with North America and Australasia where the native languages were ignored or had been exterminated by the colonists, who gave their own English names instead. We should be grateful our highest peaks aren't called Mount McKinley, Cook or Kosciusko, and be wary in case names like The Cobbler and The Ben (used by climbers) supplant the real name.

Scottish mountaineering, in the sense of climbing hills for pleasure rather than necessity, came after the Ordnance Survey had set the names in concrete, or at least on paper. The main way climbers got mentioned for posterity was through naming a rock route – from the early pioneers we have Naismith's Route, Raeburn's Buttress, Collie's Ledge and the like. But there are a few peaks named after or by mountaineers, exclusively in the Cuillin of Skye. This is not surprising in that its rocks provided one of the great tests of Scottish rock, but also because only the main peaks in the range had been named locally, leaving many of the jagged spires in between virgin at least in nomenclature.

The highest peak in Skye, **Sgùrr Alasdair** was retrospectively named in honour of Sheriff Alexander Nicolson of Husabost, who made its first recorded ascent in 1873, jointly with local shepherd Macrae. He himself had no part in the decision to name it eponymously, and indeed himself wrote of the climb;

> This corrie is called Corrie Laghain, and the tarn Loch a Laghain, and the peak, for which my companion had no name, I proposed to call Scur a Laghain …

In fact, local guide John MacKenzie said it was originally Sgùrr Viorach, from *biorach*, pointed. Nicolson made several other first ascents, including Sgùrr Dubh Mòr, and one first descent, by what is now called Nicholson's Chimney on Sgùrr na Gillean, today used as an ascent route.

Professor Dr Norman Collie was responsible for the naming of Alasdair: he himself was an accomplished climber, who gained fame in the Canadian Rockies too, and Colin Phillip proposed that the north top of Sgùrr na Banachdich be named Sgùrr a' Leighiche, doctor's peak, in his honour – this was carried out but in the modified form of his first name, **Sgùrr Thormaid** (Norman), in keeping with Sgùrr Alasdair and **Sgùrr Theàrlaich** both of which Collie had named, the latter being Gaelic for Charles. He, the Lakeland climber Charles Pilkington, is surely one of the few Englishmen to be named on a Scottish hill: he had made first ascents of Pinnacle Ridge, among others.

Pilkington in turn named **Sgùrr MhicCoinnich** in honour of the great Skye mountain guide John MacKenzie of Sconser. It's interesting that the local guide has his surname used, whilst Alexander, Charles and Norman were apparently on 'first-name terms' in the hill names! Collie (with Phillip) also named two other peaks, and had the sensitivity to use Gaelic – **Sgùrr an Fheadain** and **Sgùrr Coir' an Lochain** – although it was later found that the latter was known locally with the addition of Dubh after Sgùrr. Similarly, in the very late 19th century, geologist Alfred Harker surveyed the ridge, working for six years, and named a few of the remaining intervening peaks in the process, like **An Caisteal** and **Sgùrr na Bàirnich** (limpet).

*Sgùrr a' Fheadain, Skye, peak of the wind-gap
or water channel*

Knight's Peak, the fourth pinnacle of Sgùrr nan Gillean, is named after a St. Andrews theology professor Reverend William Knight, and there is currently a move to have the peak re-named Sgùrr Uilleam (William) to bring it into line with other first-named peaks.

Women were pushed into anonymity: a minor point on the ridge not far from the Inaccessible Pinnacle was named **Sgùrr na Cailleag** (peak of the old woman – or possibly from *caileag*, a (mere) girl), apparently after a lady with whom John MacKenzie was climbing. Whoever the lady was, he was surely no gentleman in so naming it! He clearly had an eye for the feminine figure though, for when he and Collie climbed a massive rock outcrop in Coire Lagain in 1906, he chose the name **A' Chìoch** (the breast) which was anatomically spot on, and is the root of the **Sròn na Cìche** ridge above.

MacKenzie himself was ignored in the naming of what is now called the **Inaccessible Pinnacle**, or more horribly the Inn Pinn, the only Munro where Munroists must tie on a rope. The Pilkington brothers, who made the first ascent in 1880, are sourced with the immortal description that it had

> an infinite drop on one side and an even longer drop on the other

and gave it its new, English, name. MacKenzie knew and pointed out that it was known locally as An Stac (the stack or pinnacle), which is more precise if less Tolkeinian. The 1970 edition of the Scottish Mountaineering Club's Skye guide rather grumpily writes;

> the absurd excrescence of [Sgurr Dearg's] S.E. flank, a narrow flake of gabbro that has worn better than its neighbouring rocks, fancifully called the 'Inaccessible Pinnacle'

but baulked at calling for the reinstatement of An Stac. Of all the climber-named peaks in the Cuillin, perhaps it is the one that most deserves repatriation to Gaelic.

This section is largely based on the research of Ian R.Mitchell, his article *Naming the Cuillin* in the West Highland Free Press, and his book *Scotland's Mountains before the Mountaineers* (see Bibliography).

viewpoint the single large mountain that the Cuillin is – is so high that it can hardly have been missed out, the name too must surely be Norse.

Secondly there is the fact that the Norwegian name for one of their high plateaux, from whose fiords the Vikings sailed, is the Kiolen Mountains. The afore-mentioned J.D.Forbes noted in his 1851 *Norway and its Glaciers* that the northern mountains 'were commonly called the Kjølen range', though he didn't make the link to the Cuillin. In Norway's Jotunheimen range, you will find peaks such as Veslkjolen and Kvitingskjolen, while in Iceland the range north of Hekla is the Kiolen too. Like all colonisers the Vikings brought names with them that reminded them of home – as the Scots were later to take their Lomonds and Nevises abroad – and several Hebridean hill names have doubles in Scandinavia; a range as striking as the Cuillin, high point of the Hebrides, would have been a worthy holder of this 'high rocks' name from home.

Thirdly there is the fact that the Norse names are by and large prosaic, referring usually to their more obvious features. In this context the other suggestion of a Norse derivation *directly* from *kjolr* meaning keel or keel-shaped is inappropriate (in spite of **Druim nan Ràmh**, ridge of the oars), although the metaphor of an upturned keel could apply to a ridge; whilst the name *kiolen* meaning high rocks fits perfectly this bare rocky range with scarcely a blade of grass to be seen on their gabbro sinews, and perfectly described by Thomas Pennant as

> a savage series of rude mountains.

Lastly there is the fact that the nearby island of Rum also has a range called the Cuillin, similar in rocky outline, and this suggests the possibility of a generic name, rather than one based upon a unique historical figure. The name Cuillin therefore reflects Norse powers of observation rather than Celtic legend or Gaelic imagination. Within the Cuillin there are many high Gaelic-named peaks. This may seem odd when all the other high ground is Norse. But the explanation is surely that the Vikings treated the Cuillin or Kiolen as one single mountain for their landmark purposes, stretching as it does in one long high ridge away from the sea. The Gaels named many of Skye's lower or subsidiary peaks as they moved onto the higher ground for hunting or herding, and their names are descriptive of the hill or its func-tion. In the Cuillin, as they moved up into the corries, the individual rocky peaks above them would take on significance and thus names.

Sgùrr na Banachdaich, sometimes translated from *banachdaich* as literally the smallpox peak due to the pockmarked appearance of the peridotite rocks, but more likely the milkmaid's peak from the days when the cattle were summered in the corries – the ruins of two shieling huts in the corrie, and the locally-used names Sgùrr na Banaraich or Bannachaig confirm this.

Sgùrr a' Mhadaidh is the peak of the fox, probably from foxes frequenting the corrie below, posing a threat to the beasts herded there. Names like **Sgùrr Dearg**, **Sgùrr Dubh Mòr** and **Sgùrr Dubh na Dà Bheinn**, respectively red, dark and dark two-peaked peaks, **Sgùrr nan Eag** (peak of the notch) and **Bruach na Frìthe** (slope of the wild mountainous land or deer forest) paint an accurate picture of the land.

Sgùrr a' Mhadaidh, Skye. Peak of the dog, or possibly fox. See p214,
[Natural World, Wild Animals]

One of the Cuillin's finest peaks, **Sgùrr nan Gillean**, presents a saw-toothed array of rock spires to the north; known as Pinnacle Ridge, leading to a sharp point, it is highlight of the view from Sligachan. Ostensibly a Gaelic name, meaning peak of the young men, allegedly from the number of them perishing in its attempt: however, it was suggested by a Mr Mackenzie (quoted by Colin Phillip) that it is a hybrid of Gaelic *sgùrr* with the Norse *gil*, a ghyll or gully: the word occurs elsewhere in Skye, as in **Ben Idrigill**. *Gil* is in fact a Gaelic word borrowed from the Norse, so in Gaelic it is simply peak of the gullies. J.D.Forbes wrote in 1846 of

> Scuir-na-Gillean (or rock of the young men, named, it is said, from the untimely fate met by some who attempted to climb it.) ...

His informant was old ghillie Duncan MacIntyre, but it is an explanation with the air of folk fiction clinging to it, since neither dates or victims' names were given, and rock-climbing was never a sport among the islanders before late Victorian times. The foremost 20th century Gaelic poet Sorley McLean, wrote in praise of Sgùrr nan Gillean thus:

> The forbidding great Sgùrr of danger, The Sgùrr of Skye above them all

but he was a poet rather than a historian in referring to the danger.

Another Cuillin name that has been linked with danger is **Am Basteir**, that some books and modern tartanalia pamphlets have translated as the executioner. No word like this appears in Gaelic dictionaries, although *bàs* on its own means death – usually of animals – and perhaps the story was spun by someone impressed by the fanciful resemblance of the adjacent Basteir Tooth to an executioner's axe.

The Reverend Ronald Burn, second man (and second minister too) to climb all the Munros, was fascinated by place names and had the Gaelic to talk with locals, and he wrote an item in the November 1925 *SMC Journal* comprehensively demolishing the executioner theory, submitting instead that it means deeply split or cleft. He knew of an Am Basdar in Gleann Lichd, Kintail, similar to this, down whose split

> a stone thrown can be heard jingling and rattling as it makes its long descent.

Sgùrr na Strì is the hill of strife; it is said that heirs to the local clan chieftainships, of Macleod and MacKinnon, were taken there to have pointed out to them the importance of maintaining good 'fences' or boundaries with their neighbours in order to avoid trouble and strife. There was a cruel tradition where clan boundaries were marked by the ceremonial building of cairns, followed by the severe thrashing of a young boy from each clan so that they would grow up remembering exactly where the border was! A similar story exists relating to the Seaforth boundary in Harris. Perhaps **Sgùrr a' Ghreadaidh** peak of the thrashing or whipping, refers to this too. Another simpler and less colourful explanation for both is that the 'strife' and 'thrashing' is that of conflicting and buffeting winds. Colin Phillip quotes a Professor Ker who derives the name from the Norse *greta*, clear water, and he goes on to say;

> This translation of the name is quite exceptionally accurate, for of all the clear streams in Skye, and they are more than usually clear, the Greta is the clearest, and the springs are more numerous than any of the other corries ...

Leaving aside Phillip's fulsome use of superlatives, this begs the question of why, if it is Norse, the Vikings should have singled out this one peak for naming and not the rest.

Skye outwith The Cuillin

Although the Cuillin are the main mountain feature of Skye, they are only one small but high corner of the hill ground. It may seem odd that of the 50 or so Marilyn hills on this island of Norse names, 70 per cent of them have completely Gaelic names, but this is due to Gaelic in-filling within a Norse structure. Gaelic hill names were given later, after the Norse power waned, and were applied to the island's lower hills, and – as we have seen – to the *individual* hills of the Cuillin.

The Norse named not only the highest mountain massif (the Cuillin) but also the long peninsulas (e.g. Trotternish, Waternish) and offshore islands (Raasay, Soay and Scalpay) that spread-eagle Skye out into the Minch. Many of the settlements too are Norse (e.g. Uig – from *vik*, a harbour – Carbost, Armadale). Each peninsula's high ground usually has at least one Norse hill name staking out the ground: **Ben Cleat** (from *klettr*, cliff) in Strathaird, **Ben Aslak** in Sleat, **Arnaval** (eagle fell) and **Stockval** (log mountain – a common Norwegian mountain name) in Minginish, Healaval hills in both Duirinish and Waternish: and whilst **The Storr** in Trotternish may come from stor (big) as in Norway's Storkletten (big *klettr*, cliff), it may more probably be from Gaelic *stòr*, a broken tooth or steep cliff.

The Old Man of Storr, the giant rock stack standing just apart from the hill, may have been the source of the original name, and one Gaelic alternative name for The Storr is Am Fiacaill Stòrach, the buck tooth. Further up Trotternish, along a twisting skyline ridge, is **Beinn Edra**, which in Gaelic means in-between hill (*eadar*) but in its original Norse form meant outer hill (*idri*), **Beinn Mheadhonach** to the south of it being the central hill. Intriguingly, on Blaeu's 1654 map, just south of Edergil (now Beinn Edra) is Bin Ostrafeald, clearly *austur fjall*, eastern fell, a name that seems since to have disappeared, but which may have been the name for the whole massif from The Storr through Hartaval and Flasvein. To the south, in central Skye near Portree, is a Norse triangle of hills around Glen Varragill, in **Roineval** (rough fell), **Ben Lee** (from *hlidh*, slope) and **Ben Tianavaig** from Tianavaig (*vik*, harbour) at its foot.

Close to the Cuillin, but clearly separated from it by ground barely at sea level, is **Blàbheinn** whose name has been interpreted as Gaelic Blàbheinn, *blàth bheinn*, bloom mountain, but is more likely to be the Norse *bla fjall*, blue mountain: the word order, adjective before noun, is Norse, and the *bheinn* is probably a Gaelicisation of *fjall*, and there are several mountains in Iceland and Norway with names respectively like Bláfell and Blåtind – blue, after all, is the colour of distant mountains.

Close to Blàbheinn and the Cuillin the relatively lesser hills have Gaelic names,

like **Beinn Dearg Mhòr** and **Glas Bheinn Mhòr** (big red and grey hills) and **Garbh-bheinn** (rough hill): the first of this trio is part of the **Red Cuillin**, from the pink granites of the group, whose red scree slopes are Nature's superior imitation of the Lothian oil shale bings. **Glàmaig**, the highest of the group, appears to be from the Gaelic word *glàmag* meaning a greedy woman, although feminists might prefer the alternative from *glàmach*, a greedy man. Timothy Pont's early 17th century text wrote that above the hamlet of Sconser,

> That trinket of hills ar generally called Klammaig. The hie way throw thois hills is called Bellachan Scard.

This suggests that the name Glàmaig applied to the trio including **Beinn Dearg**s **Mhòr** and **Mheadhonach** (middle), since the Bealach na Sgairde lies across them. The other red hills include **Ruadh Stac** (unsurprisingly red stack), **Belig**, whose name appears to come from *beilleag*, birch bark, or *beileach*, thick-lipped, and **Marsco**, a stunning peak with an impenetrable name. Alexander Forbes suggested in his *Place-names of Skye* that it was seagull peak from *mar* and *sgo*, but neither word is in Gaelic dictionaries. The **Black Cuillin** appears to be a geologists' term adopted by climbers (the earliest reference to the term was in 1896), to distinguish the dark gabbro and basalt rocks of the main Cuillin cirque. The **Red Cuillin** on the other hand was apparently a local name, Na Beinnean Dearga, the red mountains, whilst the 'Black-labelled' Cuillin was never a local Gaelic name ... and indeed its range includes not only a Dubh (dark) name, but a Sgùrr Dearg (red) and a **Sròn Bhuidhe** (yellow).

The English name of the pair of hills in west Skye called **Macleod's Tables**, is not so recent; it co-exists with their Old Norse/Gaelic names of **Healaval Mhòr** and **Bheag**, now **Healabhal Mhòr** and **Bheag**, the big and little flagstone fells. In 1654 Blaeu mapped it as Heillefeald. The first element of these latter names is from Old Norse *hellyr*, a flagstone (or possibly *hyalli*, a ridge of terraces), and the second element is *fjall*; the Gaelic *mòr* and *beag* (big and little) came later. Their flat or 'flag-stone' tops reflect the layer cake of basaltic rock flows that built them. (*Beag*, meaning small, is actually higher than *Mòr*, meaning big, but Mòr has the larger plateau area on top.) Legend has it that God angrily sliced off their previously-pointed peaks after a local chieftain had tried to eject Columba from the isle for preaching a sermon. Another version tells of God creating a flat bed and table for Columba after this rejection. Some say that their name means holy fell, from the Norse *helgi*, from this divine intervention, but the Vikings' names were largely prosaic, so this is unlikely. There is also the apocryphal tale of a local man, asked by tourists what the hills' name meant, answered that 'one was a helluva big climb and that the other was even more so'.

The English name **Macleod's Tables** comes from a much more recent tale of the 16th century. The story goes that when King James V entertained clan chief MacLeod in Edinburgh, the chief boasted that he had a finer table in Skye. Another version, casting MacLeod in a more seemly light, has him being provoked beyond endurance by a boastful southern lord into a wager on the topic. Either way when

the King (or Sassenach lord) was staying some time later at Dunvegan Castle, he was taken at nightfall to the broad flat top of Healaval Bheag where a banquet was laid out on the springy turf. 'This,' said the chief, 'is my table, larger and finer than yours'. Indicating the hundreds of his clan bearing torches around the feast he added ' … And these are my candlesticks'. It is recorded that the weather was fine – the Milky Way being indicated as 'my splendid ceiling' – but not whether the Skye midges were also banqueting: simply that Macleod's Tables is the name that comes

The Quiraing, Skye. The element raing also appears in the old name of Corserine, Galloway. See p176, [Southern Uplands, Corserine]

down to us for these two flat-topped hills. (The Gaelic is Bòrd Mòr 'ic Leoid).

Far away across Scotland, but Skye-bound at the time, another royal figure, Bonnie Prince Charlie, while crossing the Corrieyarick Pass, also dined at a piece of level ground, leaving the name Prince Charlie's Dining Table to outlast the crumbs. And, back on north Skye, there is yet another table, The Table at the heart of the fantastic cliffs of the Quiraing rocks. From a distance it is inconspicuous, a mere rise in at the north end of the Trotternish peninsula's long backbone, presenting slumped cliffs to the east coast. On closer inspection and penetration walkers can discover a stunning array of fantastic pinnacles and nooks, with names like The Needle, The Prison and The Table. **Quiraing** itself is probably the pillared enclosure (from *cuith raing*), and Alexander Forbes in *Place-names of Skye and adjacent islands* gave a Norse origin in *kvi rand*, or *quoy rand* (the direct ancestor of the two Gaelic words *cuith raing*): on Blaeu's 1654 map it was written Bin Quyrãga. The 'pillar' probably refers to The Needle itself.

One unusual Gaelic hill name element is found almost exclusively in Skye: *biod* or *bioda*, meaning a pointed top. There's **Biod Mòr** (big) across Glen Brittle from the Cuillin, **Biod an Athair** (sky) at the tip of Duirinish, the summit over 300 metres above its sea-cliffs, and **Bioda Buidhe** (yellow). Many of the other score of *biod* tops are, like the latter one, summits above cliffs, and many are on the west coast of the same peninsula: only three hills outside the island bear the element, one on a sea-cliff in Mull, one in the far north, and the shapely **Biod an Fhithich** (raven) beside The Saddle in Glen Shiel: the word was obviously not one of Skye Gaelic's successful exports, unlike *sgùrr*.

On the east coast of Skye and the Sleat peninsula the hills are mainly in Gaelic, like **Sgùrr na Còinnich**, peak of the moss. Nearby it are two hills both called **Beinn na Caillich**, peak of the old woman in Gaelic. Thomas Pennant climbed the one above Broadford in or about 1772 and reported

> an artificial cairn of the most enormous size, reputed to have been the place
> of sepulchre of a gigantic woman in the days of Fingal.

Beneath her is supposed to be a pot of gold, but she probably treasures more this hill name that endures. The other Beinn na Caillich nearer Kyleakin is supposed to be connected with a Norse princess who, it is said, stretched a chain across the narrows at Kyleakin to force boats to pay her taxes. Burying Norse princesses on hill tops was obviously a local pastime: **Sròn Bhiornaig** in north Skye marks the high grave of a princess whose ghost faces eternally out towards her native Norway – local tradition, related by Seton Gordon speaks of her grave being on a ledge 20 metres below the summit. Her name (sometimes spelt Biornail) apparently derives from the Old Norse *bjorn*, bear – not very lady-like. The adjacent summit **Meall na Suireanach**, hill of the maiden or nymph, is probably related and definitely more flattering.

Tiree

In this 'the land of corn', the peak of **Ben Hynish**, 140m, is from *ha-nes*, the high ness or headland, the name carried by the hamlet at its eastern foot. Blaeu's map of 1654 singled out Bin How, now **Beinn Hough**, for inclusion instead, making it a twin with neighbouring Coll's **Beinn Hogh**.

Uist (North and South)

The hills of South Uist are almost twice as high as North Uist, and can be seen clearly across the Minch from the mainland near Mallaig on a clear day, pale blue through the gap between the Cuillin of Rum and Skye. The highest point is **Beinn Mhòr**, 620m, big mountain in Gaelic: however, to Uist people the hill is always Gèideabhal, just possibly derived from *sgeite*, referring to the sparseness of grass on its slopes. Far more likely this name is a Gaelicisation of an Old Norse name from *geitar fjall*, goat mountain, for it appeared on Blaeu's 17th century map as Keadafeald. Arran's highest point, **Goatfell**, went through a similar naming process.

North Uist also has a Beinn Mhòr, but it is only half the height of **Eaval**, also

named **Eabhal,** the north's highest at 347m. Eaval's name is probably from *ey fjall*, island fell, since it is almost completely encircled by Loch Obsidary north and west and the Minch south and east, and lies in a moor studded with innumerable tiny lochs. It is thus literally an 'island-like mountain'; on Blaeu's 1654 map it was spelt Bin Aefelt, the 'ae' element sounding like 'ey', while on Thomson's 1821 map it was Eamheal. Over in the island's west is a small loch, Loch Eaval, with a dun or fort on an island in the middle – this fort, while not high, was another ey-fjall, that gave the loch its name.

Also on the Blaeu map is Gougar Hill, clearly representing **Crogary Mòr** – now called **Crògearraidh Mòr** – (the big shieling of the cattle-fold), together with Arnifeald (**Arnaval,** eagle fell, which is now called **Airneabhal**), Askrafeald (once part-gaelicised to **Askervein,** but now called **Aisgerbheinn,** and originally a namesake of Rum's **Askival,** spear fell) and Trurifealt. This last hill has been gaelicised and lengthened into **Triuirebheinn,** the puzzle lying in the Norse prefix rather than the translated Gaelic suffix. Nearby **Marrival,** now called **Maireabhal,** is the mare fell, while **North** and **South Lee,** now **Li a' Tuath** and **Li a' Deas,** hills are from *hlidh*, a gentle slope.

Returning to South Uist we find **Stulaval** (shieling fell from *stol*), **Easaval,** now called **Easabhal,** (possibly from Norse *esja* referring to volcanic stone – there is an Icelandic mountain called Esja), and **Hecla,** named as Bin Heck La on Blaeu's map: in modern Gaelic it is **Thacla.** There's another Hecla in the Hebrides (on Mingulay) and the more famous one in Iceland (known originally in the 12th century as Heklufell) a smoking volcano that on occasion erupts in incandescent fury – four times in the 20th century alone, and again in 2000.

It has been suggested that the name means cowled or hooded, from the plume of smoke or cloud that often drapes its head: in Cleasby's 19th century Icelandic dictionary the word *hekla* is said to mean a cowled or hooded frock, and that the mountain's name derived from its hood or frock of snow – though that could describe many Icelandic hills. Earlier in Norwegian history it was described in documents as *Mons Casulae*, in Latin the mountain of the monk's cowl.

However, this Latin soubriquet may be more a nickname than a translation. For there's a Heklefjell mountain in north Norway, possibly the ancestor of all the Heklas, and in Norwegian *hekle* means hackle or comb, and in Orkney near Kirkwall there are rocks called the Heckle Teeth: and while Norway's and Uist's mountains 'smoke' with cloud all too often, they are not volcanoes (not recently, anyway), and such a metaphor is a bit poetic for the Hebridean hill namers. Hecla's summit ridge does have a discontinuity that might suggest a comb.

Often climbed with **Hecla** is Ben Corodale, named after the glen on its east side: but from the mid-19th to the mid-20th century, both on OS maps and in SMC guidebooks, this was always called Feaveallach, and it is not clear why the usage changed. Feavallach could be Gaelic *feith mhealach*, hilly bog (a description fitting many Scottish hills, but not this one) or more likely has the Gaelic adjectival ending -*ach* added to a Norse Feaval, of uncertain meaning.

CHAPTER THREE

NORTH-WEST HIGHLANDS

A' Mhaighdean

A Gaelic name almost recognisable to an English speaker, it means the maiden. This is Scotland's Jungfrau, lower than its Swiss namesake but just as beautiful as it soars above the remote blue lochans of the Letterewe Forest. While it is one of a hill clan including several hills called **Am Bodach** or **A' Chailleach** (old man and old woman), this hill like its family seems to have been named with no-one in particular in mind. Across the glen to the south is a top called **Martha's Peak**, named after a herdgirl who fell to her death, but this bigger peak seems to be the 'Unknown Maiden'.

A maiden in both Gaelic and Scots cultures is also the last sheaf of corn cut in the harvest, and the outline of the peak seen from the west might suggest a bound stook in a field for its steep southern slope finishes in a near-vertical cliff. Indeed there were many Highland traditions associated with the cutting of this last stook, 'A' Mhaighdean' as it was known, especially after a good harvest. Sometimes it was dressed up like a young girl before being cut or made into a corn dolly. A bad harvest sometimes saw it clad in old woman's clothes and called A' Chailleach, the possible origin of *that* hill name. (Pronounced *a* **vY**tyan)

An Teallach

An Teallach is a sandstone-spired spectacular in Wester Ross: standing clear of other peaks, its pinnacled ridge can be seen from many points in the north-west. It is a collective name for a mountain of several separate tops (indeed the Reverend A.E.Robertson called them 'The Teallachs') with rather ordinary names like **Bidein a' Ghlas Thuill** (peak of the grey-green hollow), **Sàil Liath** (grey heel, from its quartzite screes), **Sgùrr Fiona** (white peak, from *fionn* – or wine peak, from *fion*) and **Corrag Bhuidhe** (yellow finger) – all these colours contrast with the maroon-ish-red of its main rocks. Another dizzy pinnacle called **Lord Berkeley's Seat**, spectacularly overhangs the cliffs; it got its name from the eponymous gentleman who, for a bet, sat on it with feet dangling over the edge – whatever he won that day in cash terms was but a trifle to the value of having a peak named after him for posterity! A.E.Robertson stated that it was Lord Berkeley Paget, brother of the Earl of Anglesey, who was pushed up onto the seat by Dundonnell stalker Willie Finlayson, so that he could look down on the loch – this in 1864.

No actual summit on the hill is called An Teallach, this name applying rather to the whole mountain. In Gaelic *teallach* is usually a smith's forge, or possibly a hearth, a fireplace, or even the large flat stone that backs the fireplace in a croft. In the past it has also signified an anvil or furnace. Now perhaps the shape of the precipitous cliffs backing the main eastern corrie gave locals the picture of a hearth. Or perhaps it is a more literal meaning, for there is a building at the northern foot of the mountain formerly the Old Smiddy, now a climbing club hut known as the

Clarkson Hut (in memory of a climber killed on Ben Nevis), but still recognisable in living memory with bellows and forge. Perhaps this smithy was built here because the extensive woodlands of the nearby strath were a rare commodity in a mainly barren landscape. The smithy may have given the local people the idea for the name for the huge mountain beyond.

Sgùrr Fiona, An Teallach. Wine, or white peak. See p144, [Central Highlands, White Hills, fionn]

And there may be a deeper significance, for the ancient Celts ranked the metal-working smith second only to the Gods themselves. Pont's 16th century map, and the mid-17th century Blaeu map, labelled it P Talloch, the *p* probably standing for *ben*. Later maps further corrupted this to Kalloch, and the highest top as Kea Cloch (Thomson's 1832 *County Atlas of Scotland*), and the first man known to have climbed it, John MacCulloch, knew it by this pseudonym. As Ian Mitchell's *Scotland's Mountains before the Mountaineers* points out, it was only when the Ordnance Survey thought to ask a local for its name that the maps were finally set right with the *teallach* name. **Beinn Teallach**, a newly-created 'life Munro' near Roy Bridge, has by contrast no dramatic shape nor industrial history to account for its name which may come from the shape of its craggy eastern slopes resembling a fire-place or hearth of a rather unspectacular kind. (Pronounced *an* **tya**loch)

Arkle

Along with neighbour **Foinaven**, Arkle comes high in the popular recognition stakes because of the Duchess of Westminster's two famous 1960s racehorses that bore their

names. This sporting fame belies their remoteness in the north-west, beyond the pale of the Munros and outwith the main walking areas. They are also in territory where the Norse and Gaelic tongues intermix with **Ben Stack** and **Quinag**, Laxford and Lochinver. Pont mapped it as Bin Arkilly – the *beinn* has since disappeared.

Suggestions that have been made for the name include *ark-fjall* (Norse for ark or chest mountain), and *airidh-fjall*, mountain of the high pasture. One strength of the 'ark' suggestion, apart from the shape, is that the *fj* of *fjall* would fall silent after *c* or *k*, to produce a name sounding like Arkle. One weakness of the 'pasture' name is the topography, for this is a giant Moby Dick of a mountain with a mass of whitish-grey quartzite spilling off its surfacing ridge – not much grass here. W.J.Watson, who favoured the *ark-fjall* meaning, also noted that the Gaelic *airceal*, a hiding place, might suit since there was an occurrence of that name near Loch Broom.

Baosbheinn

This highly-acclaimed but little-traversed Torridon peak is often translated as wizard's peak, from *baobh* meaning a wicked person, a witch, a fury, and – occasionally – a wizard (*fiosaiche* is a more usual word for wizard). A *baobh* can also be a she-spirit, haunting rivers, dark cousin of that other ubiquitous Gaelic creature the water-horse that rose from lochs (like Loch Avon) to spirit humans to their watery grave – such creatures occur in names in several Highland places such as Loch na Beiste a few kilometres north. Interestingly, the loch at Baosbheinn's foot is Loch na

---

Red hills

The north-west has a fair number of the Highlands' many red peaks, with at least four called Beinn Dearg and three named Ruadh Stac – indeed the Munro group near Inverlael is sometimes called The Deargs.

ruadh

Ruadh suggests those russet soft-brown colours we choose to call red, as in red-haired or Old Red Sandstone. It is found in the north-west in **Ruadh-stac Mòr**, big red stack, and others in this area such as **An Ruadh-Stac** – which Pont mapped phonetically as Bin Rowastack – where the softer tones of the Torridonian sandstone provide a warmer colour in a bog-green and peat-black landscape. **Sgòrr Ruadh**, also in this area, was mapped by Pont as Bin Skor Larig, because it stood above two passes (*làirig*). Further east, the Gaelic name for the mountain area now known as the Cairngorms is Am Monadh Ruadh, the red mountain mass, identifying the pale pinks of its granite rocks. Another reddish hue is rust, and although the Gaels lived on the land they were familiar with rust on their tools and weapons. **Càrn Mairg** in Perthshire perhaps comes from the Gaelic word for rust, *meirg*, a colour typical of the autumn slopes as the old year's bracken sours in the cold rains and crumbles in the frosts. Also in Perthshire, **Creag Roro** is from *ruadh-shruth*, the russet

h-Oidhche, the loch of night or darkness – a common name usually meaning that fish rise (to be caught) at night, but here with an interesting double meaning. However Osgood MacKenzie, who founded the celebrated Inverewe Gardens nearby, wrote that his father referred to it as *bathais bheinn*, literally forehead mountain, and the shape fits – this is the most likely meaning.

Alternatively – but very whimsically – *baos* (pronounced boe:s) means madness or lust – the latter emotion perhaps for the 'damsel' (**Tom na Gruagaich**) on the 'darling peak' of neighbour **Beinn Alligin**. (Pronounced **boe**:shvYn)

Beinn Alligin

The nearest word in Gaelic dictionaries to this name is *ailleagan*, a jewel or a darling, and the usual translation is jewelled mountain or mountain of beauty. The name is richly deserved, if unusual. The mountain's second peak **Tom na Gruagaich** is hill of the damsel, lending some authority to the mountain's claim to its chivalrous compliment of a name. 'Jewel' is an unusual name in Scotland, but it keeps good cosmopolitan company – with Les Écrins in the French Alps, the 'jewels' or 'jewel box', and the famous Kanchenjunga in the Himalaya, the 'five treasures of the snow'.

Back in Scotland **Sgòr na h-Ulaidh** above Glen Coe is from *ulaidh*, a treasure, for which there is no historical evidence, although it may refer to the way that the summit is completely hidden from the glen by its north shoulder; or more poetically

---

stream, a name suggesting iron leaking from the geology. (Pronounced **roo**-ugh)

dearg

Dearg is a blood-red colour with a hint of crimson, and is found with *beinn*, *càrn* and *meall* in over 20 Munros especially in the Glen Coe and Ben Nevis areas, and altogether over 100 hill names contain *dearg*. **Beinn Dearg Mòr** and **Beag** near An Teallach are cliffed in the soft reddy browns of Torridonian sandstone, as is **Beinn Dearg** in the heart of Torridon itself – it weathers to produce vertical, jointed crags. There are a dozen instances of **Càrn Dearg** in upper Deeside alone, for they are often found where a hard granite rock intrudes through layers of grey schist. And, confusing for Corbetteers, three Càrn Dearg hills within a few kilometres of each other above Glen Roy. Granite with a high content of the mineral feldspar appears reddish, and for instance **Càrn Mòr Dearg** screes show up as pink in contrast with neighbour Nevis' dull grey andesite rock. **Stob Dearg** (better known as **Buachaille Etive Mòr**) is tinged with pinkish rhyolite rock.

Mullach na Dheiragain may come from *deargan* or *deargan-allt*, the kestrel, literally the red one from the distinctive sheen of the bird's feathers. In a more corrupted form the colour peeps out from anglicised hill names like **Drumderg** or **Craigie Darg** in Aberdeenshire. (Pronounced **dye**rak)

ulaidh can be a darling – another treasured peak, perhaps. There's a **Meall Leac Ulaidh** near Laggan, the treasure referred to being the rich summer grazing on it.

However the pronunciation of *ailleagan* normally has a *y* sound after the *l*, and this may have led W.J.Watson to say that it was named after the River Alligin at its foot, a name in turn perhaps deriving from *ail*, a rock, as in **Ben Alder**. It could be *ail-lagan*, the little hollow of the rock; but if this is the meaning of the name, then it is more likely to refer to the mountain's eastern corries, facing the huge Coire Mhic Nobuil, than to the River Alligin which is on the western 'backside' of the hill. The name heard and mapped by Pont over four centuries ago was more prosaic: Bin Yrchory. This probably took its name from An Reidh-choire on its western side, the level corrie, from which the river Alligin flows. The nature of this old name suggests that the newer name Beinn Alligin is also a river-derived name. (Pronounced bYn **aa**leegin)

Beinn Eighe

Principal Shairp wrote of it in the 19th century, that it was

> a magnificent alp blanched bare and bald and white.

Its name means the file mountain from *eighe*, the view from Kinlochewe empha-sising its sharp skyline. The file metaphor is appropriate for this long narrow ridge in contrast to the broader shoulders of neighbour Liathach. The tops along the ridge run from **Creag Dubh** (black cliff) in the east, over **Spidean Coire nan Clach** (peak of the stony corrie), **A' Chòinneach Mhòr** (the big moss, which slopes away north from this top), **Ruadh-stac Mòr** (big red stack – atop the mighty sandstone pillars of the corrie) and **Sàil Mhòr** (big heel, which rounds it off). Pont recorded the mountain as Bin Rowstack, having had Ruadh-stac Mòr pointed out to him in the Letterewe area, and assuming it to be the name for the whole mountain: 150 years later, Roy's map recorded it phonetically as Bin Eay. (Pronounced bYn **ay**-a)

Beinn Resipol

This rugged hill in Sunart has a farm at its southern foot with the same name, and Hamish Brown has suggested that it means the mountain of the horse farmstead, from the Norse *hross bolstadr*. This would be unusual in that hardly any large Scot-tish hills are named after farms at their base (one of the few exceptions being **Beinn Achaladair**, the farm by the hard water, near Bridge of Orchy) – but it does lie in an area of post-Norse influence – Sunart is from Svein's fiord. A little to the west is another *beinn* apparently named after a farm below, **Beinn Laga**. Rezipole Hill was its first mapping, in 1733. (Pronounced bYn **re**sh*a*pol)

Ben Hope

This is Scotland's most northerly Munro, from which on a clear day you can see the Orkneys beyond the ragged seaboard and the raging Pentland Firth, named by the Vikings after the Picts who lay to their south in 'Sutherland'. So the mountain's name is appropriately one of the very few on the mainland with an Old Norse name,

from *hop* meaning a bay. As an atlas shows it lies nipped between two long sea-lochs that break deep into the land, Loch Eriboll and the Kyle of Tongue, and with the resulting peninsula slit by its own Loch Hope. The Norse *hop* was adopted by Gaelic as *ob*, as in Oban.

Ben Klibreck

Ben Hope lies about 20 kilometres from Ben Klibreck as the raven flies, but many Munro-baggers use a car to net this northerly twosome in one day. And the connection between them lies deeper in that they are probably the only two mainland Munros with Norse names. For while Klibreck could be from the Gaelic *cliath bhreac*, the speckled slope or cliff, the letter *k* gives it a Norse twang, and it lies in a chain of Sutherland hills with Norse names. It is probably Norse *klettr brekka* or *klif brekka* meaning cliff slope (*klif* is pronounced klee as in Cleveland), and there is indeed a steep slope seamed by outcrops on its western flanks. Both Gaelic and Norse meanings are at least plausible – which is more than can be said for one guidebook's 'mountain of the fish' (presumably from *breac*, trout) – and at least the name of the main summit is quite clear, for **Meall nan Con** is the hill of the dogs in Gaelic.

However the mountain's position in an area of Norse hill names surely clinches the argument for that language as an origin. Just to the south is **Ben Armine** (from *àrmann*, a hero or steward), and nearer the coast is **Beinn Horn** (possibly a horn): west is **Maovally** (*mjo-fjall*, narrow hill); and in the area are **Scaraben** (*skora-bheinn*, incised mountain, the *beinn* probably replacing an earlier *fjall*), **Creag Scalabsdale** (*skalli*, bald-headed) and **Col-bheinn** (from *kollr*, a summit) all based on Norse.

Ben Loyal (properly, Beinn Laghail)

Sometimes praised, in guidebooks at least, as 'The Queen of Scotland's Peaks', this epithet lends apparent support to a royal connection with the English-sounding 'loyal'. But reality is less deferential than the name, as we will see. Ben Loyal's striking feature is its range of castellated tops, with Gaelic names – indeed one is called **An Caisteal** (the castle) – including **Sgòr a' Bhatain** (boat, or little stick, peak) and **Sgòr a' Chlèirich** (cleric's peak). But Ben Loyal itself is more difficult to understand, sounding English as it does. W.J.Watson, who took into account the local pronunciation, wrote that it was Beinn Laghail (legal mountain) from the Old Norse *laga fiall*: he was criticising another Gaelic scholar Alexander MacBain who has said it was from *leidh fiall* (levy fell) or *lauta fjall* (leafy fell) – for woodland, unusual in Sutherland although not in nearby Tongue, clings to its western slopes. The existence of a Gaelic version (*laghail*) of a Norse name (*laga fiall*) is not unusual in Gaeldom. An 1897 'poet' in the Scottish Mountaineering Club Journal, unwittingly reversed the tendency in a series of rhyming couplets on hill name pronunciation, when he wrote of this hill:

> ... Then for sport that is raoghal
> He hies to Beinn Laoghal

Laga fiall (law mountain) is, as Watson suggested, the most likely origin, because there is a Norse tradition, strong in Iceland and with parallels in Scotland, in which hills were used for people to gather on to hear legal proclamations. Traditionally the chiefs built an altar to the god Thor on a hill top, and after prayers would hear complaints, settle disputes and issue edicts. There are also two **Layaval** hills in the Uists, and since both they and the Sutherland part of the mainland are old Norse areas, the case for legal mountain apparently rests. (Although the current local Gaelic pronunciation is *beinn laghail*, literally beautiful hill.)

This judgement has legal echoes throughout Scotland's hills. A few kilometres south is **Ben Klibreck** whose constituent word *brekka* was in Iceland often used for a hill for public meetings and legal proclamations. Further south in Gaeldom **Tom a' Mhoid** on Speyside is knoll of the justice court where the local clan chief sat in judgement. A *mod* is a meeting of significance (as well as a court), as in the Gaelic Mod: and from this word comes the name of the **Moot Hill** near Scone where King Nechtan of the Picts met and decided to follow Rome, not Iona, in the matter of Easter dates.

Tom na Croich near Blair Atholl is knoll of the gallows where an estate worker paid the penalty for murdering a colleague on the slopes of **Beinn a' Ghlo**. **Cnoc a' Chroiche** at Gairloch, situated between Free Kirk and kirkyard, was chosen apparently because of the clear 'drop' to the beach below! There are over 100 instances of **Gallows Hill** or **Knowe** in Scotland, indicating a traditional location for execution. There are several **Hangingshaw Hill**s but their name comes from the Middle English word *hingand* meaning a steep slope, plus *shaw* meaning a wood, nothing to do with execution.

In the Lowlands the name of **Castlehill** (there are at least 50 of them) is said to indicate a site of ancient justice. They are usually low hills (perhaps so as not to exhaust portly magistrates), such as the low hill near Carluke – nearby, maybe coincidentally, is the hill and village of Law. Another Castle Hill, above Campbeltown, is where the all-powerful Clan Donald had a fortress, making their laws and holding their Parliament independent of the Scots Crown. And in Skye above Glen Boreraig is the flat-topped grassy knoll of **Dùn Kearstach**, (properly Dùn a' Cheartais – justice hill (from *ceartas*).

Also in Skye near Duntulm was a hill originally called Cnoc an Eireacht, knoll of assembly, which Pennant on his 1772 tour wrote about:

> *Cnock an eirid* (sic), the hill of pleas: such eminences are frequently near the houses of all the great men, for on these, with the assistance of their friends, they determined all the differences between the people.

So the tradition of hills as legal arenas has a long history in Scotland. That most of the hill names referring to it are low is because of ease of access, Ben Loyal being the apparent exception. (Pronounced bYn **loe**ghal)

Ben Wyvis

Like a surfacing whale **Ben Wyvis** is visible from many directions, even the

Highland capital Inverness itself. In Ross-shire it is pronounced *weevus*, but often referred to simply as 'The Ben', the soubriquet of course that is borne by Ben Nevis further south. Indeed, 18th century writers often spelt the name very similar to Nevis, Ben Wevis being common, and interestingly, Dorret's map of 1750 marks the name of Ben Vevis here. Its name has been linked with the Gaelic *fuathais* meaning terror... or dismal and gloomy. Both meanings seems quite unreasonable for this long flat bulk of a hill. A now-obsolete meaning of *fuathais* is 'a great quantity', a closely related word to *uamhas* (pronounced **wa**vas) signifying a horrid deed or atrocity or equally – and here more likely – an enormous quantity. The word 'enormity' has the same double meaning in English. W.J.Watson's *Place-names of Ross & Cromarty* said that it was *beinn uais*, high: but in his later mature work he felt that majestic or awful (as in 'awe-full') was most appropriate to its massive isolated bulk, and perhaps awesome might be the best meaning. (Pronounced bYn **wee**vis)

Canisp

Unlike its neighbour Suilven, Canisp is rarely asked to pose in the many photos taken from Lochinver, lacking as it does the allure of a dramatic shape. The Reverend J.B. Johnston suggested it was from Old Norse *kenna ups* supposedly meaning well-known house roof. This is very unlikely as the neighbouring peaks mainly have Gaelic names and the Norse rarely went in for figurative description in names – and it cannot really be seen from the sea, unlike Suilven.

An earlier Scottish Mountaineering Club *Northern Highlands* guidebook points out that there are whitish quartzite cliffs spilling down its north face and suggests that its name may come from an old Gaelic word *can* meaning white. It is found in words like *canaichean*, bog-cotton, the bobbing white tufts in the moors – and is said to be the badge of Clan Sutherland. If this is correct it would take its place with the many examples of **Geal Chàrn**, **Sgùrr Bàn**, and **Fionn Bheinn** dotted over the Highlands, all 'white hills'. (See also White Hills, Central Highlands chapter p144).

Càrnan Cruithneachd

This is a fine Graham above Glen Elchaig, down to which the northern slopes drop steeply. It is often translated as hill of wheat, from the word *cruithneachd* meaning just that: but as W.J.Watson points out, the likelihood of wheat being grown, even at its foot, in these wet western wastes, is remote, and he argues for Cruithne, the Picts, the peoples who inhabited the area before the Norse and the Gaels took over. He also identified a place name Arinacruineach in Applecross, not so far away, as the shieling of the Picts.

Càrn Eige

Càrn Eige and its close neighbour **Màm Sodhail** are the two highest mountains west of the Great Glen, forming the high points of one of the great east-west ridges that run above the remote lochs of this area. The most usual interpretation of the name is as notch or file cairn, from the Gaelic *eag*, genitive form *eige*; the word can also refer to a peat-cutting tool, which perhaps lies more happily with the agricultural

name of neighbour **Màm Sodhail** (originally *màm sabhail*), barn peak. The approach to Càrn Eige from the east is along a pinnacled, narrow ridge, sometimes described as gendarmed, and at one point a stalkers' path almost becomes a flight of stone steps on a steep bit. The corrie to the north is Coire Dhomhain, deep corrie, indicating that the sides fall away steeply into it. So the idea of the narrowness of a file nicely represents the ridge's shape. However, and this is a big however, W.J.Watson and the Reverend Burn both stated that the locals pronounced it Càrn Eite, meaning extended or stretching – which it does, eastwards.

Conival

Conival is a Munro tucked aberth the bigger summit of Ben More Assynt, and seems to be one of a name clan. There are at least four instances of this name in the north-west, as well as **Little** and **Meikle Conval** hills in the north-east, and cousins **Conachro**, Cona Glen, **Conachair** and several **Conachraig**s strung across Scotland from St Kilda to the eastern Highlands.

Conival has been translated as from Old Norse *konna fjall*, or lady's peak: certainly *fjall* often became *-val* in the names of the Hebrides (as in Skye's Healavals), but rarely on the mainland. W.J.Watson, searching Gaelic, suggests early Celtic *cunos* meaning high, and suggests a meaning 'combination of lumps'. More likely, and appropriate, would be the Celtic prefix *con* meaning together or with, and *mheall* (a hill, pronounced val), for Conival and the Cona' Mhealls are all basically shoulders of lower tops of bigger peaks, and the name has the sense of a 'joined-on' hill. Three of them – Conival itself, **Cona' Mheall** in the **Ben More Coigach** group, and Cona' Mheall of **Beinn Dearg** – all lie within sight of each other, and *cona mheall* may have been a local dialect word for just such a hill. Further south, **Sròn Chona Choirein** is the nose of the joining of the corries. Near Loch Arkaig is another top **Streap Còmhlaidh** a few metres lower than **Streap** and linked to it by a narrow saddle, expressing the same 'adjoining' idea, in the sense of 'together with Streap'.

Cùl Beag and Cùl Mòr

Beag is little, *mòr* is big. But *cùl* means 'back of ... (anything)'. So the names of these two fine bodyguards to Stac Pollaidh literally mean 'big back of ' and 'little back of'. Back of what? Are they the 'backdrop' to the grander Ben More Coigach, or to lower but nearer and more spectacular Stac Pollaidh? There's another pair of Cùl Mòr and Cùl Beag in Easter Ross, very distinctive hills, backing a fertile strath: while **Culardoch** hill near Braemar is simply back of the high place. (Pronounced kool **moa**:r and **bayk**)

The Fannaichs

This chain of Ross-shire mountains appear to take its group name from the large loch, Fainich in Gaelic, washing their southern feet, and the eponymous deer forest running from shoreline to skyline. The origin of this name is obscure, and while there is a Gaelic word *fan* indicating a gentle slope, it would have a longer *a* sound,

and in any case seems inappropriate for these swooping Munros. There is a Gaelic word *fannaich* meaning to grow faint or feeble, as Munro-baggers perhaps feel on the ninth and last of the group!

Meall a' Chrasgaidh (possibly Meall a' Chrasgaich) is perhaps the hill of the crossing, guarding as it does the northern entrance to a hill-pass that lets travellers and herds cross the Fannaich ridge from north to south: on the face of it however, the name is literally hill of the box or coffer. Many of the summits have straightforward names, like **Sgùrr Mòr** (big peak), **Meall Gorm** (blue hill) and **An Coileachan** (little cock, probably the grouse). There are two **Druim Rèidh** names in this group, meaning level ridges, contrasting with the steeper slopes around them. **Beinn nan Ràmh** is the hill of oars: at the west end of the loch, it stands – according to W.J.Watson – above a stormy part of the loch, where rowing was critical for survival.

Five Sisters of Kintail

Lying above Glen Shiel, at the head of the sea-loch Duich, the view of these hills from the west is almost an 'industry standard' for Scottish pictorial calendars. Perhaps this is because its skyline resembles a young child's idealised drawing of a mountain, with a series of sharp points linked by swooping and regular curves. In reality it is not a range but one long mountain ridge, as indicated by its original Gaelic name of Beinn Mhòr, the big mountain.

Each separate peak has a Gaelic name, probably given later than the *beinn* name of the whole massif: **Sgùrr na Mòraichd** (majestic or mightiness peak), **Sgùrr nan Saighead** (arrows peak), **Sgùrr na Càrnach** (rocky peak), **Sgùrr na Ciste Duibhe** (peak of the dark chest). **Sgùrr Fhuaran** is ostensibly the peak of springs: Sir Hugh Munro, however, who climbed it in 1879 in the course of a long trip, grumbled that its slope was long and tiresome, and that its supposed meaning was inaccurate because 'never a sign of water was encountered from base to summit'. W.J.Watson was also sceptical of the springs meaning because it didn't fit local pronunciation, and suggested either *odharan* (cow-parsnip) or Oran's peak. A century earlier Dawson, engaged with Captain Colby on a surveying expedition, recorded its name as Scour Ouran – the *fh* is not pronounced in Gaelic. It is almost certainly *not* the 'peak of the wolf' suggested in one book.

Just why the range has the name Five Sisters is not very clear. The Gaels certainly did not call it this, so it is not a translation. Nor is it a very old English name, for Dr Johnson and Boswell, passing through Glen Shiel in September 1773, referred only to 'prodigious mountains on either side'. The term was however being widely used by the late 1930s, having been used in the 1931 first edition of the Scottish Mountaineering Club district guidebook. Hamish Brown in his book *Hamish's Mountain Walk* hints at the possibility that the shape of their peaks is pap or breast-like, which would make sisters the appropriate term; but again there is no record of local use of the common Gaelic name-words for breast or nipple, *cìoch* or *màm*, to suggest this. And the marked sharpness of the Five Sisters lacks the slight summit rounding appropriate to *cìoch* or *màm*, as can be seen on Sgùrr na Cìche 15 kilometres away.

Grey Hills
liath

Among many hill-names bearing *liath*, the main concentrations are in the north-west and north-central Highlands. The best known are in Torridon and the Monadh Liath range above Kingussie. **Liathach** is from *liath-ach*, greyish one: it is a square-shouldered lump of a mountain rising steeply from the glen – grey from the colour of the quartzite rock that forms its protective hard cap over the softer sandstones, and from the trailing clouds that catch and tear on its ridge, and from its grey-weathered plunging cliffs. As Thomas Pennant wrote of it in 1774:

> ... an amazing mountain, steeply sloping, composed of a whitish marble so extensive, glossy and even, as to appear like an enormous sheet of ice ...

That *liath* in a name often indicates such screes should be health warning enough for walkers, for instance on the ankle-twisting quartzite boulder slopes of **Sàil Liath**, of **An Teallach**.

The **Monadh Liath** the grey mountain, or moorland – is a massive outcrop of grey schist rock, so-called to contrast them with the Monadh Ruadh – the red mountain – across the Spey. They are also grey in the sense of dull and uninteresting, being described in an HMSO Forestry Guide as: 'They don't afford much scenery but offer hill-track access to the Great Glen'!

In the east is **Cairnleith Hill**, using the genitive form of the colour, and it may originally have been Cnoc a' Chairn Lèithe. However *lì*, as in **Mullach Lì** in the west, is not a short form of *liath*, but means instead coloured or hued. There's a delightful name in the Fannaichs, the mountain **Beinn Liath Mhòr a' Ghiubhais Lì**, big grey hill of the coloured pine. Other liaths, for instance **Càrn Liath** above Blair Atholl, mark sites of greyer metamorphic quartzite and schist rocks. (Pronounced **lyee-***a*)

The tendency to see hills as 'sisters' may have begun on the English chalk cliffs The Seven Sisters, and in Scotland the north buttresses of **Bidean nam Bian** above Glen Coe became known as the **Three Sisters of Glencoe**, after a dramatic and famous painting by Horatio MacCulloch, which hangs in Glasgow's Kelvingrove Art Gallery. On the continent, three sharp peaks on the northern edge of the Maladeta in the Spanish Pyrenees are Los Tres Hermanas de Paderna, while in Norway in the Helgeland mountains stand the Seven Sisters, daughters of a legendary king, turned to stone by the sunrise.

Near Hunterston on the Clyde coast are distinctive inland clifftops called The Three Sisters, and further east in the Central Lowlands near West Calder a group of shale bings has long been known as the **Five Sisters** (of Westwood!). Further up Glen Shiel from the Five Sisters are the less-famous siblings, the **Three Brothers of Kintail** – a rarely-used soubriquet – consisting of **Sàileag** (little heel), **Sgùrr an Fhuarail** (cold peak) and **Sgùrr a' Bhealaich Dheirg** (red pass peak). But the 'family name' for these brothers and sisters is definitely English, not Gaelic.

Foinaven

Famous, like its neighbour Arkle, for its eponymous racehorse, Foinaven is a long raw bone of whitish quartzite rock sticking out of the green and brown peat moors of the north-west. A harsh beauty certainly, but barely deserving of the name of wart mountain, the translation of the Gaelic *foinne-bheinn*, on account of its having 'three protuberances', as the Reverend J.B Johnston referred to them. The colour of its massive screes might suggest that it is a corrupted *fionn-bheinn*, pronounced *fyown vyn* and meaning white mountain, and indeed several guidebooks' indexes have mis-spelt it Fionaven as if in Freudian error.

However, although the colour name *fionn* is common in the north-west, there is little evidence for such an origin, as the local pronunciation, usually the most reliable guide, is indeed *foinne-bheinn*. Pont mapped it as Fannevein. W.J.Watson felt that it had probably begun as a Norse name – certainly it is Norse name territory, next to Arkle – and that it may have been *vind-fjall* (wind fell), the *fjall* being later translated to *beinn*. Now there is a Norse word *fann* meaning snow (as in *fann-hvitr*, snow white) – perhaps its rock screes looked like snow to the Norse – and it would fit Pont's recording. At 914m, just shy of the 914.4m required for Munro status, it is the highest Corbett, and it's appropriate that its summit is **Ganu Mòr**, probably big head from *ceann mòr*. (Pronounced **fo**n*ya*vin)

Yellow Hills
Meall Buidhe and Beinn Bhuidhe

These two stand side by side in Knoydart, dominating the near view as the boat sails into Inverie. There's another Buidhe Bheinn, not far away above Kinloch Hourn.

buidhe

Yellow. Not the modern bright yellow of the some walkers' fluorescent jackets but the soft tones of the dried grasses and bents that mat to form the mellow yellow sward on the many a **Tom Buidhe** and Meall Buidhe – there are at least 35 hills with this latter name and 22 with the former. One of this large family, **Meall Buidhe** above Glen Lyon, stands at the western end of a chain of dark heather-covered hills, and is by comparison pale yellow in tone. This colour is however most commonly found on hills along the western seaboard, especially on the south-west coast and islands: **Beinn Bhuidhe** stands in Knoydart side by side with **Meall Buidhe**, a Corbett hugely bigger in bulk than its taller Munro neighbour, but both dressed in this colour. This is because grasses rather than heathers tend to colonise the wettest hill-slopes (heather being therefore commoner in the drier east), this pattern may reflect the heavier rain falling on these Atlantic coasts.

In the east however there are some, for **A' Bhuidheanach Bheag** above Drumochter is the little yellow place (and there is a Bhuidheanach slope on **Cairn Toul** and an A' Bhuidheanach ridge on **Càrn Liath**, east of Creag Meagaidh). This Gaelic colour also peeps from anglicised hill names like **Drumbuy**, **Ben Bowie** and **Cairnbowie**, while **Monthboy** and **Monawee Hill** in Angus are from *monadh buidhe*. (Pronounced **boo**-*ya*)

Fuar Tholl

This simply means the 'cold hole' or 'cold hollow'. Hamish Brown in his book *Climbing the Corbetts* says:

> There is some lack of clarity as to which corrie of this grand hill is responsible for the name but my money would go on that grim, cliff-held eastern hollow which is *the* feature of the peak seen from Glen Carron.

The word *toll* is found also in the names of **Tolmount** (mountain of the hollow, above Glen Doll), a Munro in the Grampians, and **Toll Creagach** (rocky hollow) above Glen Affric. Fuar Tholl's earlier name, Beinn Leac Dearg – Pont mapped it as Ben Leckderg – mountain of the red rock, appears to have been more appropriate given the peak's red sandstone geology. The profile of the summit ridge from the hamlet of Lochcarron led to the mountain's soubriquet **Wellington's Nose**, after the eponymous Duke, which suggests a mid-19th century naming. (Pronounced **foo**-ur howl)

Garbh Bheinn

There are four peaks of this name, three within 25 kilometres of Ben Nevis, and of these the best-known is Garbh Bheinn of Ardgour, a rugged peak best seen against a sunset sky looking west from the Ballachulish Bridge. Popular with rock-climbers when higher peaks are wreathed in clouds, it simply means rough mountain. In the western areas of high rainfall like this, the downpours give the hills little chance to develop a greensward to smooth over their rocky bones, and hence the name. *Garbh*, rough, along with colours, is one of the few adjectives to regularly precede the noun in Gaelic. (Pronounced **ga**rav vYn)

Ladhar Bheinn

This is the highest mountain in the Knoydart peninsula, and certainly the grandest in bulk and rock architecture. It translates as hoof or claw mountain, presumably by analogy from its deep corries and encircling rocky ridges. The word order is significant, because *beinn* is usually the first word in a Gaelic hill name, but this was Norse territory (thus Knut's Fjord, source of Knoydart) and several hills have Norse word order of this type where the noun meaning hill is preceded by the adjective or a qualifying noun; **Slat Bheinn** and **Luinne Bheinn** being others nearby. Its subsidiary peaks include **Aonach Sgoitte**, split ridge and **Stob a' Chearcaill**, rounded or hooped peak. (Pronounced **loe**-ar vYn).

Liathach

In the dictionary, *liathach* means greyish, and that would be appropriate to the colour of the weathered quartzite protecting its softer sandstone. However Pont mapped it as Bin Liachann (possibly *liath-cheann*, grey head): and Thomson's 1826 map has it as Leagach (as it is locally pronounced) which might point at *beinn leacach*, slabby mountain. The *beinn* first name that Pont recorded may have been lost over time, but the old Gaelic-speaking *bodach* who W.H.Murray met one winter's day just after the war got the gender right (beinn being a feminine word) when he warned them not to climb it – 'She iss not to be tampered with!' The

mountain is so big that it hosts several tops, of which its two Munros are **Mullach an Rathain** (summit of the pulleys, perhaps identifying the shape of the rocky rugosities just north of the top) and **Spidean a' Choire Lèith** (pointed peak of the grey corrie). (Pronounced **lyee**ahoch, locally **lee**aghach)

Liathach, the greyish or slabby mountain. See p104, [Grey Hills, liath]

Màm Sodhail

The original Gaelic was Màm Sabhail; *màm* is a rounded, breast-shaped hill, while *sabhal* is a barn. Sabhal occurs in several hill names, such as **Cairn Toul** (Càrn an t-Sabhail) in the Cairngorms, and **Sabhal Mòr** and **Beag**, further north of here. There would be a contradiction here between a rounded breast shape and the flat-topped ridge shape of a barn. Nevertheless there is surely a connection between the name of one of the long south-eastern ridges dropping from Màm Sodhail towards Loch Affric, which is called **An Tudair** (properly, *An Tughadair*). This means 'the thatcher', and since the mountains were named long before the Americans got the dubious habit of naming peaks after national leaders, we can assume it refers to a roofing craftsman, who would thatch barns frequently. A Gaelic poem refers to it as 'Màm Sodhail of the grass', *Màm Sabhail an fheòir*. (Pronounced maam **soa**-al or **sool**)

Morven

There are two hills called Morven in Scotland, meaning big mountain, *mòr bheinn*. This one, near Helmsdale, is certainly the highest in the surrounding area at 706m, although not necessarily the biggest in terms of bulk, and presents a striking conical profile. In a Norse name area (it overlooks Berriedale, for instance) it and its

neighbour **Scaraben** (the divided or separated hill) show the Norse name word order, adjective before noun. It also has two English named neighbours, **Maiden Pap** (splendidly breast-shaped, but perhaps it should be Paps, since from below there appear two nipples) to the east and **Little Mount** to the west, the partner of this particular big mount.

Quinag

The local people in Assynt pronounce this mountain 'koonyak' confirming the name's Gaelic name of *cuinneag*, a milking pail or stoup, which had a wooden handle in the shape of the summit's profile. The Highlands are scattered with such domestic items as if some *cailleach* had strewn the household implements around after an argument with her *bodach*: on Speyside there's a cup – **Meall Cuaich**, in the Cairngorms a table – **Beinn a' Bhùird**, on Arran a comb – **Cìr Mhòr**, above Glen Shiel a basket and a knife – **A' Chralaig**, and **Sgùrr na Sgìne**, together with **Sgùrr Mhurlagain** – wool-basket and **An Sgruaboch** – a broom ... perhaps they were all flung out of her creel, **Beinn a' Chlèibh**, as she stormed out past the door-post, **Sgùrr an Ursainn**, past the big barn, **Sabhal Mòr**, to the cowshed, **Am Bàthach**, to collect off the pulleys, **Mullach an Rathain**, this *cuinneag*, milk pail. Many of these hills have a shape which fits their name – the upturned bowl of Meall Cuaich, the flat top of Beinn a' Bhùird – and in the case of Quinag a former Scottish Mountaineering Club guidebook says of its **Spidean Còinnich**, mossy peak, summit:

> ... the southern peak which stands out boldly like a water-spout. This peak gives the mountain its name Cuinneag in Gaelic as a narrow-mouthed water bucket.

It might be more accurate to say that it resembles the handle or lug of a traditional milk pail. Not far away in Easter Ross is **Càrn Chuinneag**, another of the same, showing how the peak's shape struck a chord in the Gaelic countryside – the peak's profile is a more likely meaning than the alternative that it comes from the shape of some pail-like hollows in rocks somewhere on its slopes. The other two main tops are **Sàil Gharbh** and **Sàil Gorm**, respectively rough and blue heels. (Pronounced **choon**yak)

Rois-Bheinn

In the far west, Rois-Bheinn lies within sight of **Beinn Resipol**, and like it has been linked to horses as mountain of horses (*hross bheinn*). Horsy names were quite important to the Norse as names like **Roishal** (Harris), **Hestaval** (a Lewis hill) and Roisnish (from *ness*, headland) show. A Gaelic alternative of An Fhrosbeinn from *frois bheinn* (mountain of showers) has been suggested but while showery would be an understatement for the wild wet weather that regularly soaks this area, *frois* usually means a shower of grain, not rain. Alternatively the Gaelic *ros*, meaning a headland, is a common element in place names, though not usually in hills, and Rois-Bheinn certainly does stand, headland-like, farthest west in its group of hills, up against the seaboard. On the other hand this same position would have made it significant as a landmark to the Norse sailors on the Minch, and the evidence probably points that way. (Pronounced **rosh**-vYn)

The Saddle

Around Kintail in Wester Ross is an intriguingly 'horsy place': here there are foals (in **Sgùrr an t-Searraich** – on the **Five Sisters** – and **Beinn an t-Searraich**), a mare (in **Sgùrr na Làire Brice** – as in **Beinn Làir** further north), another mare above Glenelg (in **Beinn a' Chapuill**), a mane (**A' Mhuing** above Glen Shiel), and both Norse and Gaelic horses (in Rosdail near Glenelg and in **Sgùrr Leac nan Each** on the Saddle). **The Saddle** itself (An Diollaid in Gaelic – another lies on a shoulder of Ladhar Bheinn) is so-named from the yoke-shape of its 1010m summit slung between two peaked tops – like its English little cousin Saddleback, and its distant relative the Sattelhorn in the Swiss Bernese Oberland – and completes the equestrian connection in this area. The concentration in this western seaboard area may be due to the Norse influence, for the Norse word *hross* occurs throughout the Western Isles, as well as in place names like Rosdail and Rois-bheinn. The Vikings did use horses, and may well have introduced new strains to the local people. Many climbers approach The Saddle's summit by scrambling up the steep ridge to the top called **Sgùrr na Forcan**, peak of the little fork. Purely coincidentally, across the corrie lies **Sgùrr na Sgìne**, peak of the knife – the fork here refers to the pinnacled outline.

Seana Bhràigh

This means simply old height or upper part. But why 'old'? Not from its rocks since they are schists rather than the ancient gneisses found elsewhere in the north-west. Perhaps old in the sense of familiar ... or 'wrinkled' with its furrowed ledges? There are several names in the Highlands with *sean*, and they are scattered mainly along the western seaboard from Cape Wrath to Kintyre, and through the Hebrides – places called (in translation) old fort, old hill, old cliff, old heap and old knoll. Over in the Grampians **Càrn Aosda** is the aged mountain, probably from *aoise*. However, the name – certainly for the main summit – may well be an error. Both the Reverend Burn, early in the 20th century, and J.H.B.Bell, mid-century, quote local keepers who said that the main top was Beinn Eag (notch mountain), while Seana Bhràigh was the rounded slope and domed hill to the north of it. The top to the east, now **Creag an Duine** (crag of the man), was known as An Sgùrr, the peak: Mr McKenzie, the keeper at Corriemulzie in 1941, claimed that its name came from a man (*duine*) who disappeared while climbing out to rescue a sheep from a ledge.

However there is yet another, stranger, possibility. In the MacFarlane Geographical Manuscripts, a 17th century correspondent (possibly Timothy Pont) says

> Charroun [R. Carron] falleth out of the great hill of Scornivar ... on the southsyd thereof ...

Now the Carron rises in the Deargs range north of the A835, and Scornivar (elsewhere in Macfarlane Skormyvarr) could well be what is now Seana Bhràigh, and indeed that the modern name may be a corruption of the old. Hidden away on the 1:25000 map, while not shown on the 1:50000 series, is a top now called **Sgòr a' Bharra**, demoted since the 17th century from naming the main summit, to indicating now the dip or cleft between two of its main peaks. It may be *sgùrr na bhàrr*

(peak of the top or ridge), or even *sgùrr na bhràighe*, peak of the upper height, a name possibly corrupted to that currently on the map. (Pronounced **she**na vrY)

Slioch

Slioch is described in the Scottish Mountaineering Club's *The Munros* guidebook as

> ... one of the great sights of the northern Highlands, well seen and much photographed from the A832 road.

Protruding up from behind a long low ridge above Loch Maree, the main body of the mountain thrusts itself up by means of sandstone buttresses, matching the usual translation of the Gaelic *sleagh*, a spear. And within the two eastern arms of its summit ridge lies Coire na Sleaghaich, corrie of the spear.

However in the 1830s *New Statistical Account* the local Poolewe minister, the Reverend Donald MacRae, wrote that 'The principal mountain of the range is Slioch or Sliabhach.' This latter word is the adjectival form of *sliabh*, the early Gaelic word for mountain, mainly confined in Scotland to the south-west, where it had been imported by Irish Celts. Loch Maree at Slioch's feet is however named after a 7th century Irish missionary Saint Maelrubha, and so it is possible that Slioch's name is also a relic of 'the old country' as Ireland was known. On the other hand, in the Wester Ross dialect *sliabhach* can refer simply to mountain grass, and early this century the locals called it An Sleaghach, meaning the spear-like mountain: the Reverend Burn, early 20th century, said locally it was pronounced 'sluggich'. A 1750 map by Dorret, wildly inaccurate in location – it put Slioch on the shores of Loch Torridon – probably reflected the local pronunciation of *sleagh* when he put 'Mount Sliach'.

Obviously a simple meaning 'mountain' (from *sliabh*) does not have the charm and striking imagery of 'the spear'; and a spear would also be able to claim international company, for the Zulu name for the South African Drakensberg range is Ekhalamba, meaning barrier of spears. Nearer home, there's a hill above Loch Linnhe called **An Sleaghach**, the spear-like mountain. (Pronounced **slee**ach)

Suilven

Contemporary photos of this striking hill are normally taken from Lochinver. From this seaward view, over a middle distance of rolling moorlands, the mountain rises up with the suddenness of a surfacing submarine, an effect enhanced by telephoto lenses. The Vikings in their longships would have seen this, and the name is almost certainly Norse, from *sul-r*, a pillar. It was probably originally *sul-r fjall*, and became part-Gaelicised to *sul-r bheinn* (pronounced *ven*), just as Skye's *Bla-fjall* became Blà Bheinn. Certainly the main summit of **Caisteal Liath**, grey castle, sits well on top of this 'pillar'.

The 18th century traveller Thomas Pennant called it the Sugar Loaf mountain, a figurative title for a hill that was quite common in those days. In 1774, John Home in his survey of Assynt mapped the hill with the legend

> A remarkable high rocky mountain called Soalving or Sugar Loaf.

There have been suggestions that it is a completely Gaelic name. One writer

suggested *soillse-bheinn*, light mountain, indicating that communications bonfires may have been lit on it, but there's no archaeological evidence for this. The Reverend J.B.Johnston's *Place-names of Scotland's* suggestion of *suil-bheinn*, eye mountain (from its shape, he said – had he ever seen it?), is even wider of the mark. There is an alternative local Gaelic name of A' Bheinn Bhuidhe, the yellow mountain, hardly an eye-catching title!

Suilven, a landmark from the sea and for the Norse for whom it was sulr, pillar. See also p64, [Islands, introduction]

In the late 16th century, Pont mapped it as Skormynag, a clear phonetic reference to the central summit Sgùrr – now **Meall – Mheadonach**, middle peak. But while the separate peaks may have Gaelic names, the whole mountain's name is clearly Norse: apart from the sheer aptness of the pillar name, there are pillar mountains in Scandinavia too – such as two called Sulur in north Iceland. (Pronounced **soo:lavYn**)

The Torridons

Several books published in the 1980s – among them an edition of the Scottish Mountaineering Club's *Munro's Tables* – make reference to 'The Torridons', and although mapmakers do not yet recognise such a range, it may well be a name for the future. At present the Torridon name applies to the glen and to the area in general. W.J.Watson thought from the sound of the Gaelic *toirbheartan* that it meant place of portage, where boats were carried across a narrow strip of land: such places normally are called *tarbert*, a related word (and there are several places Tarbet or Tarbert in Scotland) but there is no obvious isthmus here for this carrying to take place, and it's a long way to haul a longship to Loch Maree!

CHAPTER FOUR

THE CAIRNGORMS

An Sgarsoch

Sgar in Gaelic is a knot or fissure (as in wood), but the meaning of this name is obscure. One mid-19th century writer on place names, James Robertson, claimed that it meant 'place abounding in sharp rocks', but this is not at all appropriate for the topography here. This is a flat-topped hill a long way from the nearest road, but there is a tradition that it was once the site of an annual cattle fair, the Feill Sgarsaich – not that the name relates to this activity.

However this cultural importance of the hill may have caused the name's appearance on old maps, when few other surrounding hills were named. Indeed, mapmakers from Blaeu and Gordon in the 1650s onwards depicted 'Mountayns of the Scairsoch' ('10 myles long') as the main group in the area, giving the hill a central importance that it lacks today. And in the late 16th century, the great Dutch cartographer Mercator showed the Scairschioch Hilles at the hub of Grampius Montes chain: the second syllable of his mapped name, if accurate, could point at *cìoch*, breast, a common hill name element, but there is no tor on the hill of appropriate shape. (Pronounced an skarsoch)

Beinn a' Bhùird

This is Scotland's answer to South Africa's Table Mountain, in name at least. At the risk of stating the obvious, it is almost certainly called this because of its three-kilometre-long, flat summit plateau, bounded by steep cliffs on the east; Seton Gordon wrote in 1948 that 'with little difficulty it could be made a landing-place for aircraft'. The Gaelic word *bòrd* is related to the Scots or English 'board' for a table, and *bùird* is the genitive form. In the 17th century, mapmaker Blaeu recorded it as Bini Bourd, so arguably the correct Gaelic may be Beinn Bòrd. A patch of snow – The Laird's Tablecloth – lingers in summer high up in the corrie, and is the subject of a legend that if it disappears, the Farquharsons would lose their Invercauld estate. In fact it does disappear most summers, but the laird's stock answer was that it may be very dirty but it was still there under the grime! (Pronounced bYn a **voo**:rsht or bYn **bawrd**)

Beinn a' Ghlo

This is a single mountain mass, with three separate peaks of Munro status lying within it, visible and striking for kilometres around above the broad strath at Blair Atholl. In 1769 Thomas Pennant on his *Tour of Scotland*, described it thus:

> ... the great hill of Ben y Glo, whose base is 35 miles in circumference and whose summit towers far above the others.

The great height (1129m) that Pennant refers to and its tendency to catch the clouds will explain the name from an old Gaelic word *glo* meaning veil or hood, and stretched by imagination to suggest a veiled or cloud-capped summit. Hill of the mist would be a convenient shorthand. There was a witch who lived on its summit,

with the power to control the weather in order to force humans to meet her demands – so the name may have roots in legend as well as geography. In the local Gaelic its name is Beinn a' Ghlotha, or Na Beinnichean Glotha, another version of *glo*. Timothy Pont in the 16th century mapped it as Binglo and on another map as Bin Gloin, and in Grant's Legends of the Braes o' Mar it was given as Beinn a' Ghlo nan Eag (of the notches).

The constituent trio of peaks are **Càrn nan Gabhar** (hill of goats), **Càrn Liath** (grey hill) and **Bràigh Coire Chruinn-bhalgain** (height of the corrie of round blisters) – this was known to the Rev A.E.Robertson, the First Munroist, as 'the turkey peak', clearly a little phonetic joke based on the pimple on its Glen Tilt slopes called Càrn Torcaidh, from *torc*, a boar! **Airgiod Bheinn** is the silver hill, probably from the mica flakes in the schist rock.

The hill was and is sometimes spelt Ben y Glo, using a local Perthshire variant of *a'*, as in Craig y Barns, Ben y Vrackie or Ben y Hone (**Ben Chonzie**), all sometimes hyphenated. But the letter *y* is not part of the Gaelic alphabet, and it suggests that the first mapping which 'recorded' these spellings was done by an Ordnance Survey surveyor with origins or training in Wales where y is the common equivalent of the Gaelic *a'*; Englishman Thomas Pennant may have based his spelling on the sound of the local pronunciation. (Pronounced bYn a **gh**law)

Beinn Bhrotain

The old mapmakers got their pronunciation of *bh* more or less correct when they spelt this hill as Binwrodin, Binny-wroten and Beinn-na-Vrotan. Lying in the eastern Cairngorms above the mapped Coire Cath (correctly Cadha) nam Fionn, the corrie of the battle (correctly pass) of the Fingalians, it is fitting that this name too comes from ancient legend, from Brodan the fabled hound or mastiff. By repute a jet black hound, it chased the white fairy deer; and while it was probably owned by one of the Fingalians, like many aggressive dogs the specific owner preferred not to be identified. (Pronounced bYn **vroh**tYnʸ)

Beinn Mheadhoin

This means middle mountain. Early mapmakers had it as Binnamain, Biny Main and Ben Mean: *mh* is normally pronounced *v* in Gaelic, to make the second word sound like 'vane'. However Adam Watson's research, and the evidence of the old maps whose makers would have based their names on local pronunciation, indicates that locals pronounced the name with an *m*, making it Beinn Meadhon. There are two other, better known hills named Ben Vane, pronounced with a *v*, **Benvane** in the Trossachs and **Ben Vane** in the Arrochar Alps where it is piggy-in-the-middle between Beinn Ime and Ben Vorlich: their nearness to the cities probably ensures they are more climbed than this Beinn Mheadhoin in the Cairngorms, which lies at least 15 walking kilometres from the nearest roads. And this is probably the clue to its name. For it does indeed lie in the middle of this mountain range. A similarly central position is occupied by Beinn Mheadhonach near Blair Atholl, between two very deep glens.

The designation 'middle' sounds like a put-down – but it's in good international company, for La Meije, one of the jewels of the Dauphine Alps, means just that. The Gaelic word *meadhon* can also have the connotation of 'the centre, the heart', and perhaps this is a fairer translation of its position in the Cairngorm range. From it streams flow north to join the River Avon and south to join the Dee. Certainly the mountain need fear no comparison with its higher neighbours when the character of the actual summits are compared, for Beinn Mheadhoin has a magnificent tor, about 12 metres high, of weathered granite. Lying on a plateau surface spread with the granite crumbles of this semi-arctic desert with tufts of short grass clinging to it, it looks like a butte from the American West. (Pronounced bYn **vee**-oiny)

Ben Avon

The northern foothills of this mountain are washed by the River Avon on its journey to the Moray Firth, and the river and mountain probably share the name. The name Avon is the archetypal British word for a river, there being at least three in Scotland, and five major ones in England, all deriving from an ancient Indo-European root word for water, with descendants in the Latin *abona* and Welsh *afon*. But this north-east name is *not* exactly the same word, and the identical spelling is the result of Ordnance Survey surveyors, familiar with the many Rivers Avon down

---

Dappled Hills

breac
Meaning dappled or speckled, it is applied to hill-slopes where patches of scree and heather, greys and greens and browns, break out from under each other. Thus the **Beinn Bhreac** in the Cairngorms has a heathery hillside patterned with great weeping grey scars of scree; and there are 54 other mountains called Beinn Bhreac in Scotland. **Ben Vrackie** in the Trossachs, **The Brack** near Arrochar, the several **Dumbreck** hills also come from this word – and so perhaps does **Beinn Bhraggie** in the north, although it may commemorate Saint Brachdaidh.

Another **Ben Vrackie**, the Corbett dominating Pitlochry, is geologically a whirl of black schists, grey micaschists, white quartzite and greenish epidiorite, all with characteristic screes, soils and therefore plants to give it 'speckle'. Approaching it on the 'tourist path' you face a patchwork of grey screes, dark heather, and light grasses on its south-western slopes.

One authority on Gaelic folklore says that there is a hag-like creature in Gaelic legend called Cailleach **Beinn a' Bhric**, the 'spirit of the speckled mountains', who was said to disguise herself in deer-hides and be able to be a good friend or a mortal enemy to lone travellers. Perhaps some of the Beinn Bhreac and Beinn a' Bhric hills were named in order to appease her.

Another, rarer, word for speckled is *bailgeann* (from *bailgfhionn*): **Tom Bailgeann** in

---

south, writing down the nearest equivalent to the Gaelic word *abhainn*, (pronounced roughly aving or awing) also meaning a river. A 1600 spelling of the name, by traveller John Taylor, as Benawne is closer both to the original Gaelic, and to the modern hill-walkers' pronunciation as Ben Aan.

Other suggestions on the watery note have included *ath fionn* or *abhain fhionn*, white or very bright ford or stream, and a legend that it comes from Ath nam Fionn (the *th* is silent in speech), meaning the ford of the Fingalians, referring to the Fords of Avon on the river below. The legend tells of Fionn's wife being swept away and drowned while crossing here. Florin and the Fingalians exist in Celtic legend if not in historical reality, and several other hills elsewhere may well refer to them. The local Gaelic pronunciation for the strath is indeed *athfhinn*, but this pronunciation is apparently only two centuries old; and its 12th century written spelling Strathouen suggests *strath abhann*, an archaic genitive form of *abhainn*, a river.

The modern hill-walkers' pronunciation as Ben Aan recalls the hill in the Trossachs called **Ben A' n**. This latter name is probably a mistake by Sir Walter Scott for the original name *binnean*, a small peak. It might be thought that the tors on Ben Avon's summit ridge could be classed as *binnean*, but this Gaelic word is largely confined to southern parts of the Highlands, and the pronunciation would not really fit the name.

Stratherrick is composed of conglomerate sandstone, in which assorted pebbles were geologically pressed into a sandstone bed, giving it a three-dimensional speckled appearance. And *lap*, as in **Beinn na Lap** at the edge of Rannoch Moor, is also said to mean dappled, since *lap* refers to a defective colour spot, in textiles.

odhar

Odhar means dun, pale, dappled or tawny, a greyish brown colour and is pronounced 'oa-ur', (roughly as in the corrupted name of **Ben Our**). This colour name is found throughout the Highlands, though commonest in Kintyre and upper Speyside. One example **Meall Odhar** is very familiar to thousands of hill-users, though they will not recognise this colour easily, for most of them see it in the form of the winter-white lump trussed up like Gulliver in a tangle of ski-wires one and a half kilometres to the east of the Glen Shee car park. This was formerly Am Meall, Odhar Mòr, the smaller hill between it and the car park being the Beag. In Ayrshire, Lanarkshire and the Pentlands there are a **Millour Hill**, a **Melowther Hill** and a **Mealowther**, all from *meall odhar*.

riabhach

Grey or speckled but in a streaked manner, like a rain-blotched water colour, it appears in **Braeriach** (Am Bràigh Riabhach), Scotland's third highest mountain. **An Riabhachan** near Loch Monar means simply the grey one – although the name is close to being An Riabhach Mòr, the Devil! Sometimes the word is anglicised, as in Sròn Riach on **Ben Macdui**.

However Ben Avon does have a distinctive skyline because of these granite tors. As Olive Fraser's poem observed:

> Yon's nae wife's hoose ayont
> A'an In the green lift ava,
> Yon's the cauld lums o' Ben A'an
> Wha's smeek is snaw.

These tors – known also as the Bads o' Ben A'an, or literally tufts – have their individual names, the summit rock itself being mapped as **Leabaidh an Daimh Bhuidhe**, bed of the yellow stag, although the old name was **Stob Dubh Easaidh Mòr**, the dark stob above the big Essie burn. Other tops include **Clach Choutsaich** (Coutts' stone – a common local surname, and there's another on **Brown Cow Hill**), **Mullach Lochan nan Gabhar** (summit of the goats' lochan), and **Stob Bac an Fhuarain** (top of the bank of the spring,). The first of these three was also once known as Invercauld Stables, from the estate's habit of taking hill ponies there.

Another large tor, **Clach Bhàn** on the slopes above the River Avon, means the stone of the women. Legend has it that it was visited by Fingal's wife, and documented history attests that it was visited by pregnant women, as late as the 19th century, who bathed in its hollowed-out rock pools in the hope of easing their impending labour. (Pronounced bYn **a**-an^y)

Ben Gulabin

It has been suggested that its name may come from *gulban*, a beak, or the derivative *guilbneach*, a curlew (the 'beaked bird'). However, this name Ben Gulabin appears in varying spellings in several localities, and signifies an association with the legendary Fingalian heroes: Ben Gulbin is the old name of **Beinn Tianavaig** in Skye, there's a **Ben Gullipen** near Callander, a **Beinn a' Ghuilbein** near Garve, and a **Beinn Ghuilbin** near Aviemore. They are linked to Ben Bulben (Beann Ghulbain) near Sligo in west Ireland, and through that to the Irish hero Conal Gulban: above Spittal of Glenshee, Ben Gulabin is, like its Irish cousin, a steep-sided flat-topped hill, and was significant enough locally to be mapped by Pont in the 1590s as Bin Whouilby. All these hills are reputed to be places connected to the Fingalian legend of the hunter Diarmaid, his lover Grainne, and their two hounds, lying buried on the slopes. A 16th century poem set in Glen Shee, runs;

> In the glen, below Ben Gulbin green,
> Whose tulachs gleam in the sun,
> The river's flow was stained with red
> When deer fell to Fionn of the fairies
> … hear my lay… of Ben Gulbin, of generous Fionn, and Diarmid O'Doon…
> a tale of grief.

The tale in one sentence is that Diarmuid, lover of Grainne, died after being tusked by a boar after spitefully denying Fionn a sip of the hill's life-saving water. The boar is *torc* in Gaelic, which is why there's often a boar name nearby, for

instance Brig o' Turk near Callander, a Loch an Tuirc on the very shoulder of the Garve hill, and in relation to this Ben Gulabin, **Càrn an Tuirc** overlooking the head of Glen Clunie to the north. (Pronounced bYn **gool**abin)

Ben Macdui

Although second to Nevis in the land, this mountain is number one in the Cairngorms. For many years this was thought – by the locals at least – to be the highest Scottish mountain, although Blaeu's 1654 map does not identify it, naming instead the nearby Ben Bhrotain, Cairn Gorm and Ben Avon. A mountain by the name of Corintrack Mt appears roughly where Macdui stands, and Adam Watson has suggested to me that it is a phonetic representation of Coire an t-Sneachda, which from some angles to the north blocks Macdui's view out.

It was not until 1811 that Macdui was removed from its presumed pole position as a result of a survey of Dr George Keith (who, incidentally, spelled it Ben Macdouie). The Ordnance Survey of 1847 fixed this downgrading to second place (by 30 metres) in the concrete of its trig points, and in spite of the appeals of old Macdui sentimentalists. Such was the sense of outrage that there was even a plan mooted by the landowner Earl of Fife to build himself a burial pyramid of stones on the summit over 30 metres high, to carry Macdui back to the commanding height as well, presumably, as his own soul to even higher places. His family name may well have played a part in the mountain's name, as we will see.

One feature Macdui does share with Ben Nevis is the ambiguity of its name. One popular interpretation derives the name from *beinn na muic duibh*, mountain of the black pig. Set amidst Gaelic names which translated include a blue hill, a middle hill, a rounded peak and grey heights, this meaning certainly has the asset of dramatic contrast. The local Forestry Commission Guide puts this porcine meaning down to 'its shape'. However, it is unlikely, for the domestic pig was never the universal animal of the Highlands in the way that cattle, which gave their name to many hills, were. Its forerunner the wild boar rummaged in oak woods, not found here in the heart of the Cairngorms and by the 15th century when mountains were being named, their domesticated descendants were confined to the far west. In any case the Gaelic word for boar is *torc*, as in Càrn an Tuirc above Glen Clunie. There is a suggestion that the 'pig' name was first used not by knowledgeable locals but by a minister of Crathie and Braemar parish, writing of Binn-na-muick-duibh in the first Statistical Account, and that this colourful porcine explanation then took wings in subsequent years in the oft-used form of Ben Muick Dhui.

A more prosaic (but almost certainly more accurate) interpretation of the name is that it is from *beinn mac dhuibh*, hill of the son of *dubh* the black one, or hill of the sons of Duff. It's stated in the 18th century Statistical Account that MacDuff, Thane of Fife, made a grant of the parish of Inveraven – the waters of the Avon start on the mountain – so he must have owned the land. The Duff (or Fife) family owned much of the Aberdeenshire part of the mountain until they sold out to a Swiss owner in the 1960s. Duff is a common anglicisation of *dubh* – witness the several Torduff Hills in southern Scotland – and the common Gaelic prefix *mac* means son of.

Indeed one of Robert Gordon's early 17th century maps shows Cairn Toul beside it as Soul Bin MacDuff (ie *sabhal* [barn of] Bin Mac Duff. This suggestion is the most plausible, and accords well with General Roy's 1750s military map name of Ben Mach Dui; there are other Highland mountain names taken from personal names, like **Sgòrr Dhònuill** (Donald) and **Beinn Fhionnlaidh** (Finlay).

A third suggestion for the name given by one authority, Diack, was for an original form of Binnmach Duibh, with *mach* (he says) being an obsolete Gaelic suffix, leaving the rest as the simple 'dark hills'. **Clashmach Hill** near Huntly seems to have this suffix *mach* added to *clais*, a furrow.

It is certainly a mountain of colour contrasts. Famous for its legendary spectre Am Fear Liath Mòr (the Big Grey Man), it is also known for its subsidiary features Sròn Riach (speckled nose – properly, Sròn Riabhach), Fèith Buidhe (yellow bog-stream,), Sputan Dearg (red spouts), and its Lochan Uaine (green lochan). Appropriate then that the man after whose family it is almost certainly named, MacDuff, had himself a 'colour' name! (Pronounced bYn *mac* **doo**ee)

Ben Rinnes

Ben Rinnes in the far north-east recalls the names of those lower hills in the south-west, the **Rhinns of Kells**, and the **Rhinns of Islay**. From the Old Irish *rind* meaning a headland, the word *rinn* in Gaelic can mean a sharp point although the suffix letter -s is puzzling. Now while Ben Rinnes is a great rounded whaleback of a hill, it is made distinctive by the outcropping granite tors known as the Scurrans near the summit, and these skyline pinpricks are probably the reason for the mountain's name. (See under Sgoran in the chapter on Generics, for Scurran.) On old maps, from Blaeu's in the 1650s on, the mountain is often spelled Bel-rinnes, but by the early 19th century it was mapped as Beinn Rennis Hill. (Pronounced bYn **ree**nyaysh)

Bennachie

Such is the fondness with which this hill is regarded in the north-east that it has its own 'Swiss Guard' of hill-lovers, the Bailies of Bennachie. Founded in 1970, they look after its care and conservation. The hill's pointed top is familiar from many viewpoints, sitting on a wedge of high ground in the Garioch lowlands, advance runner for the distant Cairngorms. More poetically, local bard Charles Murray wrote of it:

> ... Ben Nevis looms, the laird of a',
> But Bennachie! Faith, yon's the hill
> Rugs at the hairt where you're awa'

The granite tor that protrudes from its plateau, the famous **Mither Tap**, is the goal of most walkers although the true summit is the **Oxen Craig**. This Scots name the Mither Tap (mother top) directs us to the Gaelic original of Beinn na Cìche meaning mountain of the nipples or breasts, *cìoch* (genitive *cìche*) being widely used in the Highlands for granite tors of this shape. Adam Watson recorded an old

woman who referred to the top rocks by the Scots equivalent, The Pap Rocks.
One article on the hill says boldly that,

> the Gael, coming within view of this peak, was instinctively compelled to
> exclaim Beinn-na-cìche!

In 1170 the hill was written as Benychie, and in the 14th century as Benechkey.
W.J.Watson's interpretation of the name as *beannachadh* meaning blessed (hill)
seems fanciful by comparison with the anatomical meaning, but his is only one of
many wild surmisings over the years. It has been translated as meaning the mountain of springs and also of the Tap, of rain, or sight, of the dog, of Che (a pagan god),
of God (*dia*), and even as the 'bend-up-high' hill! This last may have begun with a
19th century English traveller who decided that Benahee (as spoken) was really the
'ben up high' (in the sky?) mountain! Subsequently a local minister spread the idea
that it was 'bend up high' because its shape resembled someone bending over to
touch their toes. Certainly for a minister in last century's more prudish times, any
name would be preferable to 'the mountain of the breast' although that is exactly
what it is. (Pronounced binni**cheech**)

Braeriach (properly, Am Bràigh Riabhach)

This mountain giant has a rather unexciting name in translation, as the grey, drab
or brindled upland. The original Gaelic was Am Bràigh Riabhach, literally the
brindled upland – many local people still refer to it, correctly, as The Braeriach. The
usual translation of *riabhach* is 'grizzled' or 'brindled', words which have become
obsolete in English and mean (in modern parlance) streaked, mottled or dappled.
This description of a 'mottled grey height' may well come from the patchy pattern
of the hardy dwarf arctic vegetation that struggles to survive in the harsh conditions
amongst the granite gravel spreads on its plateau.

Of more dramatic note, in the midst of this plateau lies the true source of the
River Dee, at 1190m the highest spring in Britain, a trickle that spills over Braeriach's
cliffs into An Garbh Choire. It is this, 'the rough corrie', and the mountain's other
corries, that distinguish Braeriach. An Garbh Choire, known to many climbers as the
Garracorrie, is a deep boulder-bottomed bowl in the hillside. Off it runs Coire
Bhrochain, literally porridge corrie (figuratively pointing at the mass of broken boulders on its floor), where mists may bubble up to the very summit: alternatively,
Seton Gordon suggests it got its name from cattle falling over its cliffs and being
pulped to pieces on the rocks below – he claims to have found bones there in 1927.
Alternatively indeed, but fanciful – cattle would not be on the high plateau,
and even if they were, why would this corrie be a more likely trap for them than
others? On the northern slopes are Coire an Lochain (corrie of the little loch),
Coire Beanaidh (dull), Coire Ruadh (russet-red, from the weathered granite) and
Coire Gorm (green, from the grasses, the result of late-lying snow). (Pronounced *am*
brY **ree**avoch)

Bynack More

The peaks of the eastern Cairngorms are often crowned with huge granite tors with a local name, *barns*, possibly a translation of the local Gaelic name Saibhlean Bheinneig. The **Barns of Bynack More** lie just below the summit, and may well have influenced the name. Originally it was called Beinn (or Am) Beidhneag, and therefore are several possibilities for its meaning. *Binneag* is a chimney pot or a house roof-ridge; chimney pots are, like the Barns here, often set just beneath the topmost ridge of the roof. However the pronunciation does not fit very well. One Gaelic scholar suggests that the name is from *beinneag*, little mountain, in which case Bynack More would be the big little mountain, since *mòr* is big! (There's a `wee' **Bynack Beag** nearby). *Binneach* – towered or turreted – might fit the mountain and its tors better. The similar word *binneach* – probably the root of Cairn Bannock east of Lochnagar – meaning pointed, might suit well.

Other writers say it is from *beannag* meaning a cap, or handkerchief or headband. A Gaelic dictionary gives *beannag* (pronounced byanak) as meaning 'a corner, a skirt, or a pointed coif (headwear), worn as a sign of marriage by women': indeed it would be close to the name mapped by Blaeu in 1654 as Byn Byinck. Certainly when you look up at the mountain from the path in Strath Nethy it does appear to rise to a fine point, unusual in the rounded Cairngorms. But both the headgear similes' lack the power of the 'chimney pot' image that strikes the eye from the north. It is however a name whose meaning must remain uncertain.

Cairn Gorm

Although the smallest of the four Cairngorm 4000 footers, this is probably the best known because it has given its name to the whole mountain group. In Gaelic the range is known as Am Monadh Ruadh, the red mountain-land, from the pink colour of the granite that composes them. It became known universally in English as the Cairngorms in the last century, taking the name from this one rounded swell of a mountain that is prominent in the view from Speyside.

The mountain's name comes from the Gaelic An Càrn Gorm, the blue mountain, called this because like many hills seen from a distance it appears blue because the atmosphere has filtered out the red wavelengths from the spectrum. The change from *càrn* to cairn, a process that affected many a *càrn* in the north-east, began early in writing, for MacFarlane's 18th century manuscripts speak of 'Kairne Gorum', whilst the previous century's map by Blaue had Carn-gorum; both reproduce *gorm* phonetically.

The Cairngorms

Probably Scotland's best-known range as far as media Britain is concerned, on account of its ski developments, it takes its modern name from one mountain, **Cairn Gorm**. This peak at 1245m is the lowest of the range's quartet of 4000 footers, and lies at the northern edge of the massive plateau. The name Cairn Gorm is not

unique, for there are several examples of **Càrn Gorm** (blue cairn) some 80 kilometres to the north-west in Ross; but what does make it unusual among Scottish mountain ranges is that one individual peak's name has spread out like a ripple in a pond to become the name of the whole range, in the process submerging its Gaelic name of Am Monadh Ruadh, the red mountain-land. This name was from the pink colours of the Cairngorm granite, in contrast to the grey schists of the **Monadh Liath** range west across Strathspey. This name was lost together with much of the once-great Speyside Gaelic culture during the 20th century. On Gordon's map of the 1640s the range appears as a northern extension of what he names as The Mountains of Scairsoch, from **An Sgarsoch**.

Also submerged by the 'ripple effect' was the old name of another mountain in the range lying six kilometres south of Cairn Gorm, another Cairn Gorm; there was no room for two of the same name when one had become so famous. So the southern, lower one is now known as **Derry Cairngorm**. Both Cairn Gorms were originally named An Càrn Gorm, the blue hill ... or perhaps the green hill. If blue, it is in appreciation of the apparent colour when seen from the distant habitations at Inverey and Aviemore and if green, from its grassy slopes (in contrast to the dark cliffs or gravel spreads elsewhere in the range) – the name was of course given before the ski developments scarred the green.

Since the range had these *two* Cairn Gorms, this may have helped the growth of the new collective name for the whole range. The first reference appears to have been in an 1804 book by Englishman Colonel Thomson, who writes of,

> ... aurora peeping over the immense Cairngorms.

The ripple effect of its name spread even beyond the Cairngorms proper, to include in some books all the mountains north and east of the A9 and the Angus glens. In 1928, Henry Alexander, editor of the Scottish Mountaineering Club guidebook on the area, defended the book's title *The Cairngorms* for the whole area just mentioned on the grounds that the correct name 'the Grampians' had never found popular favour and conjured up 'no distinct mental picture', whilst 'the Cairngorms' was the name being used more and more widely as descriptive of the whole area. He does concede that the 'true' Cairngorms are limited to the mountains between the Dee and the Spey.

Although the individual mountain Cairn Gorm has retained its two-word form, the range is generally referred to as one word Cairngorms. This was not always true. For David Thomson, author of *Nairn in Darkness and Light*, writing from his notes of early in the 20th century tells of days when:

> ... the calves of my legs (were) stronger – perhaps from climbing the Cairn
> Gorms so often

By the 1920s however the name was commonly used in its modern one-word form. (See also Blue and Green Hills on p130).

Cairn Toul (Càrn an t-Sabhail)

On the southern edge of An Garbh Choire of **Braeriach** stands Cairn Toul, an anglicised version of the Gaelic Càrn an t-Sabhail, peak of the barn. (After the definite article *t-*, the following consonant, in this case the *s*, falls silent. And the same word, and the same *ool* sound in anglicised speech, can be found in **Màm Sodhail**, pronounced 'mam *sool*', above Glen Affric, though in this area *sowel* is the local pronunciation). Now a 'barn' can either be the farm building for cattle or crop storage, or it can refer to the wartlike granite tors that outcrop on other Cairngorm hills like Beinn Mheadhoin, Ben Avon, and indeed on the **Barns of Bynack More** near the top of Bynack More.

Cairn Toul, hill of the barn. For other 'barn' hills see p108, [North-West Highlands, Quinag, Sabhal Mòr], and p107 [North-West Highlands, Màm Sodhail] and p120 [Bynack More]

However although Cairn Toul is part of the same mass of granite rock, there are no tors or barns near its summit. So the description must refer to its barn-like shape, for when seen from the east, from Ben Macdui, or the south-west, its summit and corrie have the shape of a ridged roof, with a flat top framed by two angled spurs dropping away from it. This explanation is the more credible because the corrie thus framed, the smallest of the mountain's trio on the north-east slope, is the Coire an t-Sabhail. And of course, in the days of transhumance, there may have been some small barn in the corrie for storing hay or dairy produce.

Indeed the mountain as a whole is sometimes known locally as Sabhal Beinn Macdhui, the barn of Ben Macdui – and on one of Gordon's early 17th century maps it appeared as Soul Bin MacDuff. Other Highland peaks have similar names comparing them with buildings: **Sgùrr a' Mhuilinn** (peak of the mill) **Meall a' Phùbuill** (hill of the tent), **Am Bàthach** (the cowhouse or byre) and **Tigh Mòr na Seilge** (big house of the hunt).

A suggestion has been made that the name comes from Càrn an t-Seallaidh, meaning mountain of the prospect or view (as in Balquhidder's **Meall an t-Seallaidh**, which does have a striking view of three big lochs), but the pronunciation does not fit this.

A subsidiary top of the mountain, the shapely cone on the ridge running out to the north-west, is known as the **Angel's Peak**: it was allegedly named by a Victorian gentleman Copland – first president of the Cairngorm Club – as a genteel counterweight to **The Devil's Point** on the south side of the mountain. But while The Devil's Point is a polite translation of the Gaelic *Bod an Deamhain*, the demon's penis, the 'Angel' name is probably bogus, for this top's original name is **Sgòr an Lochan Uaine**, peak of the green lochan, which lies in the corrie below. Seton Gordon (not always a reliable source for place names) met with a Gaelic speaking stalker who claimed that in the 1890s he referred to it among his colleagues as Sgòr an Aingeil, more likely a Gaelic back-translation from English rather than a genuine alternative name.

Cairnwell

The skiers' mountain at the head of Glen Shee, and sharing with **Cairn Gorm** the 'distinction' of being a Munro easily completed from a chairlift. An ancient Gaelic verse includes the line:

> … *Sneachd is reath air chàrna bhalg*

> … Snow and frost on The Cairnwell
> (perhaps a feature that will be rarer in the future due to global warming).

The name comes from **An Càrn Bhalg**, literally the cairn of the bags, referring perhaps to the pouchy peatbanks on the slopes, and is locally pronounced The Cairnwall. The *balg* noun is also found in three nearby hills all called **Creag Bhalg** as well as **Blàth Bhalg** above Pitlochry.

Càrn an t-Sagairt Mòr

Càrn an t-Sagairt Mòr (sometimes spelt roughly as it is pronounced Cairn Taggart), big hill of the priest, was named after Padruig, a Braemar priest, who led his flock out to Loch Callater to pray for an end to a severe frost that gripped the land well into May. As they prayed, the ice at the Priest's Well melted along with nature's iron heart, clouds gathered over the hill, and the thaw set in. The locals named that hill after him in gratitude. Creag Phadraig nearby is probably connected to the priest's name, too. (Pronounced kaarn an tag*a*rsht **moa:**r)

Clachnaben

Lying on the eastern shoulders of **The Mounth**, where the gentle swell of the hills loses its wave power before dying out on the coastal plains, Clachnaben is a land-mark because of the huge granite tor on top. In Gaelic it was *clach na beinne*, stone on the hill. Its prominence is clear from Hamish Brown's estimates of a 300 pace circumference and a 30m height.

Conval Hills

Above the whisky distilleries of Mortlach on Speyside stand **Little** and **Meike Conval Hill**s, outliers of the **Ben Rinnes** massif. Their names have similarities with many other hills in the north-west called **Conival** or Con Mheall. These hills are often shoulders of bigger mountains, and the name probably derives from a root *con* meaning with or together. So the Conval Hills name means probably a pair of adjoining hills.

Coyles of Muick

A trio of hills above Deeside where it is joined by Glen Muick (glen of the pig), it comprises the Coyle of Muick (the wood, *coille*, of Muick), **Meall Dubh** (dark hill) and the Craig of Loinmuie. This is a relatively recent name, not used by older Gaelic speakers, and hence rather tenuous.

Cromdale Hills

The hills and haughs of Cromdale lie east of the hamlet of the same name, which in turn is from *crom dail*, crooked field or meadow, from the shape that the water-mead-ows have been carved into by the wide meanders of the River Spey.

Derry Cairngorm

Although there are several hills called **Càrn Gorm** (blue cairn) throughout Scotland, this one suffered from its close proximity to the famous **Cairn Gorm**, fifth highest in the land and namer of the Cairngorms range. Originally An Càrn Gorm (the blue hill) from its blue appearance when seen from Inverey several kilometres distant, it became known as Càrn Gorm an Doire to distinguish a from its big neighbour, (and even ignominiously as the Lesser or Eastern Cairngorm), before the Doire became anglicised to Derry.

This suffix turned prefix originally meant oakwood, or more generally, wooded (*doireach*). The woods for which Glen Derry is still rightly famous are not oaks but the beautiful Scots pines. These relics of the ancient extensive wood of Caledon are living sculptures formed of soft russet-brown bark and dark green needles, contrast-ing their soft forest carpets of bilberry with their brittle twisted limbs. If this moun-tain had to be pushed into second place by the other Cairngorm, its consolation lies in taking its newly-added forename from a beautiful glen.

The Devil's Point

By contrast with the breast – found in *cìoch* and *màm* – the male sexual organ hardly

lends itself to comparison with hill shapes in the British Isles, excepting the vertical sea-stacks known by the probably euphemistic names of Old Man of Hoy, Old Man of Stoer, and the like. However The Devil's Point in the Cairngorms, a sharp peak of scaly black slabs above the Làirig Ghrù, was originally called Bod an Deamhain or demon's penis. Early writers ducked the problem of translating the offending word into cold print, referring to it as 'the devil's -----', or simply as 'a literal translation'. In one note, appearing in Sir James Balfour's Collections, a footnote reads:

> A place called by the barbarous inhabitants, Pittindawin or Bodindeweill (that is the deivell's...) so speakes these wylde scurrilous people, amongst wych ther is bot small feare and knowledge of God.

The Devil's Point – a polite translation for Bod an Deamhain, devil's penis. See also p140, [Central Highlands, Bidean nam Bian]

Even Edward Dwelly's dictionary can only blush in Latin at *bod*, stating that it is *membrum virile* – [i.e. the male member, here in a Latin codpiece]. The 'problem' of its name was solved by the Victorian clerics and professors, the early mountaineers, whose demure English translation of *bod* into 'point' made hillwalking safe for decent people in the area, draping a veil of modesty across the name. The Gaels were not alone in identifying a penis in their hills, for there are at least two Himalayan peaks named Shivling, which means the god Shiva's penis.

125

The Grampians

This appears to be a huge range, in some atlases – for instance the *Times Atlas of the World* – covering the entire highland area east of the Great Glen. But is its name's location accurate? Author W.Douglas Simpson, in his *Portrait of the Highlands*, wrote in the 1940s of this range's name:

> It is greatly to be wished that the word 'Grampian' should disappear from our atlases and from books dealing with the Central Highlands.

Why? Because like a rainbow, the name appears to shift around the mountains and in close-up vanishes altogether. For while some books and atlases apply it to the whole area of the east and central highlands, putting Ben Nevis as its high point, others confine it to the area east of the A9 road and south of the River Dee, whilst others still cross the A9 south-west into Perthshire. A 1940 book on British Mountains noted the ambiguity in saying that the term 'Grampians':

> ... may be held to apply to the whole mountain barrier stretching between the lowlands and the Great Glen. However it is often applied to the range east of the Tay valley and south of Deeside.

To add to the confusion the late 20th century political name Grampian Region included only the north-east part of this area, headquartered in Aberdeen.

The generally-accepted modern limit of the term is indeed to the hills east of the A9 and south of Deeside. Thus a 1970s book called *Grampian Ways* is an account of the hill-paths across this area, that was and still is known as the Mounth – a name derived from the Gaelic *monadh*, mountain-land. W.J.Watson asserted a century ago that :

> The chief *monadh* in Scotland is, of course, the range of mountains now known as the Grampians, formerly the Mounth, which divides Scotland north of the Forth into two divisions...

He goes on to contrast this with the mountain spine which runs north-south through the north-west Highlands, so clearly he regards **The Mounth**, and now the Grampians – a modern term whose rise he regrets – as stretching from North Sea to Atlantic.

But the broad sweep of the 'Grampian' canvas has no near view... the 'rainbow' has no pot of gold at its end. Nowhere within its supposed domains do local people point out 'the Grampians' in the way that the Cuillin, Cairngorms or Pentlands might be indicated to a visitor. The only local use is the name Gramps for a few small hills on the south side of Aberdeen, clearly not our Grampian mountains. Not that this absence has prevented expatriate Scots from exporting the name 'The Grampians' to some undistinguished hills in Victoria, Australia.

Nor has the elusive nature of the name deterred speculation about its origin. Johnston's book on Scottish place names carries two speculations, by others: a Celtic word *gruq*, supposedly meaning curved or rounded, fitting the modern perception of

the hills' shape compared to the spiky western Highlands; and a European root-word *gra-uq* which was said to mean a hill-like place, as in the Graian Alps. In fact these latter are named after Hercules the Greek (*graecus* in Latin) who was reputed to have carried out some of his Labours in those Italian mountains.

There is also a theory that the name came from a printers' mistake in the transcription of the Roman scribe Tacitus' *Life of Agricola*, where the battle-site *Mons Graupius* (or Craupius) became Grampius, a mistake later compounded by Hector Boece, a 16th century Aberdeen historian, writing it as Grampians in his 1526 book on the history of Scotland. Boece said in his book that the locals called them, in the vernacular, Granzebain, and the 1531 translation of his work into Scots by John Bellenden speaks of the 'mountains of Granzeben', stretching from 'the fute of Dee to Dounbriton' (ie from Aberdeen to Dunbarton). Later he refers to the Tay rising 'far beyond the mountains of Granzeben'.

The name then appears on several maps in the 16th century. In 1539, the Carta Marina (showing the Baltic and North Seas) showed in Scotland *Alpes* and *Grampius Mons* either side of a sketch of hills. The map's author Oleus Magnus, a Swedish Catholic Bishop exiled to Rome, is unlikely to have read Boece, suggesting the name was more than a printer's mistake. An anonymous Italian map of 1560 has *Grampius* beside Loch Tay. In 1573 Ortelius of Antwerp produced a map of Scotland showing *Grampius Mons*, near Loch Avon, and a further *Grampius Mons, vulgo* [i.e. commonly] *Gransebain* positioned in the area of the Monadh Liath: Dutchman Gerard Mercator, a few years later in 1595, positioned his *Grampius Mons* in a similar location. Remarkably, Ortelius identified one further *Grampius Mons* in the Borders, as if the name was a generic one for hills!

Strangely, subsequent maps of the 17th and 18th century produced by Scots do not show the range – if it was a local place name, then they surely would have, being in contact with informants in the glens. They show instead ranges with names like Minigeg Mountains and Scairsoch Mountains. Neither Pont, travelling extensively in the late 16th century, nor Blaeu, who based his 1650s map on Pont's work, identified the Grampians, although Robert Gordon mentioned *Grampios Montes* in his Latin text to a later edition of the map. The name was however current to educated men – the parish ministers, writing in the late 18th century's Statistical Account, often mentioned the Grampians.

If this Granzeben name *was* authentic, and if the last part is -*beinn*, then the meaning remains obscure since *beinn*, especially in the eastern Highlands, normally comes before an adjective. So although the adjective *griangheal* (pronounced **gree-un-yal**) seems appropriate because it means sun-bright and perhaps refers to the sun glinting off the late-lying snows... however it should really be *beinn griangheal* rather than *griangheal-bheinn* to be convincing as an origin. Dwelly's Gaelic dictionary does have the word *gruaim-bheinn*, meaning gloomy mountain or dark hill, another possibility.

It is of course possible that the Romans made up the name *Mons Graupius* themselves – after all they 're-named' the **Eildon Hills** in the Borders as the *Trimontium*

(three mountains) from their shape – rather than basing their Latin word *Graupius* on a local people's name. Certainly any local name in Roman times cannot have been of Gaelic origin, for that language came to Scotland centuries after the Legions left. And the Picts who ruled that part of Scotland left us so few words altogether that it is impossible to say. Perhaps Boece simply muddied the waters by linking the Roman name and a vernacular one. However the fact that Grampians is not a locally-used name today – unlike other ancient names that have survived, like the Ochils and Pentlands – must cast doubt on its authenticity. So its origin and meaning must be as mystery-enshrouded as the site of the famous battle site of *Mons Graupius*!

Kincardine Hills

This small range above Loch Morlich, an outlier facing the mighty Cairngorms, has a name reflecting the life of the valleys rather than the mountains. For it takes its name from a small parish, from Gaelic *cinn* (the locative case of *ceann*, and anglicised to kin) meaning at the end of, and *cardenn* (a Pictish word) meaning a wood. The highest hill in the group is **Meall a' Bhuachaille**, hill of the herdsman or shepherd, and the other tops are named after cliffy outcrops – **Creagan Gorm**, blue little rocky hill, **Craiggowrie**, rocky hill of goats, and **Creag Ghreusaiche**, rocky hill of the cobbler.

Ladder Hills

W.J.Watson says that the name of this north-eastern hill range is a literal translation of Monadh an Àraidh, and backs it up with a reference to the Irish use of *àradh* (a ladder) to hills with tranverse ridges. In Scottish Gaelic the word is *fàradh*, but within this name the *f* would be silent. Indeed, on Gordon's 1654 map appeared the words 'Monagan Ary or ye mountains of ye ledder', thus giving a phonetic name in Gaelic and its English translation. The old road crossing these hills is still known as the Ladder Road. It was used by illicit whisky smugglers heading for Donside, and its steep zig-zags as it climbs out of Glenlivet from Ladderfoot may be the origin of the hill name, since the burn plashing alongside it is the Ladder Burn. **The Fara** hill above Dalwhinnie station may also be from the word for a ladder, its long summit ridge being described by Hamish Brown as 'a long undulating crest', as you would expect of a ladder lying on the ground. On the other hand, there's a word in Gaelic dictionaries *fàire* meaning a distant ridge or a skyline, equally apt.

Lochnagar

On this hill we can observe the strange sight of a loch 'running uphill', for the name of a corrie lochan has displaced the summit's original name. For the Gaelic name of this mountain was Beinn (nan) Cìochan, the mountain of the breasts, referring to the granite tors on the eastern rim of the corrie today known by the Scots names of the **Meikle Pap** and **Little Pap**, the big and little breast. On Blaeu's 1654 map the hill is Bin Chichnes, with, at its foot, L. Garr. This loch lay in the corrie far below, Loch-na-Garr on Roy's 1750 map, the lochan of noise or laughter (*gàire*). (The sound 'garr' in a mountain name might seem to point at the adjective *garbh* (pronounced garav), and certainly the granite cliffs spill a rough scree down into the loch – and

garbh is a frequently used Gaelic mountain adjective. But the form of the name loch-na-gar indicates a noun, not the adjectival *garbh*: and besides the case for 'noise' can draw on hill names like **Gàirich** and **Gleouraich**, both 'roaring' peaks.)

Gradually, over the decades, the name of the 'noisy' loch below began to be used for the peak itself: initially in 1721, then in 1761, 1806 and with gathering pace in the 19th century, it was referred to as the Top of (ie above), or Hill of, Lochan-y-gar. Englishman Thomas Pennant wrote in August 1769:

> ... I saw the great mountain Laghin y Gair, which is always
> covered with snow

Lochnagar, a mountain that has lost its original name to a feature below. For another example, see p106 [North-West Highlands, Fuar Tholl]

The transformation was completed in the 19th century, first by the Romantic Lord Byron's famous poem on 'Dark Lochnagar':

> England! Thy beauties are tame and domestic
> To one who has roamed o'er the mountains afar;
> Oh for the crags that are wild and majestic!
> The steep frowning glories of dark Lochnagar

Queen Victoria's adoption of the Balmoral estate at its foot would stamp the name change with a *By Appointment* seal. She wrote in 1848 of the,

> ... beautiful surrounding hills of Loch-na-gar.

A map of 1867 using the name Lochnagar for the lochan only, and the individual tops by their own names, was a last defiant fling for the old ways.

In addition to the two paps, the summits of the massif include the highest points **Cac Càrn Beag** (properly, Cadha Càrn Beag) and **Cac Càrn Mòr** (properly, Cadha

---

Blue and Green Hills

The Gaelic adjectives for these colours overlap to a considerable degree.

uaine

There is a Gaelic word for the bright green we recognise in the Lowlands, *uaine*, as in **Meall Uaine** south of Spittal of Glenshee. But it is rare in Gaelic hill names, with less than a dozen examples: the word *glas* meaning grey-green is commoner, because it is usually a more accurate description of the colours involved. Curiously, five of the six Gaelic 'green hills' called Meall Uaine, lie in a 40 kilometre wide belt across the southern fringes of the higher ground from Glen Shee to Glen Garry and Drumochter, the sixth lying a little further down the Garry.

Sometimes a top with *uaine* is named after a subsidiary feature, as in **Sgòr an Lochan Uaine** (peak of the little green loch) on **Cairn Toul**. The Cairngorms have in fact four examples of a Lochan Uaine, the most dramatic and yet easily accessible of which is the one in the Ryvoan Pass just beyond Glenmore Lodge. Its striking green, almost a Mediterranean turquoise, is set beneath grey screes and surrounded by dark Scots pines; the colour comes from underwater plants and algae. Legend, less scientific, has it that the colour comes from the fairies washing their clothes in it. The curiously-named **Laidwinley** hill in Angus is perhaps a corruption of *leathad uainealach*, the greenish slope.

glas

Glas, means grey (or green, when applied to new spring grass) or indeed grey-green – *liath* can also have both meanings. It may seem strange that grey and green can inhabit the same word, but on many windswept hillsides the grasses that survive, poke from amongst the grey rock screes, and the overall effect of the blend of these plants and rock is grey-green. The best-known is surely **Beinn Ghlas** of **Ben Lawers**, its slopes facing the south-west spilled with screes, crumbled from grey schistose rock.

A' Ghlas-bheinn in Kintail is simply the grey-green hill, while further north in Assynt, **Glas Bheinn**'s grey gneiss screes threaten to overwhelm the heather moors at its foot.

gorm

Gorm can mean green when applied to grass, but more usually indicates the colour nearby on the spectrum, blue or azure. There are several Gorm Lochs, and several specimens of Càrn or **Meall Gorm** across Scotland, and they are found especially to the west of the Great Glen. Ironically, while there are five examples of **Càrn Gorm** in Ross-shire, it is the lone one east of the Spey, and now corrupted to **Cairn Gorm**, that has become best known, through

Càrn Mòr), which are mistaken names on two counts. The Beag (wee cairn) is in fact six metres higher than the Mòr (big cairn). More seriously, the Cac is a corruption of *cadha*, meaning slope, or path up a slope: *cac* in Gaelic is connected with the Scots word *keech*, known to the English as faeces. Hardly the sort of name, however

lending its name to the mountain range.

Indeed this Cairngorms range, literally the blue mountains, was known for centuries as Am Monadh Ruadh, the red mountain – as it still is in Gaelic. It has been suggested that the 'blue' colour stems from the rocks – two **Meall Gorm** hills on Deeside are said to have blue-grey boulders on their slope. West of **Creag Leacach** in Glen Shee, **Meall Gorm** is definitely very green due to the base-rich rocks nourishing the vegetation. More probably the blue colour in the name *gorm* stems from the fact that *all* hills seen at a distance through the atmosphere take on a bluish tinge due to the properties of light, as the red wavelengths are absorbed by dust and the land. There are blue hills world-wide, such as Australia's Blue Mountains and the Blue Mountain in Jamaica, and poetically it is expressed in the poet A.E.Housman's memorable phrase,

> What are these blue remembered hills?

Alistair Cram wrote in the Scottish Mountaineering Club Journal of a Cuillin day;

> As is usual in our mountain landscapes, blue was the prevailing colour. That tint which seems to lend the faint air of mystery to distant hills, at once restful and intriguing.

Indeed there is a Gaelic proverb which runs:

> *Is gorm na cnuic a tha fada bhuainn*
> (Blue are the hills that are far from us)

According to Adam Watson, contemporary expert on the area, Cairn Gorm itself looks blue when seen from Nethy Bridge (but less often from Aviemore), while some kilometres south, **Derry Cairngorm** often looks blue from Inverey on Deeside. As walkers in the area know well, the distances to the peaks here are long, and this distance from habitation and therefore from perception may be responsible for the concentration of 'blues' here. They are often stony hills and therefore liable to look grey or blue. Ironically the famous semi-precious Cairngorm stone, collected for jewellery, is usually not blue, but a brown or yellow colour.

Another famous 'blue' mountain in Scotland is Skye's **Blà Bheinn**, a hybrid of Norse *blá* and Gaelic *beinn* producing blue mountain; it was probably *Blåfjall* (of which there are several in Norway and Iceland) before the last element was translated. The old pronunciation, and spelling, as Blaavin, is more Norse than the sometimes-suggested Gaelic version *blàth bheinn*, mountain of bloom.

mistaken, to set before a Queen, especially Victoria, which is perhaps why the Balmoral royals were keen to encourage the name Lochnagar!

The Stuic, the summit at the end of the north-western corrie, is from the Gaelic *stùc*, a projecting hill or round promontory, while **Cuidhe Crom** (properly *cuithe chrom*) is crooked snow wreath, which often lies on its shaded north-east slope into summer. The hill above the shallow scoop on the southern slopes of the plateau is **Càrn a' Choire Bhòidheach**, cairn of the beautiful corrie, a name that could apply equally to the granite-girt corrie harbouring the upstart Lochan na Gaire.

Morven

There are two (possibly three) hills called Morven in Scotland. One, near Helmsdale, is especially striking from the road north, but the highest Morven (literally big mountain, *mòr-bheinn*), is on the east of the Cairngorms and dominates the views around Aboyne. In 1769 Thomas Pennant on his tour of Scotland wrote:

> One of the great mountains to the West [of Donside] is styled the hill of Morven, is of a stupendous height, and on the side next to Cromar almost perpendicular ... The other great mountains appear to sink to a common size, and even Laghin y Gair [Lochnagar] abates of its grandeur.

Certainly it's a Mòr Bheinn after that praise! Its even older names were Morvine, Morevene and Mons de Morving. It is intriguing to speculate why some 'big mountains' are Mòr Bheinn while others are **Beinn Mhòr** (or the anglicised **Ben More**). The Ben Mores are the highest hills with three Munros in Mull, Perthshire and Assynt – the anglicised spelling is due to the linguistic innocence of the early Ordnance Survey surveyors. Most of the Beinn Mhòr names surviving as such on the Ordnance Survey maps are lower peaks – as low as 182m on North Uist, and 193m in Easdale – although Beinn Mhòr above Loch Eck in Cowal reaches 741m – and are more generally in the west and on the islands.

The Morven hills lie in the intermediate height range between 600m to 900m, but their significance probably does not lie in their height, nor in their location in the eastern Highlands. The word *mòr-bheinn* can be a poetic Gaelic expression for the more usual *beinn mhòr*, used in names like Mull's soubriquet of Muile nam Mòr-bheann, Mull of the big mountains. It seems odd that these two should have an archaic, poetic Gaelic name, surrounded as they are by 'foreign names': Morven near Helmsdale was probably influenced by the structure of its Norse-name neighbours like Scaraben; while Morven above Donside stands in sight of **Mormond Hill** (*mòr-monadh*), which W.J.Watson argued was a Gaelic name using a Pictish word-structure, this being Pictish territory (*monadh*, a Gaelic word, derived from Pictish *monid*).

Above Braemar is a **Morrone** (perhaps *mòr-shròn*, big nose or promontory), sometimes known as Morven: its alternative names have been the subject of considerable debate. One feature it has in common with the Aboyne Morven is that, while backed by higher mountains, it dominates the view from the village – from where the names were presumably given. **Mortlich**, a name of sepulchral sound, is from *mòr-thulaich*, big hillock, above Aboyne.

The Mounth

The Mounth is the historic name for the east-west ridge of mountains that hinders north to south road and rail travel in the eastern Highlands, forcing the ribbons of steel and tarmacadam out onto the North Sea coastal plain, or west into the Drumochter cleft.

Travellers on foot fare better with a selection of Mounth passes between these two trade routes, but these lonely ways are treated with respect by walkers. Such respect was not always accorded the old name, for atlases and books refer to the hills as the Grampians; Mounth, the older name, comes from the Gaelic *monadh*, literally a mountain mass. In north-east Scotland many Gaelic names changed – *càrn* to cairn, *creag* to craig – and the shift from *monadh* to *moneth*, *mounth*, *mound*, *mond* and *mount* (all extant usages) would not have been difficult. Further north The Ord hill near Inverness, a long ridge, was also known earlier as the Mounth, since *monadh* is a generic term.

In an old Latin document the name Muneth is recorded, being crossed by holy men with relics en route to convert the King of the Picts; perhaps the mountain called **Càrn an Rìgh** (cairn of the king) near Braemar perhaps commemorates this king, although it may 'belong' to James VI who hunted near here in the 1560s. On the other hand it may be a corruption of *ruighe*, a hill meadow or shieling. The **Hill of St Colm** (i.e. Columba) near Tarfside more definitely commemorates the first missionary to the area. And in 1400 a chronicle records the pursuit of Macbeth,

> ...our the Mounth thai chast hym than, til the wode of Lwnfannan (Lumphanan – where they killed him).

Within the range the name still lingers on in the **White Mounth** (the plateau south of Lochnagar) and the easternmost Munro of **Mount Keen** (from *caoin*, probably gentle or smooth in the sense of being unbroken by cliffs, or possibly beautiful). The Cairn o' Mounth pass, **Capel Mounth** (mare or colt mounth), **Firmounth** (*fear*, genitive or plural *fir*, man) and **Tolmount** (*tol*, a hollow or corrie), **Mount Blair** (*blàr*, a plain – it dominates the view from the low-lying Carse of Gowrie) and **Mount Battock** (Mon Battain in Pont; possibly from *bàthach*, a byre, or more likely from *badaig*, a grove – there are pine roots in the bog high on the hill) are also survivors of the name that originally stretched over the whole of this east-west ridge from the coastal plain to the edge of Rannoch Moor, where it was called Monadh Druim-uachdair, the mountain of the upper ridge. The three hills **Monawee**, **Manywee** and **Monybuie** (the former two in Angus, the latter in Galloway), are all *monadh buidhe*, yellow *monadh*.

CHAPTER FIVE

CENTRAL HIGHLANDS

Aonach Beag & Mòr

Aonach means a ridge-shaped mountain. In the case of Aonach Beag (wee ridged mountain) and Aonach Mòr (big ridged mountain), the word *aonach* precisely describes their shape. Together – for they are a pair – they form one magnificent long high ridge running from Glen Lundy near Fort William, with the outlying shoulder called **Aonach an Nid** (ridge of the nest), south to a vantage point above Glen Nevis.

However while the *aonach* is exactly right, the adjectives *mòr* and *beag* are inexact, for the 'wee' Aonach Beag is the higher of the two by some 20 metres. The whole ridge is more easily seen from the north, rather than from the narrow mouth of Glen Nevis in the south; and from the north the Aonach Mòr, being nearest to the glen and therefore foreshortened, would appear to the local people to be the higher. The coming of the Ordnance Survey and their precise height measurements could hardly be expected to upset an old traditional name. Besides, the local name has some modern backers who claim that the Mòr is of larger mass, and *mòr* in Gaelic *does* tend to refer to size rather than height. The Mòr, too, has a longer *ridge*, the Beag being more hump-shaped. (Pronounced oe:noch **bayk** *and* **moa:r**)

Aonach Eagach

This means the notched ridge, a precise description of the classic rock scramble high over rocky spires and clefts high above Glen Coe: from the north, against the light, it has the appearance of a fence of steel palings. The *aonach* proper is slung between the summits of **Stob Coire Lèith** (peak of the grey corrie) and **Am Bodach** (the old man), with the apex on Meall Dearg (red hill); the traverse is usually started or finished on **Sgòrr nam Fiannaidh**, peak of the Fingalians, legendary Celtic hunters. There's another Aonach Eagach, of similar form, not far away on the eastern summit ridge of **Stob Ghabhar**. (Pronounced oe:noch **e**goch)

Beinn a' Bheithir

Although Highland folktales are spirited by demons and water-sprites of various kinds, one of the few that seems to have left its mark on a hill name is on **Beinn a' Bheithir** above Ballachulish. Named after the Celtic goddess of winter and death (and with ministerial responsibility for wind and storm), it was believed to be the home of Cailleach Bheithir, who could be a nasty piece of interference in human lives, able, they said, to raise floods and move mountains; but when so inclined she could be a beautiful maiden with the gift of immortal youth. Her contradictory character is mirrored in the dictionary, where a *beithir* was a destructive demon of rather unspecific nature, a kind of indiscriminate vandal.

Alternatively it can mean an electric storm, a bear, a thunderbolt, or again a very large serpent. Sea-serpents play an eye-widening role in Gaelic mythology, being responsible on occasion for destroying entire fleets. The main trouble walkers have had on it though are the approaches through dense conifers on the north, where

desperate men have recommended ice-axes as machetes. The constituent Munros of the mountain are **Sgòrr Dhearg** (red) and **Sgòrr Dhònuill** (Donald). (Pronounced bYn a **vay**heer)

Aonach Eagach, the notched ridge. A test of mountaineering. See p18, [Generics, aonach]

Beinn Trilleachan

Although several Highland peaks are named after birds, surely the sweetest-sounding bird mountain is Beinn Trilleachan above Loch Etive. Better-known among southern visitors for its steep slabs where rock-climbers perch, its Gaelic meaning is the mountain of sandpipers, or oyster-catchers. The latter name is more likely, for the sheltered sea-loch Etive at its very foot would provide excellent feeding for this loud-trilling flashy bird. Sandpipers prefer fresh water, and have an alternative form *drilleachan*. (Pronounced bYn **tree**lyochan)

Ben Alder

This lies in the very heart of the Highlands, a great hunk of a mountain sending streams forth west to the Atlantic and north-east to the North Sea. Its name however is something of a mystery, perhaps because so central and high a mountain mass would have a very old, possibly a pre- or early Gaelic name. It appeared on Blaeu's 17th century map as Bin Aildir, but Pont's map on which Blaeu is based showed it as Bin Ailloir – indeed a century earlier a Gaelic poem *The Owl of Strone* called it

Beinn Allair; later it was also known as Beinn Eallar which was interpreted by W.J.Watson as *beinn alldobhar* (or *ail dobhar*) meaning hill of 'rock (and) water' or 'precipice (and) water'. This would certainly fit its corried slopes, and this 18th century description of Prince Charlie's hideout at Cluny's Cage here:

> ... 'Twas situate on the face of a very rough high rockie mountain called Letternilichk which is still a part of Ben Alder, full of great stones and crevices
>
> ('Letternilichk' is probably leitir nan leac, slope of the stones.)

Ail is an archaic word for steep rock, and *dobhair* (water), also an ancient word, would be an apt companion for it: and the name of Morar in the west, deriving from *mòr-dhobhair* (big water), shows how the element *dhobhair* can be shortened in speech just as *ail-dhobhair* here became *(beinn) allair* to the local Gaels. The position of the two words suggests too that *ail* was probably an adjectival noun (the genitive case, meaning 'of rock'), again paralleling the structure of Morar (adjective *mòr* preceding noun *dobhair*); and so the name *ail-dhobhair* literally means 'water of rock', describing the rocky chasm carved out by the burn as it tumbled down the slopes.

The subsidiary peak of **Beinn Bheòil**, between the main massif and Loch Ericht, is often translated literally as mouth mountain, from beul – as used in Cowal's highest hill **Beinn Bheula** – but the Gaelic phrase *an taobh bheòil*, meaning the fore side, points us perhaps to a meaning of fore mountain, which it is in relation to the bulk of Ben Alder seen from the loch. (Pronounced bYn **y**alar)

Ben Cruachan

Often known simply as Cruachan, in the 14th century it was recorded as Crechinben, an attempt at the Gaelic name Cruachan Beinne. A *cruachan* is a conical hill, often one standing atop a broader mountain mass (as *cruachan beinne*, 'heap on the mountain' suggests), and this meaning describes the main peak's shape perfectly. From Ardnamurchan and other vantage points, Cruachan stands out clearly as one of a high trio, Ben Nevis, Bidean nam Bian and itself.

The main ridge has two main summit cones, and the lower of these being **Stob Diamh** (properly Daimh), peak of the stag, and an outlying top is **Beinn a' Bhùiridh**, peak of the roaring (of the autumn stag rut). The other summits are **Stob Dearg** – red top, also known as the Taynuilt peak from the village to the west – **Meall Cuanail** (hill of the flocks), **Drochaid Ghlas** (the grey bridge), **Stob Garbh** (the rough top) and **Sròn an Isean** (promontory of the chick). (Pronounced bYn **kroo**achan)

Ben Nevis

This is known to climbers simply as 'The Ben'. This is so because it is the highest in the land, the Queen of Scotland's mountains, *beinn* being a feminine Gaelic noun. As if in deference to its unique status, none of the high peaks beside it is a *beinn*, being instead *càrns* or *aonachs*, *mullachs* or *stobs*, *sgùrrs* or *binneins*. Although it is only one amongst over 1000 Scottish *beinns* or *bens*, this one alone could bear the

definite article 'the' without need of further explanation. The Gaels, however, did not call it A' Bheinn (The Ben), in the way that other hills like An Tòrr and An Stuc were named. Instead they left us a puzzle in the word Nevis.

The earliest versions of the name appear as Neevush (1532) and Nevess (1552). Timothy Pont's 16th century map gives Bin Nevesh, while Blaeu in 1654 renders it as Bin Novesh. A century later the military mapmaker William Roy, who completed the first accurate map of Scotland for the government, concurred with Ben Nevis, so Thomas Pennant who toured the Highlands some years later must have done so without the aid of Roy's map, for he writes:

> ... Fort William is surrounded by vast mountains, which occasion almost perpetual rain: the loftiest are on the south side – Benevish soars above the rest and ends, as I was told, in a point ... whose height is said to be 1450 yards.

But what does Nevis mean? Unlike other nations' highest peaks, like Mont Blanc, Chomolungma (Everest), or Snowdon, whose meanings are quite clear to their local peoples, the origin of the name Nevis is misted over by time as much as its top often is by cloud.

The commonest explanation is that it means evil or venomous mountain, from *nimheil* or *nibheis*. Certainly, a late 16th century Gaelic poem *The Song of the Owl of Strone*, refers to it as Beinn Nimheis. When the yearly toll of death and injury, to tourists, walkers and serious climbers, is added up, this name seems ominously appropriate. But the name was given long before mountaineers came to dice with death on its cliffs. The doyen of Gaelic place name study, W.J.Watson, who wrote in the era before mass tourism, argued in his *History of the Celtic Place-Names of Scotland* that the 'venomous' name came from the River and Glen Nevis at its foot. This was by repute a barren glen, described by one Gaelic poet as,

> ... A glen on which God has turned his back: the slop-pail of the great world.

Another rhyme tells of:

> *Gleann Nibheis, gleann na gcloch,*
> *Gleann am bi an gart anmoch;*
> *Gleann fada fiadhaich, fàs,*
> *Sluagh bradach an mhioghnais.*

> Glen Nevis, glen of stones,
> A glen where corn ripens late;
> A long wild waste glen,
> With thievish folk of evil habit.

W.J.Watson said the name Nevis was an anglicisation of an old Gaelic form *neimheas* (latterly *nimheas*, or *nimheis*) from *neimh* meaning poison or venom, derived from an Old Irish root *nem*, venom. Now it is true that names of rivers are

often the oldest, being major natural obstacles to early peoples. And the 'evil' name certainly fits upper Glen Nevis, today deserted by all inhabitants bar a few campers braving its marshy pitches. And elsewhere in the world there are 'wicked' peaks such as Mont Maudit, a shoulder of Mont Blanc. Coincidentally there is a genuinely 'evil' hill in lower Glen Nevis, the **Cnocan Mì-chomhairle** (knoll of the evil counsel) where a gathering of Mackintoshes plotted an attack on the MacSorlies. And the pronunciation of *nimheis* (*nee-vash*) certainly fits the earliest, 1532, spelling. Loch Nevis, 40 kilometres away, derived from the same root, also has an evil reputation in Gaelic folklore.

However, W.J.Watson's explanation doesn't provide a completely cut-and-dried 'solution' to our mystery, for there are clues pointing in a different direction. The mountain's huge cliffs and corrie face away from the river; and how likely is it that the highest mountain in Scotland, outstretching even its nearest neighbours by 120 metres, and rising literally from sea-level, should be named after a not-very-large river, when few other Scottish mountains are?

Watson himself dismissed the suggestion by the Gaelic scholar Alexander MacBain that Nevis comes from an old European root-word *neb* meaning cloud or water, as found in the Spanish river name Nebis or Nebya. Yet Ben Nevis stands in a prime position to tear open the underbelly of every grey Atlantic cloudwave, thus giving its footfort town the highest rainfall total of any in Scotland. (This watery meaning might also suit Loch Nevis.) And since Ben Nevis was probably one of the first mountains to be named, being so high, it may well have had a pre-Gaelic name (perhaps from this European root-word *neb*) to which the Gaels then applied their most similar-sounding adjective (*nimheis*).

Other plausible Gaelic heirs claimant to the Nevis estate include *nèamh* meaning the sky – or indeed Heaven – and its adjective *nèamhaidh* (pronounced nye:vee) meaning heavenly or divine: in similar vein, the book *Companion to Scottish Culture* has proposed *neimhidh*, sacred, as the name's origin. More profane is the suggestion in some books of *beinn-nimh-bhathais*, the mountain with its head in the clouds, or the mountain with a cold brow. Both of these possible meanings are good descriptions of a summit completely clear on only a handful of days each year, and with snow lying for over half the year on top, and almost permanently in the gloomy heart of its northern corries. Other less plausible suggestions for the name have included derivations of Gaelic words *uamhais*, dread, or *ni-mhaise*, literally no-beauty, and *neamh*, supposedly meaning a raw biting wind. Further the word *neimh*, besides meaning venom, can also refer to the sting of a cold frost.

Earlier, mention was made of the mountain's familiar name, 'The Ben'. (Or as the old Scottish Tourist Board put it '... the Real Big Ben ...'!) In one sense this simple name, The Ben, avoids the agony of choice involved in selecting from the many possible meanings. Perhaps, however, the ambiguity of the name itself is apt, for the mountain herself is enigmatic: her reputation attracts not only the hardest of climbers but also the most soft-soled of casual tourists; presenting on the one side the largest cliff face in Britain, and round the back a heavily eroded tourist path

which zigzags up a slope with all the charm of an elephant's flank; and offering on both sides and in all seasons superb days or foul, mountaineering epics or pedestrian pechs. (Pronounced bYn **neev**ash)

Ben Starav

Rising straight up out of Loch Etive, this fine mountain's name gives few clues away. Is it from *starbhanach* (pronounced starvanach) meaning a well-built fellow or animal, or from *starra*, a block of rock ... or more probably, from *starabhan* (pronounced **star**avan) meaning a rustling noise? After all, only a few kilometres away at the head of Glen Etive is **Meall a' Bhùiridh**, hill of the roaring.

Bidean nam Bian

Bidean nam Bian is literally the peak of the hides or animal pelts. But Seton Gordon says that Canon MacInnes of Glencoe, scholar and native Gaelic speaker, had said

The Three Sisters of Glen Coe, shoulders of Bidean nam Bian. For other 'sisters' see p103,
[North-West Highlands, Five Sisters of Kintail]

that it was in Gaelic originally Bidean nam Beann, the peak of the mountains or the 'chief of the hills'. This is certainly a more plausible name, for it is a large sprawling mountain with many subsidiary tops, a landmark from many points on the west coast.

However the name that appears on Pont's 16th century maps of the area, which he repeats in three overlapping fragments, is Pittindeaun or Poddindeaun or Boddindeaun – clearly the same name with phonetic nuances, the Gaelic *p* often being sounded like English *b*. This means penis of the demon or devil, *bod an deamhain*, and is exactly the original name also of what is now called **The Devil's Point** in the Cairngorms; very possibly the modern *bidean nam bian* is a corruption of the original *bod an deamhain*, a corruption the good Canon would have been secretly happy to go along with.

Roy's military map of 1755, a century and a half after Pont, had it as Biddanabian, a possible stepping-stone from the original to the descendant. Within the mountain's sprawl are a number of subsidiary peaks: **Beinn Fhada** and **Geàrr Aonach** are respectively the long and short peaks, and together with **Aonach Dubh** (dark) their steep north faces above Glen Coe make up the **Three Sisters**, after a famously stunning picture – with the inevitable deer in the foreground – by Horatio MacCulloch hanging in Glasgow's Kelvingrove Art Gallery. Hidden behind them are three Stob Coire peaks – **Stob Coire nam Beith**, **Stob Coire nan Lochan**, and **Stob Coire Sgreamhach**, respectively birch, lochan and loathsome corries. (Pronounced beedyan n*a*m **byown**)

Binnein Shuas & Shìos

These two lovely sharp peaks lie between Loch Laggan and Lochan na h-Earba, almost on an island. The former, the higher, is famed for its rock climbs. In Gaelic, *suas* normally means up or upward while *sìos* is down, but in parts of the north-west coast around Gairloch they mean respectively south and north, and in Wester Ross respectively east and west. However in Perthshire (and in Sutherland) they are respectively west and east. Here, Binnein Shìos lies a little north-eastwards of Binnein Shuas, and its location would therefore be fine to the locals, or a passing Gairloch man. The reason for the locational variation around the country lies in the relationship to the general direction of flowing water, upstream or downstream – and here, we are east of the watershed. (Pronounced beenyan **hoo**us and **hee**us)

Black Mount

The Black Mount is the narrow-spined but wide-limbed plateau lying west of Rannoch Moor and encompassing such peaks as **Clach Leathad**, stone slope, **Stob Ghabhar** and **Meall a' Bhùiridh**. **Creise** is probably from an old Gaelic word *creas*, meaning narrow, which describes the ridge along it well – it probably lost its generic *beinn* or *meall*. Black Mount is a straight translation from its Gaelic name An Monadh Dubh the colour in its name coming perhaps from the dark peat and heather of Rannoch Moor which it overlooks – including the **Black Corries** hills (**A' Chruach**, the heap, at its centre) and the Blackwater River draining it westwards.

Thomas Pennant, passing here in 1769, spoke of a Black Mountain here, but located it north of the true position.

The Black Mount is deeply gouged on its northern flanks by corries, one of which, Corrie Bà, is reputed to be Scotland's largest in terms of cubic 'bite': this casts deep shadows in the evening, another possible source of its name. Facing as they do north and east, they hold snow late, and one of them is the site of a ski development known, ironically, as the White Corries. At the foot of the ski road, to complete the Russian Doll effect, is the whitewashed Blackrock Cottage.

Boar of Badenoch

Hogging the western skyline at Drumochter Pass together with his mate **The Sow of Atholl** the Boar's name is based on the Gaelic original An Torc (the boar) and it stood in the Badenoch estates. From the north (i.e., in Badenoch) its huge convex ridge is indeed of hog's-back shape. (In southern Scotland similarly-shaped hills are known as 'soo's backs'.)

In 1773 one map showed it as Bin Torc and it is supposed to be haunted by the spectre of a boar, a native species that was hunted to extinction – perhaps here – over 500 years ago. The Sow of Atholl is however the product of a marriage of convenience, name-wise, for her maiden name appears to have been Meall an Dobhraichean hill of the watercress; she marked the northern limit of Atholl lands, on the south side of the pass. The Reverend Burn passed here in 1917 and was told that the true local name was Muc Athollach, i.e. the Atholl Sow.

Buachaille Etive Mòr & Beag

In Glen Coe the famous Lost Valley – so-named because it is a glacial 'hanging valley' lost to view from the main glen – was where the MacDonalds hid away their still-hoofed hamburgers! At the eastern mouth of Glen Coe just beyond its watershed with the Coe stand Buachaille Eite (Etive) Mòr and Beag, the big and little herdsmen of Etive; the individual peaks' names were **Stob Dearg** and **Stob Dubh** (red and dark peaks), so perhaps the 'herdsman' was an ironic name given by the wary drovers edging their herds past here. Cattle-herding (not to mention cattle-thieving) was an important part of the Highland economy, before the black cattle and the humans were driven out by 'The Great Sheep' in the Clearances.

They are sometimes translated as 'shepherd', which may be true in the Biblical sense of watching over the glens. But given Gaeldom's reaction to the hated Clearances that introduced sheep, – 'Woe to thee, O land, for the Great Sheep is coming.' – shepherd seems less likely than herdsman. The name is old, for Timothy Pont wrote in the late 16th century of "the twa Bochaletyrs". (Pronounced boo-ucheely*a* ay:ty*a* **moa:r** and **bayk**)

Càrn Mòr Dearg

Càrn Mòr Dearg is the junior partner of Ben Nevis, facing across to its huge northern cliffs. It is joined to it by a narrow swooping ridge, of Alpine difficulty in winter, and known appropriately as the Càrn Mòr Dearg Arete. It means big red cairn, and

all three terms in its name are relative to the surrounding hills. *Càrn* emphasises the conical shape of this hill, compared to the broad-shouldered *beinn* of Nevis and the long ridge of Aonach Mòr. *Dearg*, red, picks out the pinkish hue of its granite rock screes in contrast to the grey andesite cliffs of The Ben across Coire Leis. And while the Mòr might be thought to refer to its absolute height as Scotland's number seven peak, it is of course outstretched by both its neighbours on either side. In fact its 'bigness' is in relation to the two other summits on the long north-running ridge which it heads, known as the middle and little red cairns – **Càrn Dearg Meadhonach** and **Càrn Beag Dearg**. Indeed there are two other Càrn Dearg hills across on the western side of the Ben Nevis massif, one of them above Fort William reaching not far short of the Mòr itself. (Pronounced kaarn moa:r dyer*a*k)

Creag Meagaidh

This is a massive hill above Loch Laggan, with a name rather less than grand: W.J.Watson said it was a form of *creag mhigeachaidh*, crag of the boggy place, derived from an old Celtic word *mig* (the Angus hill **Meg Sweerie**, and Creag Megen above Loch Muick, come from the same word). Near the summit is an enigmatic pile of stone called Mad Meg's Cairn, but it seems unlikely that she is connected with the name, even though early 20th century Scottish Mountaineering Club Journal writers called it Craig Meggie.

In the 1890s, The Reverend A.E.Robertson, who went on to become the first Munroist, wrote that local people never used the *creag* name but called it the Coire Arder range, and he quotes a lady writing in 1789 referring to 'the lofty Corryarder'. (Coire Ardair lies at the heart of the mountain.) And an earlier 1869 memoir of Captain Colby (military surveyor) says that he called it Bui-Annoc, presumably from *buidhe aonach*, yellow mountain ridge – although this probably refers not to the highest point but to the A' Bhuidheanach ridge on Càrn Liath, east of the main corrie.

Even earlier, in MacFarlane's Geographical Manuscripts, 'Creag Megevie' is described as 'a mightie steep craggie hill'. And of course, such a huge mass of mountain could sustain several names on different parts – some of these remain on high (but not the highest) ground: **Càrn Liath** (grey cairn) and **Stob Poite Coire Àrdair**, peak of the pot of the high corrie, *poit* being a nice description of this long deep corrie. (Pronounced krayk **me**gee)

Drumochter hills

Drumochter is the high pass that takes the A9 and rail link into snowdrift country in winter: it comes from *druim uachdair*, the ridge of the upper part. Although there are hills on both sides the term is usually used for those west of the road, between it and Loch Ericht, although the author has heard the pejorative term 'the Dreary Drumochters' applied to the Munros on the east side. The highest is **Beinn Udlamain**, whose name is obscure – *udalan* is a swivel joint, possibly the ball-and-socket. Its neighbour **Sgàirneach Mhòr**, has a splendid name, *sgàirneach* meaning howling, or more plausibly a stony hillside, or even the sound of falling stones – this will refer

to the rocky corrie on its north face, one of the few cliffs in these rounded hills.

A' Mharconaich is the horsy place, while Geal-chàrn, white cairn, is one of two dozen of this name in this area (from its pale grasses): its former claim to individuality, its tall tottering chimney-like cairns visible from the A9, no longer stand. In Pont's 16th century map it was called Corrie Charn Hill. One cairn that has withstood time is the massive one on Beinn Mholach, hairy mountain, in the south of the group; now an obscure Corbett, it may once have had greater significance as a boundary, for it appears on early 19th century maps of Scotland as the only hill of the group to be named; on Pont's 16th century map, it appears as Bin Vourich, so it may originally have been *beinn bhùirich*, hill of (stags') roaring.

Easains

A very small range consisting of just two large mountains rising out of Loch Treig. They take their name from the higher one, Stob Coire Easain, peak of the corrie of the little waterfalls, spilling down the steep slopes to the loch. The other half of the range is Stob a' Choire Mheadhoin, peak of the middle corrie. Although comprising only these two summits, the ridge they crown is ten kilometres long. There's another almost identically-named Stob Coire an Easain nearby in the Grey Corries. Just adjacent to the mini-range are the steep rocky twins Cruach Innse and Sgùrr Innse; *innis*, genitive *innse*, means island (source of the Scots equivalent *inch*) but can also mean a meadow or resting place for cattle. Since they stand above the Làirig Leacach, the stony pass often used by drovers, it was probably these drovers who named them the meadow heap and peak.

Grey Corries

This is the chain of high mountains that runs along Glen Spean, eastwards from the Ben Nevis area. The ridge sheds long slides of ash-grey scree to north and south and the northern corries in particular have a bing-like bareness to them, weeping grey. Geologically these mountains are a mixture of quartzites, a whitish rock that also explains the name of nearby Stob Bàn and Beinn Bhàn, from the Gaelic *bàn* meaning white, and greenish-grey mica-schists, and some limestone, three apparent sources of 'grey'. On close examination, however, much of the summit quartzite is tinged and veined with a rose pink, and much of the greyness seems to be due to the lichens growing over the surface of the stones. The Gaelic name Na Coireachan Lèithe formerly used by the peoples of Glen Spean, does not appear on maps, only the English translation. A similar anglicised fate befell An Monadh Dubh a few kilometres south at the Black Mount.

The Grey Corries' highest peak is Stob Choire Claurigh, perhaps the most modest of the top 20 Munros, for its name refers to the corrie beneath it, identifying itself only as the Stob, or stubby top, above it. It has been suggested that the word *claurigh* derives from the Gaelic *clamhras* meaning brawling or clamouring – generally disturbing the peace. Peaks elsewhere in the Highlands have such meanings, among them Gleouraich above Loch Quoich, meaning roaring or bellowing; autumn hillwalkers will know the heartfelt bellowing of stags at rut echoing in dark

White Hills

There are three 'whiter shades of pale' in Gaelic, with *bàn*, *fionn* and *geal*. Often translated simply as white, they have in fact distinct nuances. While both *bàn* and *fionn* mean pale, white, wan or fair – and *fionn* hints also at the colour lilac and at the condition cold – *geal* (pronounced gyal) means white, clear or bright.

White is the world's commonest and oldest element in mountain names: Mont Blanc, Aconcagua, the Weisshorn, Elbruz, Mauna Kea, the Cordillera Blanca, and many more are 'white peaks' in other tongues, but mainly on account of snow and ice. However the main cause of a white appearance in the Scottish summer hills is either whitish rock or lighter vegetation. **Sgurr Bàn** (on **Beinn Eighe**) and **Stob Bàn** in the **Mamores** both occur where bands of whitish quartzite rock spill down the slopes in long scree curtains; quartzite is chemically too pure to provide many nutrients as a basis for soil and vegetation to grow, so it often appears naked on the weather-whipped hill summits. These quartzite hills of the north-west are sometimes mistaken from afar for snowfields by summer tourists, but in the past other thoughts occurred.

Ortelius' 1573 map of Scotland shows adjacent ranges *Montes Alabstri* (alabaster, or white gypsum, mountains) and *Montes Marmorei* (marble) in the north, a feature refined by Blaeu's map 60 years later into the 'Marble Mountains of Sutherland' and the 'Alabaster Mountains of Ross-shire'; while as late as 1852, a book by Buchanan speaks of '… mountains of white marble' as the only noteworthy feature of the area. The 'marble' mountains of Sutherland could refer to the pale grey quartzite massifs of Arkle and Foinaven (pp95 & 105), while Rossshire's 'alabaster' hills could be Beinn Eighe (p98).

bàn

Bàn is the commonest of the three Gaelic whites in mountain names and, like *fionn*, is overwhelmingly a word of the south-western Highlands and inner islands, with examples of **Beinn Bhàn** and **Càrn Bàn** stretching from Applecross to Arran. In the south the word often appears in the corrupted form in hills like **Tombain**.

fionn

Fionn is found mainly in the cold, sharp watery light of the north-west and on Skye, as in the Fannaichs' **Fionn Bheinn**. Fionn Bheinn's name seems to come from its long damp slopes above Achnasheen covered in light grasses and mosses, in contrast with the dark moors south of it. Curiously, although *fionn* is an uncommon colour word, it is one of the few which often precede the hill name, as in **Fionn Àrd**, **Fionn Mhàm** and Fionn Glen, suggesting that the colour is a very old name element. In southern Scotland the word often appears as 'fin', as in Fife's **Drumfinn** or Lothian's **Torphin**.

Elsewhere it may be confused with Fionn, the Celtic hero, as in **Suidh' Fhinn** on Skye, but Fionn or Finn's name was in fact itself derived in Irish legend from the Irish Gaelic word for fair or white. The Reverend Ronald Burn, second Munroist, was told locally in the early 20th century that the hill was where Fionn had killed some children, and had to flee with his mother, whose legs he then dropped in Loch Luragainn; the story does not ring true. Elsewhere it has been suggested that the pinnacle **Sgùrr Fiona** (of An Teallach), usually translated as from *fionn*, may in fact come from *fion* meaning wine, and while this may

seem unlikely – in this the heartland of whisky – wine was in fact a common drink of the Highlands, through the French connection, until the early 19th century. Thus 18th century traveller Thomas Pennant wrote that,

> These crags are called Sgur-fein, or hills of wine.

Perhaps the local people saw in the array of pinnacles a resemblance to the necks of the stone wine pitchers imported by ship.

geal

Although *geal* is a common Gaelic word, it is only used in hill names in the Spey and Laggan valleys. In this area a walker who sets out to climb **Geal Chàrn** will have 14 hills all called Geal Charn to choose from, and four of them are Munros. These four lie within a radius of 16 kilometres, and all visible from each other, and are rounded grassy peaks. Their fair, pale colour is a result of late-lying snow (here in the central Grampians they are a long way from the Atlantic's thawing influences), for this prevents the growth of the darker heather at the expense of the lighter grasses. Heather needs a snow-free growing season of several months. In a 1909 Scottish Mountaineering Club Journal, William Garden wrote of the summit of the Geal Charn above Pattack:

> ... one of the most singular I have seen ... a vast but shallow depression ... in which a huge snow field deposits itself annually ... the melting snows irrigate the surrounding groud ... and there are the most verdant stretches of pasture all over the summit, unbroken by a single stone.

Another interesting example of this is the **Brown Cow Hill** on Donside where a late-lingering crescent of snow, known as the **White Calf**, melts off in mid-summer to leave a crescent of light-coloured grasses stencilled into the surrounding heather.

There are also several hill names incorporating the phrase *clach geala*, white stone: the northern Munro **Eididh nan Clach Geala** means nest or web of the white stones, describing the intricate patterns of quartzite blocks shifted into geometric shape by frost movements. The Reverend Ronald Burn says some locals called it Meall Lochan Sgeiriche, but that name may in fact be the lesser northern summit, one kilometre away from the main peak, and overlooking the deep glen holding that lochan.

Only two or three of Scotland's hill features are named by reason of late-lying snow, unlike the famous 'whites' abroad, Mont Blanc and the Weisshorn. There is a top in the Monadh Liath named **Sneachdach Slinnean**, properly Slinnean Sneachdach, snowy shoulder, a shoulder indeed of the aptly-named **Càrn Bàn**. Similarly **Cairn Gorm** has a Fiacaill and Coire an t-Sneachda, snowy ridge and corrie. **Cuidhe Crom** atop **Lochnagar**, translates as the crooked snow wreath (properly *cuithe chrom*), describing the white crescent there that lingers into early summer. In the Borders lies the splendidly-named **Gathersnow Hill**, at a mere 689m: but at that height, as one 19th century writer noted ...

> The white-croon'd law blithe spring can thaw.

...so perhaps that is just its winter name, shed in spring, for it also called **Glenwhappen Rig** on the map.

evening corries. A bare stony corrie such as this mountain's has a powerful amplifying effect on noises. **Sgùrr Chòinnich Mòr** and **Beag** (mossy), and **Stob Coire an Laoigh** (calf corrie) complete up the range.

The Mamores

This chain of Munros starts across Glen Nevis from 'The Ben' and uncoils east for several kilometres, rearing and falling and throwing out several spurs. A full traverse is a major mountain day even in summer, and in this context J.B.Johnston's *Place-Names of Scotland* suggestion of *magh mòr*, the big plain, is completely out of place. Much more likely is *màm mòr*, big breast (shaped hills).

The name Mamoir appears on Blaeu's mid-17th century map, although it is not clear whether it refers to the area, the range, or a single hill: if the latter, an obvious candidate would be the dominating hill in the western end of the group, **Sgùrr a' Mhàim** (peak of the breast), and it's noteworthy that the large southern outlier is **Màm na Gualainn** (shoulder), both based on this same word *màm*. Among the other big hills in this switchbacking group (and not covered elsewhere in this book) are **Sgùrr Èilde Mòr** (properly Sgùrr na h-Eilde Mòr), big peak of the hind, **Am Bodach**, old man, and **Na Gruagaichean**, the maidens – this was formerly A' Gruagach, a singular girl, but there are in effect twin tops, hence the name expanded. **An Gearanach**, the complainer, and its near neighbour **An Garbhanach**, the tough one, sound like a couple of old grumps who would be in good company with Am Bodach.

Monadh Liath

This is literally the grey mountain mass, its colour distinguishing it from Am Monadh Ruadh, the red mountain mass, of the Cairngorms on the other bank of the Spey. The reds of the latter are the pinkish granite rocks: the greys of the former the schists and gneisses. One mid-19th century writer on place names, James Robertson, suggested they were grey because often misty – certainly they do lie west of the Spey, and therefore backing into the prevailing Atlantic winds.

There have been accusations in the walking press that the range is also grey in the sense of featureless and dull, lacking sharp summits and abounding in vast peat moors. Hamish Brown in particular has made it his business to rebut the charge, pointing out there are no dull hills, only dull people, and praising its stretches of high-level walking. Munro-baggers and Corbett-collectors tend to nibble only at its southern and eastern fringes, where colour names add sparkle, like the several **Càrn Dearg** (red) and **Geal-chàrn Mòr** (big white) summits; **Gairbeinn** (from *garbh*, rough) describes the terrain; while **Càrn an Fhreiceadain**, hill of the watcher, has an old stone deer-watchers' hut just west of the summit.

Further into the massif, the terrain is a sargasso of peatbogs drained by burns, but has some intriging hill names. The Corbett **Càrn na Saobhaidhe** (foxes' den) is one of eight occurrences in the Highlands, of which six are found here in the Monadh Liath. **Burrach Mòr** appears to be the big caterpillar, while **Calpa Mòr** is the big calf (of the leg – like the several **Lurg Mhòr**, big thigh hills). **Meall a' Ghuirmein** is an

unusual colour – indigo – while **Ileach Bàn** appears to mean the white Islayman. **Sgaraman nam Fiadh** has a hill-generic not in the dictionaries, although it looks like a variety of *sgòr* or *sgar*, peak, of the deer.

There was a Gaelic mnemonic to help the locals in the Newtonmore area remember the names of the peaks at the edge of the *monadh*, from Kingussie round to Lochan Uvie near where the Tromie joins the Spey:

> **Creag Bheag** chinn a' ghiubhsaich, [at Kingussie]
> **Creag Mhòr** bhail' a' chrothain [at the sheepfold]
> **Beinn Bhuidhe** na Sròine [of the nose]
> **Creag an Loin** aig na croitean [at the crofts]
> **Sìthean Mòr** dhail a' chaoruinn [at the field of rowans]
> **Creag an Abhaig** a' bhail-shias [at the lower farm]
> **Creag Liath** a' bhail-shuas [at the upper farm]
> Is **Creag Dhubh** bhiallaid [and … to the front]
> Cadha an Fhèidh Lochain Ubhaidh [the pass of the deer]

The hill names are in bold, and all but one you can still find on the map – the location of Creag an Abhaig (terrier) you must guess at. Who said the Monadh Liath were dull? (Pronounced monagh **lyee-***a*)

Meall a' Bhùiridh

This Gaelic attention to natural detail is apparent in peaks like Meall a' Bhùiridh – there are two, one on either edge of Rannoch Moor – the hill of the roaring, from where the rutting autumn stags bellow soulfully through the lengthening black nights. There are a dozen peaks in the Highlands of this name, or its variant **Meall a' Bhùirich** (or the anglicised **Ben Vuirich**). (Pronounced myowl *a* **voo**:ree)

Pap of Glencoe

Approaching Glen Coe from the west along Loch Leven, this striking breast-shaped peak above the mouth of the river is precisely-named. It is however a translation from the equally accurate Gaelic name, **Sgòrr na Cìche**, into Scots rather than English.

CHAPTER SIX

SOUTHERN HIGHLANDS

Argyll's Bowling Green

This name is not on the Ordnance Survey map, but is or was well-known amongst locals. It refers to all or part of the peninsula between Loch Long and Loch Goil, also known by walkers as Ardgoil. W.H.Murray (local man, as well as a leading 20th century Scottish mountaineer) referred to it in his *Scotland's Mountains*, and the term is still used extensively in tourist information. Travellers on the West Highland railway train edging along above Loch Long look west to this knobbly peninsula, a ruckled piece of land. Names lying within it include **Clach Bheinn** (stony peak), the simple **Garbh** (rough) and **Tom Molach** (shaggy hill), all precise about the ground. Irony is thus often thought to have been the origin of the current name – the 1823 edition of *Scottish Tourist and Traveller* said it was so-named 'in derision from the extreme irregularity and bleakness of the mountains'.

It may possibly have had a straightforward Gaelic origin in *Buaile a' Ghrianain*, cattlefold of the sunny hillock, *grianan* being a fairly common Gaelic hill name; the whole area of course belonged to the Duke of Argyll. But a full investigation of the name in a 1913 Scottish Mountaineering Club Journal article by F.S.Goggs concluded that it originally applied to a small level patch of ground beside the Duke's Path, where the duke rested en route from the Portincaple Ferry to Loch Goil, and that it was then mapped in 1735 (perhaps 50 or so years later) by Carrington Bowles as applying to the whole peninsula, other mapmakers then following suit: early 19th century maps by Langlands and Thomson named it, and whilst the Ordnance Survey from the mid-19th century chose not to record it, the fine Bartholomew's half-inch map series displayed it well into the 20th century.

Many kilometres north, the summit of **Ben Tee** (west of the Great Glen) was known last century as **Glengarry's Bowling Green**, even although, as Victorian writer Edward Ellice says, there is 'scarcely a square yard of green of any sort' among its summit rocks.

Arrochar Alps

A few jack-lengths from Argyll's Bowling Green lie the 'Arrochar Alps'. Containing Munros **Beinns Ìme** and **Narnain** and **Ben Vane**, they are however dominated in fame and feature by the slightly lower peak of **Ben Arthur**, **The Cobbler**. This, with its three peaks jagging the sky, could well be a 'horn' in the Bernese Oberland when under snow and the name Arrochar Alps is the acceptable face of the Scots 'Wha's like us?' syndrome.

It was apparently given to the area in the 1930s by climbers from the Clydeside unemployed who escaped there for weeks on end from urban misery. Articles on the area in the Scottish Mountaineering Club Journal at the turn of the century never used the term 'Alps', referring instead to 'the Arrochar group' or 'the Arrochar mountains' which, wrote W.W.Naismith in 1895, 'will probably have been brought (by the new railway) within a couple of hours from Glasgow'. The term 'Arrochar Alps' was first used in print in 1946 by author and climber Ben Humble who had climbed a lot there

in the 1930s, and although the 1950s SMC guidebook was too strait-laced to use this new coining, the name caught on and is now widely used.

Beinn Dòrain

Beinn Dòrain is a striking mountain towering over Bridge of Orchy. Its slope rises from the railway, steepening towards the summit in a crescendo of concavity. Streams scour out multiple parallel gullies on its face as they skid down. Its main claim to fame in Highland culture lies in the 18th century poet Duncan Bàn MacIntyre's celebration of the mountain in his epic work *Moladh Beinn Dòbhrain*.

A century earlier, Walter MacFarlane's manuscripts had referred to it as Bin Dowran and Bindawran, phonetically-based. There are two usual candidates for its name; most often canvassed is dòbhran (pronounced **doa**:ran) meaning otter – creatures often feature in Gaelic hill names and this would be a strong contender, and indeed there is a **Beinn Dòbhrain**, otter mountain, near Helmsdale. Or else it could be mountain of the streamlets from *dobhar* (diminutive *dobharan*) which would fit its gullied sides. **Ben Alder** across Rannoch Moor also contains *dobhar* (*beinn ail-dobhar*) and this connection, together with these striking streams, makes this meaning more likely. The two candidates are related, for the otter can be known as *dobhar-chu*, water-dog.

There's also *dòrainn* meaning pain or anguish – certainly what some walkers experience on its relentless slopes. Just such a meaning is referred to in an old Gaelic song, which has (in translation) the line, 'There's aye keening on Beinn Dorain', *keening* being the Scots for crying. A commentary on the song, written by an expert in the 1940s, says that the mountain was known for making sounds at night – continuous murmurs like a child or creature in pain – when a wind got up before bad weather. Perhaps it was caused by the wind soughing over the many gullies, a huge natural chanter – the mountain of pain indeed. (Pronounced bYn **do**:ran)

Beinn Ìme

This is the highest peak in the 'Arrochar Alps', nowadays not so well-known as The Cobbler just south-east of it. On Roy's 1755 map it was the only peak in the group named (as Beiniam) and this was true on the earliest map of the 19th century too. Its name means butter mountain, from *ìm*, genitive *ìme*, butter, and the name will refer to the days of transhumance when herds were pastured in the hills in summer, and butter often made there on the high shielings. It is no accident that the bridge on the A83 to the west is Butterbridge, an old name, and that the burn foaming down from The Cobbler to the east is the Buttermilk Burn.

Beinn Narnain

The Cobbler's 'left-hand mountain', and often ignored beside its lower but more dramatic neighbour, Beinn Narnain's name seems at first sight as enigmatic as C.S.Lewis mythical land of Narnia; most books say of it 'origin unknown'. The only similar name in Scotland is Nairn, a town on the river of the same name, which is said to come from an ancient European word for water, with cognates rivers Nar and Naro in the Mediterranean lands. But Nairn is 160 kilometres from Beinn Narnain and a connection is impossible.

However in an 1895 volume of the Scottish Mountaineering Club Journal, there is a reference to its old name Ben Varnan, and this may help us solve the mystery. For *v* is usually the Gaelic pronunciation of *bh*, and a *beinn bharnan* would resemble *bheàrnan*, the notches or gaps, pointing at the rock fissures around its eastern Spearhead Arete cliffs.

Timothy Pont in the late 16th century appears to have mapped it as Bin Clhlarachan, though the location is difficult to pinpoint and the name could suggest Beinn Chorranach, three kilometres north-west: one of his many cartographic qualities is that he often drew accurate little profiles of distinctive hills, and Pont's hill is shown with a flat top and a steep cliff to the right, which is the exact appearance of Beinn Narnain from the south and east. If this is indeed this hill, it might suggest an original meaning from *clàrach*, smooth or bald – certainly it has a plateau top.

Ben A' n

(Sometimes Ben A' an). When Sir Walter Scott wrote his epic poem *Lady of the Lake* he effectively created the Trossachs as a tourist attraction, and also brought this sharp little peak into the spotlight – but made a bad mistake with its name in the process, creating a 'Ben' where none had stood before! A fine viewpoint from which to look down on Loch Katrine and the surrounding woods and hills, it probably gets more visitors than any other Scottish hill of its modest 533m height, and in fact it is not really a separate hill at all but a pointed bump on the shoulder of **Meall Gainmheich** (sandy hill). From below however it is a striking sharp little peak, and Scott wrote of it:

> ... While on the north, through middle air,
> Ben-an heaved high his forehead bare.

The map spelling of Ben A'n has the bracketed alternative of Binnein, indicating that it might originally be from Am Binnean meaning the small pointed peak. There is a hill called **Binnean nan Gobhar**, goats' peak, not far away across Loch Ard. Walter Scott's Ben-an may also be the simple diminutive *beannan*, little mountain ... there's a **Beannan Beaca** in the Monadh Liath (though this may be an Ordnance Survey misprint for *beanntan*), an **Am Beannan** above Loch Rannoch, and the many **Bennan** hills in Galloway ... and certainly it is the Trossachs' 'little mountain'.

The Cobbler (Ben Arthur)

This lovely and much-climbed mountain has two names, The Cobbler and Ben Arthur. Several hills have two names, one referring to the whole mountain, the other to a summit upon it. This is the case here too, The Cobbler being the central peak of three, but one that has spread to refer to the whole mountain almost displacing the older name Ben Arthur or Beinn Artair. Like a popular person with a formal title and a nickname, the frequent use of the latter makes use of the former impossibly stiff-necked, and only maps and guides ever draw our attention to the official mode of address. Ironically this formal name with its 'Ben' would appear to be more Gaelic than the English nickname, but in fact the truth is the reverse, that the latter is a translation from Gaelic while the former may well commemorate an early British king.

The suggested origins of Ben Arthur have included *beinn artaich* (stony mountain), *art mòr* (or Old Welsh *arth mawr*) meaning big bear, and even a Latin root in *arare*, to

plough, supposedly from Arrochar village below it! These 'star-gazing' names (with their great bear and the plough) are of little value compared to the more obvious root in the name *Artair*, Arthur. Timothy Pont's late 15th century map records it clearly – complete with an accurate sketch of the skyline profile – as 'craggie hill, Suy Arthire', a phonetic representation of Suidhe Artair.

The Cobbler, the name of the sharp central peak now is used for the entire hill. For other 'craftsmen', see p189, [Mountain Characters, Craftsmen and Musicians]

Suidhe, as a hill name generic, is usually applied with saints or noble people. There are several Scottish hills named after the legendary British King, including two called **Arthur's Seat**. W.J.Watson describes a rock on the west side of Glen Kinglas as Aghaidh Artair (Arthur's face), and there's no reason why this crown-shaped hill should not join them. It is said of King Arthur that when the Romans left Britin and the heathens invaded, he tried to defend it from Cornwall to the Clyde: this mountain, at the head of sea-Loch Long, would mark the northern marches with the men of the north. Or, it could be from another Arthur, a 'local boy made good', a son of the 6th century King Aedan of Dalriada. *Beinn* clearly replaced *suidhe* as the generic, later.

The Cobbler's name is more straightforward. One suggestion is that it is from *gobhlach*, forked, from its shape. There is a mountain called **Beinn Gobhlach** near Ullapool with a serrated summit ridge (reminiscent of a factory roof), but its pronunciation **goa:l**ach is not much of a basis for the word cobbler. A 1928 book, *Place-names of Cowal* by Maclean, asserted that Ben Goblach was the local Gaelic at that time, and that The Cobbler was an Englishman's attempt to cope with the Gaelic; unfortunately for Maclean's credibility, there is no Gaelic word *goblach*, the correct *gobhlach* being pronounced without the *b* sound. In any case much earlier evidence suggests that The Cobbler is in fact a simple English translation of an old local Gaelic name, for as John Stoddart wrote in 1800, in his book *Local Scenery and Manners in Scotland*:

> This terrific rock forms the bare summit of a huge mountain, and its nodding top so far overhangs the base as to assume the appearance of a cobbler sitting at work, from whence the country people call it 'an greasaiche crom', the crooked shoemaker ...

An early contributor to the Scottish Mountaineering Club Journal had an interesting theory for how the shape was identified and named. Writing in 1901, William Inglis Clark noted that in the eastern Alps peaks whose summits 'terminate in perpendicular pinnacles' are sometimes named *Schuster* (cobbler) and that a prime example was the Dreischusterspitze (three cobblers' peak) in the Tirol. He speculates:

> Is it possible therefore that the name may have originated by some traveller returning from these Dolomitic regions and seeing a fancied resemblance in our Scottish 'Dolomitas'?

Fancy indeed, that Gaelic-speakers would take on board an English-speaking traveller's description of a remote corner of the Alps! As for the Dreischusterspitze, the only Scottish peak it remotely resembles might be the pinnacle ridge of the Cuillin's Sgurr nan Gillean. This author's enquiries at the local Italian tourist office were met by the explanation that it was named because 'it was first climbed by three local cobblers', although this was not confirmed in print (and may be cobblers in another sense!). So The Cobbler's name origin need not be sought abroad: the answer is the simple one, that Gaelic culture with its wide range of names for the hills, and its powers of imagination, came up with an excellent image.

Although to a modern eye, looking for a cobbler (a trade almost vanished from our towns) on the mountain is a bit like scanning the clouds for pictures, another SMC Journal writer of early this century was able to point straight at the central peak:

> ... on account of the very striking resemblance of the topmost blocks, when seen from Arrochar, to a little cowled figure sitting with his knees gathered up, like a cobbler bending over his work. He faces north, and over against him sits the ponderous and altogether disproportionate figure of his wife ... like an old woman in a mutch (a night-cap), stooping with age.

It's a measure of how 20th century eyes have lost the ability to 'see' the hill-shapes that the three peaks have had the names The Cobbler, **The Last**, and Jean his wife or lass transposed over the years, as this table shows.

Year	Author	South Peak	Centre Peak	North Peak
1899	SMCJ	Jean, his Lass	The Cobbler	Wife **or** Cobbler's Last
1964	Poucher, W	Jean, his Wife	The Cobbler	The Last
1988	Brown, H	Jean	The Last	The Cobbler

Certainly Stoddart's 1800 quote could point to the North Peak which is clearly overhanging, but it more probably and correctly points to the Centre Peak, which is the true summit. There is a tradition that a new chief of the Clan Campbell, the Duke of Argyll, had to prove himself by climbing to the top of the Cobbler's Cowl (hood), which was the summit stone, and the keyhole on this rock which generations of walkers have wriggled through to get onto the top was known as **Argyll's Eyeglass**. The North Peak is known to climbers as the Ram's Head from its shape.

But standing by the shores of Loch Long, now that you know to look at the *Centre Peak*, you should see the cobbler hunched over his last.

Ben Lawers

Ben Lawers is a single peak that has given its name to the range of six Munros, standing high above Loch Tay, often referred to collectively simply as Ben Lawers. There are two suggested origins: the Gaelic word *labhar* (pronounced **la**var) meaning loud or noisy in the manner of a stream; and the Gaelic *ladhar* (pronounced **lu**-ar) for a hoof or claw.

The 'hoof' or 'claw' explanation might seem to fit better both by its pronunciation compared to the modern name Lawers, and because of the overall shape of the massif, with great ridges and spurs sweeping round like talons to enclose corries. And other names on the massif hint at this hooked shape: **Meall Corranaich** has several possible interpretations (including *meall coire rainich*, bracken corrie), but among them is hill of the sickle (*corran*); a top just beyond the main peak is **Creag an Fhithich**, cliff of the raven; while on the far side lies Gleann Da-ghob, glen of two beaks or two forks. There's another 'hoof mountain' in **Ladhar Bheinn** in Knoydart in the west. And there might seem to be a connection between Ben Lawers' apparent 'claw' name and Lochan nan Cat, lochan of the wild cats, lying in the deepest of these corries.

However the word *ladhar* often refers to paws rather than claws, albeit paws with claws. And there are some other awkward facts confronting a 'claw' meaning, such as the name's English plural form ending in 's' (the Gaelic plural would end in -an); and the absence of the proper form (if it is mountain of the claw) as *beinn an ladhair*.

And there are strong arguments for *labhar*, loud. This same Lochan nan Cat feeds the Lawers Burn, a substantial stream running down to Loch Tay; it is loud certainly, especially when fed by spring snowmelt or summer storm, its background clatter throwing the rest of the great silence into relief. Beinn Labhair was the spelling and local pronunciation recorded by W.J.Watson, by folk-song collectors, and by dictionary-maker Edward Dwelly at the start of the 20th century. The loud stream in question was called Labhar by Alasdair mac Mhaighstir Alasdair, the great 18th century poet and scholar. The three local land divisions of the resulting name of Labhar district, based on the stream name, became The Lawers as their collective English plural form, and this would also explain the 's' of Lawers.

'Loud' or 'noisy' mountains are not unusual in the Highlands, as names like **Gleouraich** (roaring) or **Lochnagar** (loch of noise) indicate, and indeed there's another stream called Uisge Labhair flowing west from **Ben Alder**, a noisy burn rumbling over rock staircases down to Loch Ossian. And *beinn labhair*, the loud mountain, would be a correct Gaelic form. All these details shout a 'loud' meaning from the hill tops.

Lawers' other peaks include **Beinn Ghlas** (grey-green mountain), **Meall Garbh** (rough hill), **An Stùc** (the rocky cone) and **Meall Greigh** (usually interpreted as the hill of the horse stud or cattle herd from *greigh*; but one older version has it as Meall Gruaidh, meaning the cheek, or profile).

Ben Ledi

Throughout the year the car park at the foot of Ben Ledi is packed, and the path to the top crawls with walkers, attracted by its fine shape and the views it commands over

the Central Lowlands. This is not new, for in 1794 the local parish minister in the *Old Statistical Account* wrote:

> By reason of the altitude of Ben Ledi and of its beautiful conical figure, the people of the adjacent country to a great distance, assembled annually on its top, about the time of the summer solstice, during the Druidical priesthood, to worship the Deity. This assembly seems to have been a provincial or synodical meeting, wherein all the congregations within the bounds wished to get as near to Heaven as they could to pay their homage to the God of Heaven.

Two possible origins of the name arise from this. One – currently featured on the local tourist information boards – is that it is the Mountain of God (*beinn le Dia*) which would certainly fit the history just related; *le* is a preposition meaning with or in the company of and *Dia* is pronounced **dyeea**. (Incidentally the iron cross near the summit has nothing to do with this. It was erected in 1987 to commemorate policeman Harry Lawrie killed in a helicopter crash on Ben More, during a mountain rescue.)

However the local pronunciation of a century ago recorded by Dwelly as (Beinn) Lidi or Lididh, with the stress on the first syllable, indicates that '*le* Dia' (stressed on the second syllable) is nonsense. Besides, the 'mountain *with* God' (*beinn le Dia*) is a curious use of a proposition, and the 'mountain of God' which would have made more sense, would probably have used the genitive formulation of *beinn Dhe* ... which it hasn't.

The other and more probable meaning is from *leitir* or *leathad*, a slope, from the way its long southern ridge climbs at a steady angle all the way from the valley floor leading the eye up to the summit. *Leitir* also is closer in pronunciation to Ledi than *le Dia*. W.C.MacKenzie in his 1931 *Scottish Place-names* hinted at this 'slope' meaning when he used the old-fashioned word declivitous for the hill, and there is a similar name in **Beinn Leòid** in Sutherland, hill of the slope. A century ago the Ordnance Survey Gazetteer said that the hills' name came from *beinn shlèibhte*, mountain of mountains or moorland, or mountain girt with sloping hills.

Curiously enough, the only word in the old tongues of Scotland that compares exactly in form and sound to the present name is *ledi*, an Old Norse word used in Shetland to mean a viewpoint, which would be highly appropriate for our hill here. But as there are no other Norse names within the bounds of Ledi's horizon, it cannot be accepted.

Religion had at least one sad outcome on the hill. Lochan nan Corp on its northern flanks is the lochan of the corpses, where a funeral party en route over the hill to St Bride's Chapel on Loch Lubnaig, was crossing the frozen loch when its ice gave way to swallow the body and the bearers.

God, or gods, are rarely mentioned in hill names, but **Loudon Hill**, a striking prominent hill in East Ayrshire, may come, according to W.J.Watson, from the pre-Christian god Lugus, the name then being *lugdunon*. Lugh of the long arm, a god of light, was widely worshipped in Celtic lands, as a force for good.

Ben Lomond

Like Ben Ledi, Ben Lomond is a landmark on the southern edge of the Highlands, visible from many Lowland spots. This gives credence to the idea that, like Fife's **Lomond Hills**, it comes from the Cumbric word *llumon* meaning a beacon or blaze or light,

giving the hill an ancient telecommunications function. It can after all be seen from Glasgow right across to Stirling and beyond, in a sizeable chunk of Scotland's populated lowlands.

The Gaelic *luimean*, a barren hillock, might also seem appropriate as it rises near-naked above a heavily-wooded base. The name has been one of the Highlands' more successful exports, with expatriates naming hills around the world after it: there are Ben Lomonds in New Brunswick, Tasmania, New South Wales, New Zealand and Utah. The last named, also standing like the Scottish one proud above lowlands (in this case nearly 3000 metres above Ogden on the Great Salt Lake at the 'Top of Utah'), features in the opening credit of Paramount movies, the original company's owner having come from there.

Ben Lomond, the beacon hill, with Ptarmigan to its left. See also the Lomond Hills of Fife, p166, [Central Lowlands, Lomond Hills]

Ptarmigan, the name given to Ben Lomond's distinctive western ridge overlooking Loch Lomond, is the name of the archetypal bird of the high mountains, and was shown as far back as Roy's map of the 1750s. Pont, a century and a half earlier, had mapped it as *mealden ptermachan*: this might suggest it was originally *meall nan tàrmachan*, hill of the ptarmigans.

Ben Lui

Correctly pronounced **loo**-ee, this might lend strong credence to *luaidhe*, lead (the mineral) for there are old lead mines on the flanks of **Beinn Chùirn** (hill of the cairn) and **Meall Odhar** not five kilometres away, whose heavy metal poisons make barren the hillside above Tyndrum, and also in the north-east corrie of the mountain itself. And 'lead mountain' would have a cousin in **Beinn Iaruinn** iron mountain,

30 kilometres north at the head of Glen Roy.

But the Tyndrum mine was first opened in 1739, and the local people would have given a hill as striking as Ben Lui a name of its own long before the 18th century. And indeed, Pont's late 16th century map, compiled over a century before the mine opened, mapped it as Bin Luy. There is another hill (not far away, above Glen Lyon) called **Beinn Luaidhe** where lead mining *did* take place, but it is a lesser top of the 'left-over' variety that were named much later.

Another Gaelic word producing a similar sound is *laogh* meaning calf or fawn (and Beinn Laoigh is the form we find used by local Gaelic speakers) and there is a strong Gaelic tradition of giving the hills names of animals (neighbouring **Beinn Oss** may be elk mountain). The resemblance of the mountain's gently two-horned summit to the head of a young calf, and the protuberance on the northern ridge called Cìochan (nipples of) Beinn Laoigh, almost certainly indicate that it is indeed mountain of the calf. However one animal can be definitely ruled out, for although James Hogg 'The Ettrick Shepherd', passing by in the early 1800s, managed to spell it Ben Leo, there were never lions here!

Dark hills
dubh

Dubh means dark or black. This is by far the commonest Gaelic shade with over 200 hill names to its credit. Over a dozen major tops include **Sgùrr Dubh**, **Meall Dubh** and **Tom Dubh**, and in the west there's a trio of hills called **Ciste Dhubh**, literally dark chest (or more ominously black coffin!). The dark or black may refer to the heather which covers some hills more than others, or to the blacker rocks that outcrop on it, or to the way the light falls on a particular hill or corrie. For instance **Aonach Dubh** in Glen Coe is a steep north-facing wall, with the sunless black cleft of Ossian's Cave on it barely visible in its shadow. While **The Dubhs** at the southern end of the Cuillin ridge – a relatively easy day, celebrated in the Scottish Mountaineering Club Journal poem's alliterative line:

> ... So now when they seek but a day's relaxation,
> With no thought in the world but viewing the views,
> And regarding the mountains in mute adoration,
> They call it not 'climbing' but 'doing the Dubhs'

... are where the giant slabs of gabbro, a darker volcanic rock, are most noticeable. Several other *dubh* hill names incorporate creag or coire (crag and corrie), naturally shadow-filled features, as in **Beinn Dubhchraig** or **Stob Coire Dhuibh** (of Creag Meagaidh). In southern Scotland the word *dubh* has been altered to the less pleasing *duff* – as in south Edinburgh's **Torduff**, and the **Tarduff** hills in the Ochils and the Campsies – and is often found paired with a Torfin, white hill.

There are several hills with names like **Deuchary Hill**, which W.J.Watson argued was from *dubh-chathraigh*, black broken peat hags, a common occurrence on flat-topped hills. There are several such names in the southern Cairngorms (one also known as **Mealna**

Ben More

Originally Beinn Mhòr (and still thus in Gaelic), this translates simply as big mountain. There are two Munros with this plain name, the other being on the island of Mull. On the mainland there is another Beinn Mhòr in Kintail in the north-west, but it is better known as the Five Sisters of Kintail, whilst in the further north-west beyond Ullapool **Ben More Assynt** and **Ben More Coigach** have incorporated the district name to distinguish them. (Assynt is from the Norse *ass* for a rocky ridge, while *coigeach* is Gaelic for a fifth share, a land division).

Offshore again, a plain **Beinn Mhòr** is the second highest hill in Lewis, being at 570m less than half the height of the Perthshire Ben More, the term *mòr* being, of course, relative rather than absolute, indicating its large size relative to its neighbours. This Ben More is the highest peak in the Crianlarich area. From a wide area of the Southern Highlands the mountain and its twin Stob Binnein (or Stobinian) are unmistakeable, their fine cones drawing the eye to them, and many photographic panoramas are centred around their symmetry.

Letter, hill of the slope *meall na leth-tir*) and some in the eastern Borders – like **Deuchrie Dod**.

The Vikings had 'dark hills' too – **Murkle** in Caithness is from *myrk-holl,* the root of our word murky.

donn

This, the colour brown, is found mainly on lower hills around the Clyde estuary, the earliest Gaelic-speaking area. There are two pairs of **Meall Donn** and **Cnoc Donn**, one on either side of the Kilbrannan Sound in Arran and in Kintyre. **Maol Donn**, the brown headland on Arran, refers to the colour of its Old Red Sandstone rock, but the other hills of this colour are on granite and so it may be that their 'brown' refers to the tangle of heather on the hillsides. Certainly the **Meall Donn** above Thundergay is thickly matted with heather in contrast to the nearby hills with their screes. It's surprising that there aren't more *donn* names in a country where heather is second only to the thistle as the national plant. Even the Lowlander Rabbie Burns noted the colour:

> We'll sing auld Coila's plains and fells,
> Her moors red-brown with heather bells.

There is a **Beinn Donn** near Oban on grey schist rock, and the colour probably comes from its heather; the hill seems to mark the northern limit of hills with *donn*. Above Loch Maree stands the grey quartzite of the Bonaid Dhonn, brown bonnet, over which plunges the waterfall from **Beinn a' Mhùinidh,** literally mountain of pissing.

Ben Vane

There are several Ben Vane hills on Scotland's maps, in Fife, Argyll and Perthshire, the 'vane' being an anglicised pronunciation of *mheadhoin*, middle or central in Gaelic. When Pont mapped the one above Loch Lomond, late 16th century, on hearing the locals' pronunciation he mapped it Bin Vian, which is quite a good phonetic form. **Vane Hill** in Fife is between the Lomonds and the Cleish Hills, Ben Vane in Argyll between Beinn Ìme and Ben Vorlich, and **Benvane** in the Trossachs is piggy-in-the-middle between Ben Ledi and Beinn an t-Sìthein. There is no apparent geological or language reason to accept the alternative suggestion that Benvane is from *beinn bhàn* meaning white, and indeed it has dark cliffs when seen from the south. Ben Vane in Fife is a shoulder of **Benarty Hill** (possibly from old Gaelic *art*, stony – it is seamed with small cliffs), and this Ben Vane is sometimes called locally 'The Footstool of The Sleeping Giant' of Benarty.

Ben Venue

Towering above the heart of the Trossachs and Loch Katrine, this means small mountain, for *beinn mheanbh* is pronounced in Gaelic very like the anglicised 'venue'. At 729m it might be large in its own immediate neighbourhood and 'the dominating height above Loch Katrine', but it is the smaller cousin of other Trossachs peaks like Ben Ledi, and dwarfed by hills of the Ben More (big mountain) group a few kilometres north. From the Stirling area, looking along the line of the Highland edge, it is distinctive as one of three – Ben Ledi, Ben Venue and Ben Lomond – but is clearly the smallest. A scholar at Edinburgh University has suggested that this hill is the one referred to in a 17th century Gaelic poem, where it is called *cnoc mòr meanbh-chruidh*, the great hillock of tiny cattle; this is a poetic term for goats or sheep, or equally a reference to fairy cattle, perhaps linked to the name Coire nan Ùruisgean, corrie of the goblins or milk stealing sprites, on its northern flanks.

A recent author, Ralph Storer, has suggested mountain of the caves as its meaning. A cave in Gaelic is *uamh* (pronounced oo-av), *uamhach* is 'abounding in caves', and there are indeed caves near Coire nan Ùruisgean, but the sounds 'wavuch' and 'venue' are not very alike. (For comparison, far to the west are two hills called **Beinn na h-Uamha** and **Bràigh nan Uamhachan** both cave mountains, quite uncorrupted in name. And, only a few kilometres away above Glen Artney, are **Uamh Mhòr** and **Uamh Bheag**, the latter a late addition to the Grahams and named after a cave on its south-west slopes.)

Another suggestion for this name is milk mountain, *beinn a' bhainne* (pronounced vannya), which would fit the name's sound reasonably, and has cognates a few kilometres west in **Beinn Ìme** (butter mountain) and **The Cobbler**'s white-foaming Buttermilk Burn … but why would it be called milk mountain (in the days before EU food surpluses)? Perhaps because, as the old edition of the Scottish Mountaineering Club guidebook to *The Southern Highlands* says of the hill:

> It shows a bold front to the Trossachs, rocky and deeply shadowed most of the year, and after rain is seamed by waterfalls.

These waterfalls fit well with the name of the Coire na Ùruisge, for Highland burns in spate foam a milky-white favoured by sprites. However local pronunciations of the name, collected last century, suggest that it is indeed *beinn mheanbh*, the small mountain.

Ben Vorlich

Which one? So the walker is often asked – the one above Loch Earn, or the Loch Lomond one? – for they lie in sight of each other and are both Munros. There are more explanations suggested for the name than there are hills, though. Given that *mh* in Gaelic is pronounced *v* in English, the suggestions have included Beinn Mhòr Loch (mountain of the big loch) and Beinn Mhòr-Luig (mountain of the big corrie or hollow, which is close to the local pronunciation early last century, and as with many hills fits the shape of its scooped-out corries).

There is also the possibility of the mountain of the bay, Beinn Mhuir'lag, (literally mountain of the sack-shaped sea bags from *muir bhalgan*), and Beinn Mhòr-Leacach (big stony mountain) – the Reverend Burn in his 1918 diary claimed a local shepherd had told him it was *beinn mhòir lic* (hill of the big stone). All of these fit the scenery, but none has the beauty of another suggested origin of the Perthshire (Loch Earn) one from *mùrlach* meaning kingfisher. There are many other 'bird' peaks in the Highlands, and this suggestion might sit well with Pont's mapping as Bin Vouirlyg, and the 1794 spelling Benvurlich. However, before the twitchers arrive, it should be noted that the kingfisher is a bird favouring slow-moving rivers (not tumbling Highland burns) and is a very rare sight in the mountains, having bred rarely and even then only in the west.

So the truth is probably more prosaic, lying in the geographical explanations. Of these, the mountain of the 'sack-shaped bags', (or in a word 'bays') is most likely. Both mountains have a farm at the foot called Ardvorlich, the height above the bay (on the loch), although it has to be said that the one at the foot of the Ben Vorlich on Loch Lomond is a more distinct bay than the Loch Earn-side one. Not far from Loch Earn, on Loch Voil, lies Muirlaggan, which one researcher found to be *muir bhalgan*, another of these poetically-described bays.

At the west end of Loch Arkaig is a mountain with a similar name, **Sgùrr Mhùrlagain**, probably a northern cousin of the Vorlichs. And Loch Morlich near Aviemore is probably a family member. The Ben Vorlich above Loch Earn is visible, together with its neighbour **Stùc a' Chròin**, over much of the Forth basin, and not surprisingly Pont sketched their profiles, naming them Bin Vouirlyg and Struik Chron.

Schiehallion

Schiehallion is often featured in calendar photos taken from the birch-fringed shores of Loch Rannoch in douce Perthshire, from where it appears as a shapely cone. The regularity of its shape, the result of weathering of its homogenous quartzite rock, attracted the Astronomer-Royal Maskeleyne here in the 18th century to conduct experiments on the earth's mass. And its shape gives credence to one of several suggested meanings for its name, that of *sine chailinn*, breast of the maiden. But in Gaelic the usual word for a breast is *cìoch*, found all over the Highlands, and besides, the mountain's cone 'disappears' when viewed from most other angles; Schiehallion from the Glen Coe hills is said to have 'an unusual truncated appearance.'

A more likely meaning of the name is *sìth* (or *sìdh*) *chaillean*, the fairy hill of the Caledonians – W.J.Watson inclined to this. *Sìth* is found in names like Glenshee or the hill **Shee of Ardtalnaig** south of Loch Tay, and *sìthean* (fairy, or pointed, hills) are

found all over Scotland. Furthermore Perthshire was the ancient heartland of the Caledonian tribes, known to the Romans – thus Dunkeld and Rohallion, both lying within 32 kilometres, are respectively the hillfort (*dùn*) and fort (*ràth*) of the Caledonians.

In 1642 the spelling of the mountain's name as Schachalzean (the *z* representing an old Scots letter pronounced *y*), and the Schichallion form of the name prevalent well into the 20th century, stress the *chailleann* part of the names. In the mid-19th century the local minister wrote the name as Sich-caillin in the New Statistical Account, close to the present spelling. And fairy pointed hill of the Caledonians is certainly a fine name for this very individual Munro. General Roy's military survey of 1755 maps the hill as *Shihalin or Maiden Pap*: Roy referring to it as Maiden's Pap is not a translation but a good comparison, and obviously an alternative local soubriquet.

However, Pont's map, based on surveys in the late 16th century, appears to record the mountain as Kraich, although the name is written well down the flanks of the hill's sketch: this could point at an alternative name, perhaps *cruach* (heap), or possibly *creachann* (a bare summit). In fact Pont was probably naming **Craig Kynachan**, the hill between Schiehallion and the main glen to the north-east, which was picked up by the later maps such as Blaeu's as Kainachan Forest. Ian Mitchell's chapter in *The Nation Survey'd* argues that Pont's purpose was to give directions to people heading west from Loch Tummel to Rannoch; Craig Kynachan effectively lies on the northern flanks of Schiehallion when viewed from the main glen. (Pronounced shee**hal**y*an*)

Stùc a' Chròin

A local Victorian minister, the Reverend MacGregor of Balquhidder, believed that Stùc a' Chròin's name meant the hill of moaning, or a 'lesser hill jutting out as it were from a greater one'. (The word *stuic* can mean a projecting hill.) The 'greater one' in this case will be Ben Vorlich, all of 10 metres higher, and divided from it by a deep pass one and a half kilometres wide. Certainly this gap is hidden from Balquhidder to the west, but from most other points it presents the clear image of two fiercely independent peaks, and from many spots in the Central Lowlands Stùc a' Chròin appears as an equal but independent twin … certainly not a 'lesser jutting-out' one. Another Reverend, the place names' writer J.B.Johnston, thought that *chròin* came from *crann*, tree or plough, (though it is difficult to see why), or from an old Irish word *cron* meaning a round hollow. The commonest modern explanation is *cron* meaning harm or danger. (There's another hill called **Beinn a' Chròin** a few kilometres west at the far end of Loch Voil.) But this word *cron*, also meaning hurt, has a short 'o' sound whilst the mountain name has a long 'o'. And the key to its meaning may therefore lie in a spelling recorded a century ago as Stuc a' Chroan, which would probably be from *cròthan*, a little sheepfold. After all, it stands at the northern head of the deep crag-ringed Gleann a' Chròin which would act as a natural sheepfold, and one of the tops above it is **Meall na Caora**, hill of the sheep. (Pronounced stoo:chk *a* **chroan** or **chro**-an*y*, from chrothain)

Stob Binnein

Variously known as Stobinian, or Am Binnein, this mountain forms a pair with Ben More. It has a beautiful and distinctive summit, a long cone sliced off at an angle just below its apex; this shape has led to suggestions that its name comes from the Gaelic *innean* meaning anvil, a comparison it would be easy to agree with especially when

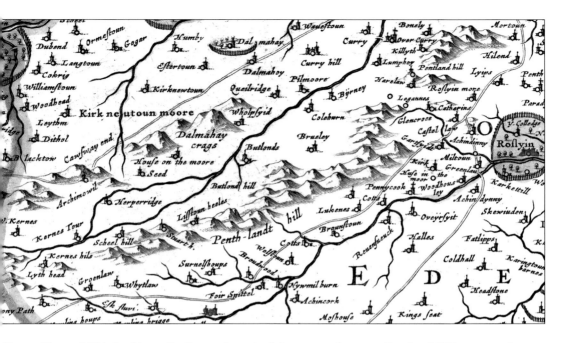

Above: Blaeu, 1654, Lothians. In the north-east of the range, the name Pentland Hill appears for one hill, while Penth-landt hill appears alongside the chain of tops further south-west, now the Pentland Hills. See p169, [Central Lowlands, The Pentlands]

Below: The huge sprawling prehistoric cairn on Carnethy Hill, probably from Cumbric carneddau, rocky heaps. See p170, [Central Lowlands, Pentland Hills]

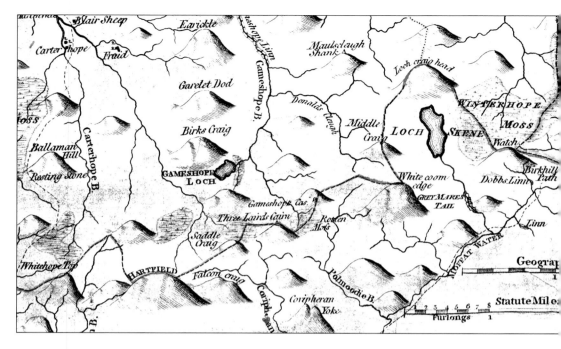

Above: Armstrong, 1775, Peeblesshire. An accurate map made just 75 years before the Ordnance Survey. Hartfield is now Hart Fell, Coripheran Yoke is Saddle Yoke (or indeed Carrifran Gans across the burn); White coom edge is now simple White Coomb, whilst simple Watch is now Watch Knowe. Maulscleugh Shank is now Molls Cleuch Dod, Three Lairds Cairn is Cape Law, and Middle Craig is Firthybrig Head. Birks Craig is now a lost name, and only Saddle and Falcon Craigs remain unchanged. See p174, [Southern Uplands, Introduction]

Below: Pykestone Hill, Borders, from the eruption of sharp boulders near the summit. See p175, [Southern Uplands, Broughton Heights

seen from the Crianlarich area. It would be in respectable company. The Cobbler and An Teallach (the forge) are other instances of craftsmen and their tools in Highland hill names, while furth of the Highlands, some tops in the **Cleish Hills** of Fife are known as **The Inneans** from Gaelic; and in Ireland the hill Mullagahoney means peak of the anvils. Half way round the world on the San Fernandez islands in the Pacific is a flat-topped hill called El Yunque, the anvil; it too has a Scottish connection, for on its top for four years sat Fifer Alexander Selkirk, model for Robinson Crusoe, scanning the horizon for ships. Not so far away in Glen Coe a projecting rock known as The Study is a corruption of the Scots *stiddie*, an anvil; and near it, although not marked on the map, is **Inneoin a' Cheathaich**, anvil of the mist.

Ben More and Stob Binnein. For stob and binnean, see p59 and 23,
[Generics, stob and binnein]

More prosaically it may simply be *stob*, meaning a peak, and *binnein*, meaning a pinnacle or conical peak, come together. However the most usual use of *stob* in peak-names refers to features *below* the top. In this part of Perthshire, **Stob Coire an Lochain**, **Stob Invercarnaig** and **Stob Garbh**, all refer to the corries, farms or ground beneath them, which would make Stob Innean or Stob Binnein the 'odd one out', since the 'anvil' here – or the *binnean* – refer to the summit itself. Alternatively the older name of Am Binnein (the peak) may have been the original version; the Stob, the actual summit alone, may have 'taken over' ownership of the name from the previous landlord of the whole mountain, Am Binnein. W.J.Watson wrote that *binnean*, although a diminutive form of *beinn*, 'always denotes a peaked hill by no means diminutive in size. The Binnean in Glendochart is 3,821 feet in height.'

However, these possible meanings fade away if you view the mountain from west of Crianlarich, perhaps from a bridge over the Fillan, for you'll be left in little doubt that the Gaels saw what you see in its summit outline... a smith's anvil.

CHAPTER SEVEN

CENTRAL LOWLANDS

It might seem strange to devote a chapter to hills in the Scottish Central Lowlands. But while they are lowlands geologically (a rift valley between the Highland and Southern upland faults) they contain many hills, individually or in ranges, largely of volcanic origin – and more importantly they are on most Scots' daily horizons. Living and moving around Edinburgh, for instance, there are the hills within the city boundary like Arthur's Seat, the Pentlands looming over the south side, and the Fife Lomonds across the Forth: while Glaswegians will recognise the Campsies and Kilpatricks, and hills like Neilston Pad to the south.

The concept of a *range* of hills, with a plural English or Scots form (the Ochils, the Pentlands, the Campsies) seems to have first appeared in the late 16th or early 17th century. Prior to that, both in the old languages of Cumbric and Gaelic as well as in Scots, the mass (that we now perceive as a plural group) was named as a singular mountain or hill. Thus, the Ochils was previously Mons (singular) or Sliabh Ochel, while as late as 1654 Blaeu mapped the Pentlands as Penthland Hill. The concept of a group depended perhaps on increased mobility and travel, whereby one group could be compared with another, rather than the individual hills being on one's lifelong village horizons.

Arthur's Seat

The legend of King Arthur and his Knights took Britain by storm in the 12th century, and places were named in their honour all over the land. In Scotland there's Arthur's Cairn in the north-east, a possible link in **Ben Arthur** (The Cobbler) in the west, and **Benarty Hill** in Fife, an Arthur's Seat on **Hart Fell** in the Borders, as well as this Edinburgh landmark of the same name. This sleeping volcano looks from many angles like a resting lion, but it got its noble name many centuries before Scots explorers brought back news and images of the 'king' of the animals.

In the 12th century, Giraldus Cambrensis in his medieval Latin wrote of *Cathedra Arturii* (Arthur's Throne) here, and in 1508 it appeared in Kennedy's *Flyting* as Arthurissete. 12th century documents refer to Craigenemarf here (Creag nam Marbh, dead men's crag), and in the same century may have given rise to the fanciful name documented as Mount Dolorous. It may indeed have been the local name for the whole hill, although it now (in English translation) refers only to Hangman's Rock down by Duddingston Loch.

A very unreliable book on names in the Lothians suggested an origin in *àrd thìr suidhe* (high land seat), but this reverses Gaelic word order and is unsound. Another more improbable suggestion was *àirde Thor*, Thor's Height, after the Norse war god, but the Gaelic word *àirde*, a height, common in the west of Scotland, doesn't occur anywhere else in the Lothian area.

The main summit, Arthur's Seat, is surrounded by later names in Gaelic, Scots and English. The Gaels named **Dunsappie Rock** and Loch (*dùn sèapach*, crouching

or tailing-off hill-fort, or *dùn sopaich*, fort of tufted or wispy grass). The Scots gave names like **Whinny Hill** (whin or gorse hill) to one long rib and **The Lang Rig** to another, while **Haggis Knowe** (where St Anthony's Chapel stands) is probably from *haggs* meaning broken ground, after the ancient field terraces here. **The Dasses** (ledges) form a ridge above Hunter's Bog, while the splendid name of the northern gully cleaving the western face of the main hill is The Guttit Haddie (gutted haddock); this was scoured out by a downpour in September 1744, and was also known locally as the Speldrin (a dried, split haddie).

Englishman the Earl of Salisbury, who came up with Edward III in 1335, may have had the **Salisbury Crags** named after him: certainly, in the 12th century it was simply Cragge, while in the 15th – well after his visit – it was Salisbere or Salisborie Crag. However Harris' *Place-names of Edinburgh* argues that it means willows hill, *salis bre* in Cumbric or *sales berg* in Anglian, there being several willow place names nearby, and that the name applied to the whole western part of the hill of which the crags were part. Nearby, the basalt columns of Samson's Ribs commemorate the Biblical character who certainly never came here any more than King Arthur himself did. But the power of the legend carried his name to the very summit.

Braid Hills

The Braids lie along the southern side of Edinburgh, a gentle first wave of hills before the real crest of the Pentland Hills beyond. Three golf courses are able to run parallel along its slopes, and the name therefore could appear to be from the Scots word *braid* meaning broad. The name first appeared in the 12th century as the estate of the Anglo-Norman Sir Henry de Brade; Stuart Harris's *Place-Names of Edinburgh* reckons that his name came from his estate, and that the estate's name probably derives from Gaelic *bràghad*, a neck, throat or by analogy a gully.

The Braid Burn's most distinctive feature is the narrow glacier-gouged gully it cuts through at the foot of the Braid Hills, between them and Blackford Hill, in an area now known as The Hermitage. The nearly-highest point of the range at 208m has the fine Scots name of the **Buckstone Snab**, a *snab* being a rocky projection or the brow of a steep rugged slope.

Cairnpapple

Some 4000 years ago this top in the Bathgate Hills was home and religious centre to a group of Beaker Folk. They looked out at other tops, islands of security in a sea of watchfulness, like nearby **Cockleroy** and **Torphichen** (raven's hill). About 400 years ago the local people were calling it by its present name. It was written as Kernepapple in 1619, and mapped as Cairnpapple in 1684, as Cornpapple in 1737, but as Cairn Napple in some early 19th century maps. In 1919 its height of just over 300m gave to West Lothian the honour of having 'the lowest highest point' of any of the old Scottish counties. Today the site is an ancient monument, its cairn sheathed from the elements by glass and metal, with a ladder descent to the subterranean burial area, but overlooked by a large and ugly radio beacon.

The name may be from the Scots *papple*, to bubble up or boil, for the hill sits amid a bumpy landscape like the frozen bubbles of a volcanic crater, but the word order is not Scots: it would be Papple Cairn. There are however several nearby Gaelic names – Torphichen, Ballencrieff Farm and **Knock Hill** (from *cnoc*, a knoll): the Gaelic word *pabail*, priest's village, is found in Lewis, and at Papple Village in East Lothian ... and there was a medieval preceptory nearby at Torphichen, so 'hill of the priest' fits nicely. On the other hand, Professor Barrow argues that it is one of several names in eastern Scotland (eg Peebles, Papple) containing the Cumbric word *pebyll*, which originally meant tent or temporary shelter, and by association shieling, where cattle were summered.

Cockleroy

Looking down on the ancient and royal burgh of Linlithgow and its well-preserved mediaeval palace, this hill top was the site of a hill-fort centuries before the settlement below. The royal connection in the town has led to suggestions that its name meant the cock, or top, of the king (*le roi*), but if so it would be the only French name among Scots hills. (Indeed on William Forrest's map of 1818, it is named as Cuckold le Roi!) More likely is the Gaelic *cochull ruadh*, (red cowl, hood or cap) the colour coming from the hues of its lavas. (In the Highlands there's a Munro called **Beinn a' Chochuill**, near Dalmally.) On Pont's late 16th century map it was shown as Coclereuf, and on General Roy's map a century later it was Cocklerewhill – both Gallic in sound, perhaps, but Gaelic in origin.

Looking north from Cockleroy the Firth of Forth can be seen over the tops of the **Erngath Hills**. These hills' name is from *airde na gaoith*, height of the wind (or *earann na gaoith*, portion), rather a grand title for ground that rises to all of 75m. Known in the 14th and 15th centuries as Arnegayth or Ardyngaith, and in more recent times as the Irongath Hills, the name is more often used by Bo'ness than Linlithgow folk. Looking south-east, the low range of hills is the Riccarton Hills: an outlier of these, but not the highest, is **Binny Craig**, a strikingly sharp point with a western precipice – so striking that it was one of the few local hills named on Pont's 16th century map – he called it Bynnin Law. The hill confirms W.J.Watson's assertion that hills called *binnean* (a diminutive of *beinn*) are always peaked hills: it is also a stunning viewpoint midway between the Ochils and Pentlands.

Campsie Fells

This layer-cake of basalt lava flows is well seen looking north from the Clyde Valley, presenting a steep-sided but flat-topped appearance like an Arizona mesa. It is also commonly known as the Campsie Fells, a name which first appeared on Roy's map of 1755, and in print in the 1790s Old Statistical Account, where the Reverend Gibb of Strathblane parish told us of

> that part (of the hills) known as the Campsie Fells.

As the Reverend went on to indicate, the Campsies are properly only the higher and southern part of the whole mass of hills, an 'island' between Blane, Forth and

Dumgoyne, one of several hill-forts whose dùn name is now spelt dum, see p35, [Generics, dùn]

Kelvin valleys; but since then the other groups like the Touch and Kilsyth Hills have been swallowed up in the 'Campsies' name.

The word *fell* is of Norse ancestry (from *fjall*, a mountain) but English parentage, for the word was born and brought up in Cumbria. Many hills in south-west Scotland adopted the name, but the Campsie 'Fells' is very much the late baby of the family, and probably reflects the growing status of English among the Scots gentry ... like the Reverend Gibb. It is also adrift by 60 kilometres from the nearest other *fell* name (viz. Culter Fell, itself 15 kilometres north of other *fell* hills), which underlines the fact that this 'Fells' was a late and essentially artificial name. Pont's late 16th century map simply records 'The Muir of Campsie' above the hamlet and church of that name, west of the Mekil Binn hill (Meikle Bin) and Craignyich (probably *creag nan each*, cliff of horses), now Laird's Hill.

This flat-topped range is dimpled by the sharp cone of the **Meikle Bin**, Scots for big hill (from the Gaelic *beinn*), and its junior, **Little Bin**. (Meikle Bin's former name is discussed in the Generics chapter, under *bin*.) Less distinctive but a few metres higher is the range's highest point **Earl's Seat** (Erlefell on Blaeu, 1654), named probably from the Earl of Lennox whose castle stood on the southern flanks of the hills. Other Scots or English names in the range include **Black Hill** and **Brown Hill**, **Hart Hill** and **Holehead** (at the end of a 'hole', Scots for hollow): and the **Laird's Hill** and **Laird's Loup** above Kilsyth where legend tells of a horsebacked Highland laird falling fatally while fleeing for his life.

Gaelic names include **Slackdhu**, from *slochd dubh* the dark pass or summit, and **Tomtain** from *tom an teine*, hill of fire (Tomtein in Pont).

Dumgoyne's name leads us back in time, to the days when a Scotsman's home was his castle... or else! For the several hills beginning with *dun* or *dum*, indicate a hill top fort. (*Dùn* usually changes to *dum* before letters *b*, *p*, *f* or *m*.) **Dundaff** and **Dumbreck** are the dark and speckled forts, **Dungoil** and **Dunmore** forts of the stranger and the big fort – this latter, on the edge of the northern corrie crags, has an authenticated fort identified on the Ordnance Survey map. The outlying western hills of Dumgoyne and **Dumgoyach** are perfect defensive sites, with steep slopes on all sides; the higher one, Dumgoyne, is possibly from *goin,* wound or lance. The little knobbly peak on its side is **Dumfoyne**, perhaps *dùn foinneach*, wart-like hill-fort.

Kilpatrick Hills

This range is full of little hill-forts (*dùn*), with names like **Duncolm, Dumbuck, Dunbowie** and the lost Dun Eillin (now **Birny Hills**). **Doughnot Hill** is no confection but probably another *dùn* name - it was mapped in 1654 as Douennet. The highest point is **Duncolm**, hill-fort of (Saint) Columba, one of Patrick's patrons. On the north slope of these hills lies **The Whangie**, a deep rock fissure once popular with rock-climbers and said to have been caused by the Devil flicking his tail as he flew past. It is in fact a landslide, one of many on the flanks of the Kilpatricks and Campsies and the rock formation allows people to walk through long narrow clefts behind the main rock face. The name may derive from Gaelic *uinneag*, a window, or possibly from the diminutive of Scots *whang*, a leather thong or strap, from the cliff's appearance from below. Alternatively, in Scots *whang* means a slice (as in a whang o' cheese) and it may relate to the freestanding slice of rock created by the fissure.

Lomond Hills

Not to be confused with Ben Lomond above Loch Lomond (out of which flows the River Leven), the Lomond Hills of Fife rise steeply above Loch Leven. Is there a connection? Are the eastern and western Lomonds cousins, and do the names Leven and Lomond come from the same parent? The case for the family tree was well put by W.J.Watson in his book on Celtic place names. Quoting from a 10th century document which speaks of a great lake Lummonu in the land of the Picts (Fife), 'called in English Loch Leven', he attributes the names to the pre-Gaelic *llumon* meaning a beacon or fire, with the loch and river names being derived from the mountain. The location of both Ben Lomond and the Lomond Hills would suit a beacon role admirably, rising suddenly up from plains as they do: the Fife Lomonds are visible from Edinburgh to Dundee, while Ben Lomond can be seen from many parts of the Lanarkshire and Glasgow area. And from Stirling Castle Rock both the Lomond Hills and Ben Lomond can be seen.

However, dissenting voices blur the clarity of this message, arguing the case for a root in the Gaelic *leamhan* (pronounced leven) meaning elm, or *loman*, a banner or shield. This seems unlikely for three reasons. Firstly, while there are often trees in

Gaelic hill names, these names' form is usually of the possessive a' (or an) form as in **Beinn a' Chaorainn** or Cnoc an Iubhair, which Ben Lomond does not have. Secondly, the Lomond Hills fall more within pre-Gaelic hill name areas (the Ochils, the Pentlands), while Ben Lomond is on the Highland fringe. And finally it would require quite modern thinking to 'see' a shield here. Since Fife was one of the flagships of the Pictish kingdom, and the Lomond Hills its mainmast, the beacon hills would be both functional and appropriate.

In the early 17th century the massif was simply Lomond Hill; only in the 19th century did the two peaks become East and West Lomond (pictured above)

Within the range **Bishop Hill** refers to the Bishopric of St Andrews which from the 12th century owned all the land hereabouts. **Maiden Castle** on the shoulders of **West Lomond** may be an Arthurian name referring to its spectacular prehistoric hill-fort, while **Maiden's Bower** by tradition represents a spot where a jilted girl pined her life away.

The Ochils

This name dates back to before Gaelic times, from *uchel* meaning simply 'high' in the ancient language of Cumbric. The earliest references are to Cindocellun (*cind*

ochil) in AD 700, Sliab Nochel in 850, Oychellis in 1461 and Ocelli Montes in 1580. An ancient Irish tract says that St Serf had his cell somewhere between 'Mount Ochel' and the Firth of Forth.

To the early peoples of central Scotland these hills would seem mountainous, being higher than the Campsie Fells, or the Pentland and Lomond Hills. From a distance they rear up from the Forth plains with the steep line of an approaching ocean breaker, but on closer inspection they are revealed as a series of quite distinct hills separated by deep glens and gorges. One of them **Dumyat**, standing slightly proud of the group, means 'the fort of the Miathi' (*dùn Miathi*), the ancient tribe who took to it for defence – they were mentioned in Roman documents (as the Maetae) as early as the 3rd century AD. The actual Stone Age fort is not quite on the summit, but 500 metres south-west, and is separated from the hill-mass by a defensive ditch. It looks precipitously down on the Forth plain below, and across to **Myot Hill** above Denny 15 kilometres away at the edge of the Campsies – which also has a fort, doubtless manned by and named after the tribe.

Although the range's name, and Dumyat, are pre-Gaelic the individual hills have Gaelic or Scots names. The highest point **Ben Cleuch** appears to have a Gaelic first element followed by the Scots word *cleugh* for gully, since its southern slopes fall steeply and evenly down into the deep gash of the Daiglen. However, mixed Gaelic-Scots names are very rare, and the hill was known as Benclach in 1783, Ben-cloch in 1790, Benclach in 1848 and Bencloich in 1869, all of which point to the Gaelic *clach* (genitive *cloich*) meaning stone or rock – and it does indeed have a stony summit area.

Ben Ever might appear to be from Scots *ever* or *over*, meaning upper (hill), but the word order is wrong (it would be Ever Bin) and Gaelic and Scots are rarely found inside one name. There is a Gaelic word *eibhir*, granite – which the rock is certainly not – so the name is a little obscure. **Ben Buck** is from *boc*, Gaelic for a buck deer, while **Tarmangie Hill** is from *torr na mainge*, fawn's hill. **Craig Leith** above Alva, is *creag liath*, the grey crag, while over the range above Glendevon **Ben Shee** is the fairy hill from *sìthean*. **Mellock Hill** in the east is from *meallach* meaning lumpy (or *mullach*, summit). **Whitewisp Hill** is named, according to the Ordnance Survey Names Book (compiled by the mid-19th century surveyors) from a light patch of grass just south of the summit, although local tradition has it that there's a late-lying snow patch in spring; indeed, Lady Alva's Web on Ben Cleuch was named, according to the Old Statistical Account of the 18th century, because:

> Snow frequently remains here far on in the summer and assumes the appearance of a fine linen web or lace work.

Above the steep southern edge is a top with a dull local name Middle Hill but on the map a splendid Scots name **The Nebit**, literally the nosed one, a name more complimentary than **Scad Hill** to the north which appears to be from the Scots *sca'd* meaning scabbed. **Andrew Gannel Hill** sounds like a man's memorial, and the Ordnance Survey men were told locally it was named after a man who died in a storm nearby. It has been suggested that it is a corruption of the Gaelic *an sruth*

gainmheail meaning the sandy stream, but 18th century references to Andrew Gan Hill and Ganhill undermine this.

Mailer's Knowe is *not* some kind of postman's knock but possibly a similarly garbled form, of Meall Odhar, the dun-coloured hill, although *mailer* is a Scots word for a tenant farmer, *mail* being rent money, and blackmail a variation. Last but not least **Wood Hill** above Tillicoultry may sound ordinary as well as merely English, but there's nothing ordinary about the fine ribbon of beech and Scots pines that fights its way up the packed contours to 450m: the trees were planted in 1725 by Sir John Erskine of Alva.

Pentland Hills

The Pentlands run north-eastwards from the Biggar area, starting as a gently swelling moorland, rise to its high point Scald Law in a switchbacking ridge, and end suddenly with the steep drop of Caerketton's northern screes falling away towards Edinburgh city. Its ridges and its dramatic 'north wall' have earned it the affection of many hillwalkers who grew up in the capital, as the titles of books like *The Breezy Pentlands (1910)* and *The Call of the Pentlands (1927)* indicate.

The element *pen* is common in Wales, with hills like Pen-y-fan (the height of the slope) in the Brecon Beacons. Some kilometres south in Scotland lie the hills of **Penvalla** and **Penveny** near Stobo and there is another **Pentland Hill** near the border with England. So it might seem logical, indeed pleasing, if these fine hills' name had a similar origin. Unfortunately not – they are named after a nearby lowland settlement.

The name first appears in written form in 1150 at Pentlant, a farm or hamlet north of Penicuik, a couple of kilometres east of the hills. Although the settlers of this area at the time were Anglians speaking Old English, they adopted many place names from the Brittonic or Cumbric people who had preceded them. These had spoken Cumbric, the ancestor of modern Welsh, and Pentland is probably from their *pen llan*, meaning height above the enclosed land or church – we are not far from the historic Roslin Chapel here; *llan* is pronounced 'chlan' or 'thlan' as in modern Welsh.

Blaeu's 1654 Atlas contains the first map to apply the name to the hill, and interestingly both he, and Adair 30 years later, show a (singular) Pentland Hill in the north of the range, probably one where the cattle from Pentland hamlet were driven in summer to pasture. Blaeu also shows the (plural) name Pentland Hills applying further south (he spells it Penth-landt Hill, and the hamlet Penthland, thus suggesting the Cumbric pronunciation), and it is most likely that, by happenstance, the name spread from the one hill attached to the original hamlet, to the whole range.

The first written appearance of the name applied to the hill range as a whole is in a record of 1642 relating to Alexander Fowlis of Colinton (just north-west of the range) giving him the right to pasture his beasts and gather his firewood '… super Pentlandhilles …', a Scots name set into the Register of the Great Seal's Latin context. Maps from the 18th century onwards simply show the collective name,

applied to the whole range, indicating that it had passed into common speech.

Three of the highest hills in the range also appear to have Cumbric names. **Caerketton** is fort (*caer*), possibly of the refuge or the retreat: there is a prehistoric fort on the eastern shoulder of the hill, and the name was probably transferred to the summit above it, in the same way that the location of the hill-fort and souterrain a few kilometres to the south has been 'transferred' to the summit above it, in **Castlelaw Hill**. **Carnethy Hill** above Penicuik was suggested as Caer Nechtan, the fort of King Nechtan of the Picts, by Will Grant, author of *The Call of the Pentlands*, but there is no evidence for this romantic idea. More likely is *carneddau*, rocky heaps, a name now applying to the high mountains of North Wales north of Snowdon, and pronounced in Welsh roughly carnethey. The summit of Carnethy has an enormous sprawling stone cairn covering many square metres, now heaped up into cairns and shelter (see below).

Carnethy is pipped by three metres for the position as highest hill by **Scald Law**,

Man-made Cairns

Cairns built by walkers are relatively recent, and tend to be on the very summits for obvious reasons, the lapidary equivalent of planting the flag. For instance, the first Munroist, the Reverend A.E.Robertson, claimed to have built the first cairn on the summit of the **Geal Chàrn** near Pattack, and most of us at some time will have carried a stone to add to a summit cairn. The story of some of the better-built cairns – such as the huge one on **Beinn Mholach** – is told in *Just a Pile of Stones?*, this author, in TGO, May 2008, pp78-81.

Cairns built by men have a long tradition in Scotland. Prehistoric man built cairns or barrows, largely for burial or depository purposes, and some of these are on hill tops: in the Pentlands, **Carnethy Hill**, **East** and **West Cairn Hill**s all have these sprawling prehistoric cairns on top, and their names reflect this.

In Galloway, a fair number of hills whose name includes the generic cairn have chambered or other ancient cairns on top, among them **Cairnerzean Fell**, **Cairnscarrow**, **Cairn Edward** and **Cairn Pat**. A weak 19th century echo of this is found around Balmoral, where some hills have been topped by memorial cairns to past members of royalty – such as **Prince Albert's Cairn**, **Princess Alice's Cairn**, and so on – the names are little used locally, being preserved only on the map.

Cairns in the man-made sense take on a significance not just on the summits. Within living memory cairns were erected outside houses to mark a death, and these are often identified by the diminutive name *càrnan*: for instance **Càrnan Ghrulin** on Eigg, beside now-abandoned crofts. High above the River Dee at Monaltrie is a cairn called **Càrn na Cuimhne** the cairn of remembrance. Clansmen marching past it on the way to a Chief's war had to deposit a stone here, and pick it up upon return, thus ensuring a 'body count' of those who did not return. Seton Gordon claims that the cairn's very name became the

Scots for scabbed or patchy hill, referring to the smears of scree in its eastern corries. (There are several hills of this name, or Scaw'd Law, in the Borders). Will Grant's book states that its name means poet's or bard's hill, from its past – the Skalds were Scandinavian bards – but he produces no evidence for this claim, and it is besides outwith the main areas of Old Norse names. The most striking hill in the southern Pentlands has a Cumbric name, for **Mendick Hill**, distinctive with its two-stepped summit ridge, has a first element from *monith*, a hill-mass – the word is still used in the *mynydd* form in many Welsh hills.

There are a number of Gaelic hill names in the Pentlands, but it is very much a Celtic fringe: to the north are small hills derived from *torr*, a small hill, thus **Torgeith**, (from *gaoith*, windy), **Torphin** and **Torduff**, (the latter two being a white and dark hill pair *fionn* and *dubh*). **Craigentarrie**, (from *tarbh*, bull), **Craigengar** (hill of the hare) and **Torweaving** probe the western flanks, while in the extreme south **Dunsyre Hill** is *dùn siar*, western fort – you can still see the ancient cultivation

---

battle cry (*sluagh-gairm*, or slogan) of the Braemar clansmen. Its alternative name is **Càrn na Coinnimh**, meeting place, where the Farquharsons assembled for battle.

Càrn nam Marbh, cairn of the dead in Glen Lyon, was where bodies of plague victims were piled and buried. It is crowned by Clach a' Phlaigh, stone of the plague, and was the site of a great bonfire of whin at the time of Samhain or Hallowe'en, round which the local people danced sun-wise. In the Borders near Greenlaw, **Twin Law** hill has twin cairns on it, said to commemorate where two brothers slew each other.

Upright and soundly built cairns, or in some cases upended flagstones, are known in Gaelic as *fir bhrèige* or false men. Sometimes they are natural pinnacles left by erosion, as in Torridon's **Sgùrr nan Fhir Duibhe**, literally the peak of the dark men on the Beinn Eighe massif – Bodaich Dubh Beinn Eighe – known in translation as **The Black Carls**; and sometimes they are man-made cairns said to have been erected to divert invading armies' attention from the enemy in hand.

Meikle Firbriggs on Deveronside is named after one of these 'false men' stones, and near Tyndrum is **Càrn Buachaille Brèig**, the hill of the false shepherd: that there are another nine Buachaille Brèig names scattered across the Highlands suggests that it is a generic name rather than one commemorating one erring shepherd. They weren't just for pastoralists' use: Ian Fraser recollects from a Gairloch childhood that fishing positions were established by rowing the boat to line up with a *fear-brèig* on the hillside nearby.

In the Southern Uplands, shepherd's cairns are often placed not on the summits but at the point where a shoulder curves over, so as to act as skyline markers for navigation: sometimes the hill name picks up on them, as in the several **Cairnsmuir** or Cairnsmore hills.

terraces on its slopes. The only other Gaelic name in the range appears to be **Gask Hill** above Loganhouse, from *gasc*, a wedge of high ground – which it is.

There are actually over 150 hill names in the range, and many of them, especially the lesser ones, have good Scots hill names with generics like *law* and *mount*, *kip* and *rig*, *knowe* and *seat* – and many of these are covered in the Generics chapter (e.g. **West Kip** and **Faw Mount**); while English has more prosaic names like **Black Hill** (named for its heathery cover) or **Turnhouse Hill** (from the hamlet at its foot). This transparency of the hill names in Scots and English would have disappointed a mid-17th century writer David Buchanan of Edinburgh who wrote a text on Lothian for Blaeu's Atlas in which he said:

> This more raised part of the region is commonly called Penlan, badly pronounced by the ignorant as Pentland; the name is a compound and means High Land, for *Pen* or *Pin* or *Bin* is high (hence alpes Peninae, by contraction Appenines, are high peaks) and *Lana* is land, dwelling (from Hebrew *lun* to inhabit) ...

To be fair to the antiquarian gentleman, place name study was not really even out of nappies by then!

Renfrew Heights

Not so much a hill range, more a rumpled block of high moorland south of Greenock in the crook of the Clyde estuary. Encompassed by today's Clyde-Muirshiel Regional Park, there are few habitations within it, and no traditional local name for the area. The designation Renfrew Heights has the chalkdust air of old geography textbooks to it, although a 1944 Scottish Geographical Magazine called the range, more poetically, the Mistylaw Hills – it didn't catch on.

Its individual high points all have Scots or English names, with only a few corrupted Gaelic names like **Knock More** (from *cnoc mòr*, the big knoll). The names are in the main simply descriptive, like **Misty Law** or **Brown Hill**, though the intriguing **Cockrobin Hill** may well be the site of a famous murder! The highest point at 521m is the **Hill of Stake**, that may come from the Scots word for the stalk (after deer), or just possibly from the Norse *stakkr*, steep, since there are a few Norse names just south of here.

Nearby is **Irish Law**, watching over to the Emerald Isle across the mouth of the Clyde, where its role is echoed by Paddy's Milestone, the nickname of Ailsa Craig. One distinctive outlier is **Neilston Pad**, standing at 260m above the small town of that name: in the Old Statistical Account of the 1790s, the local minister wrote of what was then called Neilston Craig, that it was

> vulgarly called the Pad from having its appearance in the form of a pillion ...

When you view the hill from the north, you will see that the vulgar were spot on.

Sidlaw Hills

This is the low range of hills behind Dundee and its famous Law. Indeed the second

element of the range's name obviously comes from this same Scots word for a hill. The first element of the name possibly comes from the Gaelic *suidhe* meaning a seat, or level shelf, and one of the highest hills being called **King's Seat** bolsters this idea. The best-known hill in the range, made famous by Shakespeare's *Macbeth* and the predicted destination for Birnam Wood on the march, is **Dunsinane**, possibly *dùn na sine*, fort of the nipple, from its shape. The highest hill in the range **Craigowl** is from *creag gabhal* (forked cliff): David Dorward's book *The Sidlaw Hills* makes the suggestion that the name comes from the way the old road from Dundee to Glen Ogilvie forked at the foot of the hill.

Touch Hills

The Touch Hills lie south-west of Stirling, part of the Campsies range. Their name, locally pronounced the 'Tooch' Hills (the ending as in 'loch'), is a corruption of *tulach*, meaning a knoll or hill, a Gaelic word (from an Old Irish root *tul*) that is common in the Southern Highlands and very often has the English 'hill' appended to it.

Traprain Law

This East Lothian hill has seen a lot of history, having been occupied on top from late Stone Age times to Roman times. Once a hill-fort of the Votadini tribe, it was apparently known as Dunpender, meaning the hill-fort of the spear shafts (*din peledyr* in Cumbric). In the 14th and 15th centuries it appeared in documents as Dumpeldar (1368) and Dunpender Law (1455). The name Traprain is of Cumbric origin from *tref*, a farm or simply a place, and *pren*, wood or a tree. The name was extant in the 14th century, and although it's not clear why or exactly when it replaced the more genuine hill name Dunpender, it was probably transferred from a nearby farm within whose bounds it fell.

CHAPTER EIGHT

SOUTHERN UPLANDS

The term Southern Uplands is rather dry, but has now been taken out of the geography classroom and into popular parlance by the long-distance footpath The Southern Uplands Way. Geologically it is delineated along its north side by a fault line running from Dunbar in the east to Girvan in the west, although hills like Tinto are technically a little north of this line: in the south the border with England does not correspond with their drop to the plains, but it will define this chapter's coverage. The high ground enclosed really consists of several smaller ranges of hills (the Lammermuirs, the Eildons, the Lowthers, and so on) which form the barrier between Scotland and England – southern uplands for the central Scots, but northern uplands to the English.

The hills of this area are particularly vulnerable to having had their name changed over the centuries. Over half of all the hills recorded in the maps of Blaeu (1654) and Roy (1755) have either been changed in form (not simply spelling) since then, or have been lost (i.e. fallen out of use completely). Even hills recorded in the late 18th century (e.g. on Armstrong's map of Peeblesshire, 1775) have experienced nearly a third being changed, while those of the early 19th century surveyors such as Thomson (1820s) show a fifth have altered. (Since the Ordnance Survey carried out its mapping in the mid-19th century, the rate of change has ceased, as if their one inch maps were Tablets of Stone from Mount Sinai.)

Why should these hills (the smaller ones in the main) have changed? Firstly, hills have more than one side, and from different valleys, locals may have had different names, and it was a matter of chance which one was recorded by map-makers. Secondly, in the sparsely-populated valleys, where few people knew a hill-name, if one farmer moved away or his family died out, an incoming farmer might well bring a new name. Thirdly, hill-names had little legal status and were rarely documented, as they were on poor land of little value to landowners. And last but not least, hills often have several summits or noses, with separate names, and it is easy for those down in the valleys below to get them mixed up or transfer the name to the adjacent summit.

Broad Law

The second highest hill in the Borders at 840m, this is one of a line of *laws* (a Scots name for a hill) linking **Cairn Law** to **Dollar Law** and **Notman Law**. 'Broad' could apply to the shape of many Border hills, with gently rounded summits providing spacious rooftops above the steep valley walls, but this one was particularly so: as Captain Armstrong noted in 1775, this hill

> ... might admit of a circuit horse-race of 2 miles without the smallest inequality of surface ...

At one time the hill was known as Broad Law of Hairstane from the farm below north-west: this farm is nowadays known as Hearthstane, and from it a bulldozed

road leads up to the plateau where, rather than a horse-racing circuit, we have the more practical but more intrusive air navigation beacon on top.

Broughton Heights

These hills lie just north-east of the village of Broughton. Some of the subsidiary tops have names referring to the vegetation cover, such as Broomy Side, Green Law and Green Side, Brown Dod and Clover Law, and others to farm practices such as **Wether Law** (wether, a castrated ram), Cow Hill, Hog Knowe and Woolshears Hill. The highest summit in the group at 570m is known as **Pyked Stane Hill**, from the ancient cairn near the top: in the Old Statistical Account the Broughton minister says of Pyket Stane that it is a 'rude collection of stones to distinguish the united marches' [i.e. boundaries]; while the neighbouring Kirkurd minister refers to 'a small cairn called Pyked Stane, the boundary of three parishes'. (**Pykestone Hill**, a few kilometres south, by contrast seems to be a natural grouping of pointed boulders near the summit.) For the whole area is studded with prehistoric forts, enclosures and settlements, and there are several hill names that hark back a millennium or so to when the pre-Anglian, pre-Gaelic speaking peoples dwelt here. *Pen*, as in **Penvalla** and its neighbouring hill **Penveny** is based on Cumbric *pen*, a head or hill, while **Trahenna Hill** and **Dreva Hill** derive almost certainly from Cumbric *tref*, a farm or habitation. On a map of 1775, which shows most local hill names accurately, the top now called Brown Dod is named as Penairs, a further indication of Cumbric naming. Flint Hill may well refer to the practice of using flints for arrowheads and tools.

Cairnsmore of Carsphairn, of Fleet and of Dee

These three hills lie in the south-west. The first, generic, element Cairnsmore might lead one to suspect a Gaelic origin – especially in this corner of Galloway – from *càrn mòr*, big hill, but the letter *s* would signify a hiding rat. And indeed, the earliest map of Blaeu (1654) records the first two hills as Kairnsmoort and Karnsmoor hills, while Ainslie (1782) has them as Cairns Moor and Cairnsmuir, thus showing that their name is in fact Scots for a *muir* (an area, often on high ground, where beasts could be grazed in summer) marked out by *cairns*, thus the *cairns' muir*. Cairnsmore of Fleet for instance has two big prehistoric cairns at the highest point and at the outlier called Knee of Cairnsmore, as well as several others mapped.

Cairnsmore of Carsphairn is above the hamlet of that name, although on Roy's 1755 map, it was Cairnsmuir upon Deuch, from the nearby river. Similarly, whilst Cairnsmore upon Fleet is above that river, in Roy's map it was named after the river on the other side, as Cairnsmore upon Cree. Cairnsmore of Dee seems to be a late name – it was not even recorded on early 19th century maps – and may have been in imitation of the better-known two: it has the alternative, older, name of Black Craig.

Cairn Table

This was one of the first two hills to be named in the medieval documents of the Register of the Great Seal, in a 1315 document that also mentioned **Tinto**, the two

being defining markers on a land transaction – they are both distinctive hills in their own way. Cairn Table's name is pretty transparent, being a flattish-topped hill with two ancient cairns either side of the summit. One of them, reflecting the industrial despoliation that has affected the Muirkirk area below, has been re-shaped into a war memorial.

Cheviot Hills

The Cheviots, and **The Cheviot** hill, mark the present Scottish border and lie largely within England. The name is probably better known in Scotland as a breed of sheep held responsible as agent of the hated Clearances, a foreign intruder into Gaeldom. The sheep took its name from the hill area, and it lies too far south-east to be of Gaelic ancestry, so it is Sassenach in every sense of the word. The earliest references are to Chiuiet (12th century), Chyviot and to Montes (mountains) Chiueti and Chiuioth. Together with Criffel near Dumfries, it was one of the first two Scottish hills to be named on a map, a map of 1360 known as the Gough Map: this suggests these two hills were very significant in marking the medieval border with the troublesome Scots. W.C.MacKenzie in his *Scottish Placenames*, claims that their meaning is 'watching hills', but gives no evidence in support, although they do lie in ever-vigilant Border country.

Another suggestion from J.B.Johnston is from the French *chevet* meaning a pillow, appropriate to their gentle swelling shape perhaps, but very unlikely linguistically. A possible origin lies in the Cumbric word *cefn*, a ridge – places like Chevening in England come from this word: the Anglian settlers pushing up the east coast plains in the 7th century would have observed The Cheviot as a high hill terminating a long ridge from the west, and may have adopted the Cumbric *cefn* name in clothing it in Old English.

Corserine

In Blaeu it was mapped as Krosrang Hill, and in Roy as Krosraing Hill. The range it is in is known as the **Rhinns of Kells** (from the parish name), and this may point in the direction of *rinn*, a point or promontory, as in the Rinns of Galloway. However the older form of the name looks more like the Gaelic *raing*, a row or column, with the specific *cors-* being a metathesised *cross*, indicating cross-running or transverse ridges.

Criffel

Most of the many *fell* hills in southern Scotland came as loan-words, in that the Old Norse word *fjall* had been anglicised in the Lake District into *fell* there, before it spread across the border. Criffel however first appeared (in a form Crafel) on a 1330 map, a date much earlier than the first recording of *fell* as a Scots loan-word. So it could be, like Goat Fell and many others in the Hebrides, a hill-name actually given by the Norse. Maxwell suggested it derived from *kraka fjall* – crow fell – citing Blaeu's Crafel and the later Scots Crawfell; indeed the ministers of Colvend and Kirkbean parishes spelt it in the Old Statistical Account as Crowfell and Crofell respectively,

although the contemporaneous New Abbey entry has it as Crifell. J.B.Johnston preferred a derivation from Old Norse *kryfja*, split. Whatever its meaning, it is a very distinctive hill 590m above the Solway flats – and thus a landmark for the Viking sailors – and not surprisingly was one of only five southern hills mentioned in the medieval record the Register of the Great Seal.

Culter Fell

This hill takes its present name from Culter parish which it stands in, and the hamlet of Coulter below. It is an unusual *fell* name, for it is 15 kilometres north of any other fells, almost all of which are south of the east-west watershed. The *fell* generic here, and the use of the words *beck* and *gill* for streams on its sides (Kings Beck and Lang Gill burns), suggest a farmer or landowner from northern England settled here. Its older name is much more dramatic: Pont's map of the late 16th century names it as Filfell. It turns out that this is a contraction of Fiends Fell, a contraction possibly meant as a literary exorcism by Pont – or more likely his local informants – avoiding naming the devil (or his associates). There was another Fiends Fell, the highest hill in the English northern Pennines – perhaps the immigrant farmer brought the whole name – but in the 17th century it was re-christened (and christianised) as Cross Fell. In Scotland however this was still known as Fiends Fell as late as the early 18th century: as a description of a stream north-east of the hill in the *MacFarlane Geographical Collections* relates:

> Holms Water … Upon the head of this fertile Water, above Glenkirk, is a mountain called Fiendsfell … [where] the eagle hath nestled past memory of man.
> (Vol. III, 152)

In the same volume of MacFarlane, undated but written probably early to mid 17th century, a description of the Clyde and its tributaries refers to a 'height' called Couter Stane as the Camp Water's source, and 'Coulter heichts' as one of the 'chief hills' of Lanarkshire – the Culter Fell name, mapped and named as such for the first time by General Roy's Survey a few years later in 1755, was thus arguably given mid-18th century.

Dollar Law

This hill's name has nothing to do with the town of Dollar at the foot of the Ochils, 75 kilometres away, and is mysterious. Alexander Pennecuik, who wrote in the early 18th century wrote that:

> A facetious old herd gave me this strange etymology: that the country folks in pursuit of some English depredators overtook them on Dollar Law, and being defeated were heard to mourn their hapless fate, crying 'Dool, for ever mair!'

A classic example of folk etymology, which Pennecuik spotted, but we are none the wiser – the old forms include Dollerlaw and Dollarburn, but they are no help in deciphering it.

The Eildons rise 300 metres above the Tweed plain, their three peaks a landmark for the Romans who called them Trimontium

Eildon Hills

This trio of conical hills above Melrose in the Borders has captured the imagination for centuries. Almost two millennia before Sir Walter Scott chose it as his favourite view – to the eternal gratitude of the Borders Tourist Board – the Romans from their nearby camp at Newstead referred to it as Trimontium, literally the three mountains. Approaching them along Dere Street from the south-east, the three peaks achieve their maximum separation on the horizon. In legend its shape was put down to the Devil cleaving it in three on the challenge of a local wizard. Other legends tell of King Arthur and his warriors sleeping below 'in Eildon's Caverns Lost': while a local man, Thomas of Ercildoune, foolishly followed a fairy down a secret passage into the hills to the court of Faery, and paid the penalty of seven years capture.

But long before the Romans, the northern peak was a hill-fort capable of sheltering up to 2000 people in times of crisis. And there can be little doubt that the *don* part of the name is from *dun* (or *din*) meaning a hill-fort in Old English or Cumbric (see *din* and *dun* in the Generics chapter). The oldest forms of the name go back to Aeldona in 1119 and Eldune in 1143; the Gaelic *ail* (a rock or cliff) has been suggested for the first part of the name, but there is not really a cliff on the hills, and more importantly the hills are outwith the main Gaelic-speaking areas: Cumbric (Old Welsh) or Old English are more likely origins, and the Old English *eald* (or *aeled*) *dun* meaning old hill-fort seems apt linguistically and historically. Only a few kilometres to the west just beyond Peebles are two hills with similar names, the **Black** and **White Meldons**. They too have hill-forts on their summits and ancient

settlements on their flanks, and may originate in the Cumbric words *maol din*, bare hill-fort (although *maol teine*, bare hill of fire, has been suggested). Melrose village itself, at the foot of the Eildons, is believed to be from Cumbric *maol ros*, bare moor.

Hart Fell

A hart is a male deer. This is one of the highest Borders hills, the seventh-highest of the Donalds and fifth-highest of its Marilyns, and one of only half a dozen significant enough to be mentioned in the mid-17th century in the Register of the Great Seal. According to author Nikolai Tolstoy, author of *A Quest for Merlin*, this hill was the site of the Arthurian figure Fergus' 'Black Mountain' and at one point was the home of Merlin the magician himself. The hart, noble beast and prince of the animal kingdom, was the creature into which Merlin could magic himself on occasion, hence the hill's name ... allegedly. Today, the only memorial of this legendary wizardry is the hill's lower shoulder named **Arthur's Seat**. There is however little to substantiate this claim, and it is doubtful if it has any connection with the name, which is one of a group of *fell* hills in the high country in the north of Dumfriesshire.

There is another Hart Fell in southern Dumfriesshire, and **Artfield Fell** in Wigtownshire was mapped as Hartfell by Roy in 1755. Now the *fell* names of both these shires came as loan words into Scots from northern England, and it is interesting that in the Lake District there is a Hartbarrow hill, a Hart Crag, a Hart Hill, and two Harter Fells: the *-er* ending of the latter (from Old Norse *hjartar*) indicates that these were named when a Scandinavian language was still spoken; and this may link all these hills up historically with the **Hartaval** hills in Skye and Barra. Never mind Arthurian legend, the animal was more important in Norse culture.

Hart Fell, highest of the fell hills in the Borders. See p37, [Generics, fell] and p203 [Natural World, deer]

Lammermuir Hills

Over 1000 years ago these hills were mentioned in documents as Lombormore (before 800), and later as Lambremor (1114). Whilst there is a definite similarly with Gaelic's *lompair mòr* (big bare surface), and it would fit the landscape, these low south-eastern hills rippling Lothian's horizons, are however on the very fringe of former Gaelic-speaking areas. In the 17th century David Buchanan of Edinburgh wrote in a commentary for Blaeu's Atlas that the name was from *Lau* or *Loff* deriving, he said, from the Greek *lophos*, lofty, but this is antiquarian nonsense – and who would call them lofty? The truth is that Old English language (current from the 7th to mid-12th centuries) words *lombor* and *lambre*, meaning lambs, fit the name and the hills' agriculture well, as well as the linguistic environment, and a moor (Scots *muir*) was an area of higher ground for summer pasture for the beasts. (Buchanan claimed that *muir* was also from Greek, *mauros* – this is apparently true of the Moors who conquered Spain but certainly not of *moor*, which derives from German.)

There are hills within the range called **Lamb Hill**, **Lammer Law**, **Wedder Law** and **Hog Law** (wethers are castrated rams, and hogs are unshorn yearling sheep), for they made good pasturing country, being not too high (maximum 537m.) nor too cliffy for the sheep. The highest hill is **Meikle Says Law** whose pair is Little Says Law nearby, just as to their immediate south lie a simple Meikle Law and Little Law: in

---

English and Scots colours

In southern Scotland, hills with Scots or English names have a limited range of colours compared to Gaelic, for while there are enough Black Hills and White Hills to make several chessboards, all the other colours together would struggle to make up a team of pawns. Black Hills are very common, – there are 120 mapped – usually coloured by their dark heather crop: for instance, the Pentland Hills have two Black Hills, a Black Mount and a **Black Birn**, as well as a White Hill. A *birn* is an area of springy grass, or a summer sheep pasture – the Lothian equivalent of a Highland shieling. The **Black Hill** above Balerno, was described by writer George Reith in his 1910 *The Breezy Pentlands* in this way:

> ... the Black Hill descends abruptly towards us (in the Green Cleuch) in what looks like cataracts of road metal ... (and from Scald Law) ... the steep dark sides of Black Hill, looking for all the world like a dirty patched gipsy tent.

Not a very politically correct comparison ... however today, a century later, the hill is still clearly darker than its neighbours, because of these dark grey screes and heather cover. The **Black Mount** near Dolphinton is blanketed with heather and thus clearly darker than the rolling fields and improved sheep-grass at its foot, and indeed the White hill top on its shoulder. Probably the Black Hill whose name is most familiar to the man on the three-piece suite is the transmitter of that name near Airdrie in central Scotland where his STV programmes are beamed from; its name comes from the dark volcanic rocks that outcrop

Scots *sae* can mean a tub, pail or vat, although its dull gentle slopes hardly inspire such a picture in the mind. Further south-east, **Twin Law** is named after two huge cairns, about 100 metres apart on the summit, said in legend to be named after twin brothers, separated at birth and who as adults on opposing sides slew each other.

The Leadhills

In southern Lanarkshire the village of Leadhills stands amid the hill range known as the Lowther Hills, though the immediately surrounding ones are The Leadhills. They are pitted with small mines, worked from the 13th century until early 19th century. The individual hills' names probably predate the lead mining for they bear very un-mineral titles like **Dun Law**, **Broad Law** and **Hart Law**, however thankfully for posterity there is one small hill called **Mine Hill**.

Lowther Hills

Dominated by the **Green Lowther** hill with its high radio beacon for aircraft navigation, the meaning of its name is obscure. They are significant hills, being near the headwaters of the Clyde and Nith, respectively northern and southern routeways, and the name features in old maps. Timothy Pont in the 1590s mapped the range as Lothlers (or Lodders – the handwriting is difficult to read), and on his Clydesdale map he identifies Dun Law, Loders Hill, Whyt Lodders and Wadder Law in a line,

near the top.

White Knowe near Broughton is covered in pale bent grasses in contrast to the dark heather tangle on nearby Brown Dod, and most of the nearly 200 **White Hill** specimens are similarly pale. The Ochils have the mellifluous **Whitewisp Hill**, named from its late-lingering snows.

For the rest of the colour spectrum the Renfrew Heights, the Kilpatricks and Campsies, Ochils, Lomonds and Sidlaws, Pentlands and Lammermuirs can collectively muster 60 **Brown Hill**s (mainly in the west) and several Green Hills and **Green Laws**. There's also four **Blue Hill**s, one near Aberdeen marking the eastern fringe of the Mounth, a **Blue Mull** in Shetland, and a **Pinkstone Rig** near Douglas in the Borders (possibly a corruption of pin stane rig). There are a dozen **Red Hill**s in the south-west and north-east, and even two **Yellow Hill**s, one in Fife and one near Greenock.

A handful of **Dun Rig**s or Laws completes the range, which is hardly the Gaelic colour rainbow, even though they once spoke the language here too ... hills like **Drumfinn** (from *fionn*, white) and **Tarduff** (from *dubh*, dark) in the Ochils and Campsies are faint echoes of the old tongue. And there are some distinctive Scots shades too, like the several hills called **Scawd Law**, Hill or Bank (from *scaw'd* meaning scabbed or dappled in the manner of the Gaelic *breac*) and the simple **Faugh** near Moffat is Scots for dun, or pale-red, hill.

with Over Windgate Slap between the latter two. This slap, or pass, is still clearly there, and if White Lowther was now **White Law**, this could suggest that **Wadder Law** was the old name of what became **Lousie Wood Hill** (and later, by cartographic misprint, Louise Wood), probably from a southern Scots word for the burr on certain plants. On the other hand the order of the hills is a little confused with **Dun Law** mapped south-west of the others – it is in fact north-east – and **Wether Hill**, a shoulder of **Lowther Hill**, may be his Wadder Law. What Lowther or Lodder means is however a little obscure. J.B.Johnston suggests an origin in early Irish *lothur* meaning a canal or a trench, though it's difficult to see the connection unless it refers to the north-south route up the Nith valley.

The Merrick

This is the highest hill in the south-west at 814m and is often climbed from the tourist honeypot of Glen Trool at its foot. It is, in consequence of its height, number one in the Donald Tables, as well as being number seven in the Corbett Tables. Enough of this name-dropping!

Most names in this part of Galloway are of early Gaelic origin, the area having been colonised from Ireland from the 6th century onwards, and the higher hills' names are no exception. The Merrick (Maerach Hill in Blaeu's 16th century map) probably comes from *meurach* meaning pronged, branched or fingered (from *meur* a finger). Sheriff Nicolson of Skye, a Gaelic scholar, said it meant idiomatically 'the highest knuckle of the hand' and that its five branching ridges with deep glens in between were like a huge hand. Later writers called it – rather unfairly – the 'Awful Hand', and recently the hills were actually mapped the Awful Hand range – which is a pretty gross soubriquet.

The explanation for *meurach*, an adjective, standing on its own without a 'parental' noun, is the fact that it appears to have been 'orphaned' early on – another of Blaeu's maps shows it with the alternative name Bin (*beinn*) Maerack, which indicates the parental generic *beinn* was falling out of use in Galloway at that time: so the true name is *beinn meurach*, branched or spreading mountain – an excellent description of its sprawling ridges. The southern ridge contains **Bennan** (little mountain) and **Benyellary** (*beinn na h-iolaire*, eagle mountain), the western ridge **Benmore** (*beinn mòr*, big hill) and **Kirriemore Hill** (*coire mòr*, big corrie). The loss of the generic *beinn* also explains why (from the 18th century onwards) it is called <u>The</u> Merrick, the English definite article replacing the absent Gaelic parent.

Minto Hills

These twin steep little hills near Hawick rising about 100 metres above the surrounding gently rolling countryside, and therefore very prominent locally, take their name from the Cumbric *monid*, a mountain or hill (related to Gaelic *monadh*, Welsh *mynydd* and Scots *mount*), possibly plus Old English *hōh*, a heel, used figuratively (and common in English place names) for a hill-spur. More plausibly, since there are two distinctive peaks, the name derives from the plural Cumbric form *mynynddau*. The earliest references are to Munethov in 1166.

Moorfoot Hills

This name if taken at face value would be contradictory. For a place at 'the foot of moors' would obviously be a plain or valley, not hills. The contradiction is resolved by the oldest occurrence of the name in 1142, when it was referred to as Morthwait or Morthuweit. The second element is of Norse origin in *thweit*, in common use in northern England as *thwaite* meaning a clearing or meadow. Thus the whole name means simply meadow on the moors, a prosaic description of the reality of a high moorland fit for grazing. Not surprisingly, as the Scottish Mountaineering Club's *Southern Uplands* guide writes:

> ... the highest summits are less a range of hills and more an elevated plateau with few distinguishing features.

The highest hill is **Windlestraw Law** at 659m, a name referring to the long thin-stalked grasses that rise towards the top. **Blackhope Scar** and **Whitehope Law** are named after the *hopes*, Scots for the valleys that wind deep into them: the colour in the former's name is a warning against the awful peat-hags that you may encounter when bagging it.

The other sizeable hill in the range is **Dundreich**, sometimes called Jeffries Corse – although this is really the eastern summit. *Dùn* in Gaelic means a hill-fort as does *din* in Cumbric: there is an ancient cairn on top but more significantly there is an old fort at the western foot of the hill, on a knoll called The Camps, which probably gave its name to the hill, rising as it does rather finely above it. It is more likely a Cumbric than a Gaelic name, since the latter were few and far between in these parts, while the Cumbric presence is attested by nearby names like Penicuik and Tranent. The *dreich* part of the name is certainly not from the Scots word meaning wearisome or dreary, though those conditions may well be felt on some of the other boggier Moorfoots. The suggestion contained in the Old Statistical Account, by the minister of Eddleston, that it was Dundroigh, druids' hill, owes more to fancy than fact. W.J.Watson thought it to be *dùn dreach*, fort of the (hill) face.

Queensberry

Queensberry's summit may rise to an unassuming gentle point, but its height puts it amongst the Donalds and the Grahams, and it is a landmark from many points on the Solway Firth headwaters and Dumfriesshire plain. On a promontory of higher ground between the Nith and the Annan rivers, it also commands the entry to the main natural routes to the north. Not surprisingly then that along with **Tinto** (which effectively guards the northern exit of one of these routes) it is one of the very first hills to be mentioned in historical documents, specifically the Register of the Great Seal in 1633 (Count of Queensberrie) and 1648 (Queinsberge). The latter reference gives us a possible clue to the name, because the *berry* element in this and other hills probably derives either from Old Norse *berg*, a hill, or from Old English *burh*, fort. Some of the other *berry* hills in southern Scotland have forts or ancient remains on top – thus **Goldenberry Hill** on the Firth of Clyde, **Bizzyberry Hill** and **Gallowberry Hill** near Biggar, **Tarnberry** and **Turnberry Hills**, and **Arbory Hill** and

Castle Hill (respectively, on Blaeu's map, Herber Hill and Garaberry Hill) above Abington.

Although there is no fort nor other remains mapped on Queensberry, this does not exclude the possibility that it may indeed have been an important defence site, since archaeology is always turning up new remains and may yet do so. Other *berry* hills like **Strawberry Hill** above the Fruid Reservoir east of Crawford, and **Nutberry Hill** north-east of Muirkirk, (Knutberry in Blaeu's map) could also yet reveal prehistoric secrets.

Shalloch on Minnoch

This is an odd name for a hill. Hamish Brown says that it means the heel of the Minnoch ridge, presumably from *sàil* or *sàileag* (heel or little heel). But on this lonely sprawling hill, north of The Merrick, is a separate lower top called Shalloch, and with a southern ridge called Rig of the Shalloch. This is not the usual position of a *sàil* in hills, for they usually round off a ridge with a long steep drop down to the glen, and besides *sàil* is a word of the far north-west. Shalloch could be from the Gaelic *sealg* (pronounced *shellag*) meaning a hunt, and indeed just across the shallow valley to the west lies a hill called **Eldrick**, from *eileirg*, a deer trap, and a few kilometres away is **Mullwharchar** from *meall na h-adhairce*, hill of the huntsman's horn (or *adharcach*, horn-shaped).

However, Blaeu's 1654 map of Galloway, based on Pont's work, mapped a farm on its west as Schelach of Meannoch, and indicates the hill itself as Bellachgy Hill. The first part of that old name is obviously *bealach*, a pass, and may refer to the Nick of Carclach gap just south of the summit: the name may have been *beinn a' bhealaich gaoithe*, mountain of the windy pass. A similar process of farm names coming to replace the old hill names seems to have overtaken the two tops immediately south, **Tarfessock** and **Kirriereoch**, both named after farms to the west. Blaeu's map suggests that the former may have been Bin Meanach (from *beinn meadhonach*, middle hill, which it is), and the latter Suachtoun Hill or Meal Tuaichtan hill (after Loch Twachtan which still lies in its eastern corrie).

Tinto

Tinto stands a little clear of the main northern wave of the Border Hills. Being clear of the pack, and high enough to be registered as a Donald (i.e. – above 610m) and possessed of a gentle conical shape, it is a fine landmark far into industrial Lanarkshire and rural Midlothian. This prominence led, centuries ago, to its use as a beacon hill, and the name is probably from the Gaelic *teinnteach*, fiery. It was possibly a Roman signal station, for a Roman road runs over its shoulder, or a Druidic fire site, which tradition locates on the huge cairn on its summit. The tale of its ancient use could easily have been kept alive by word of mouth for centuries, passed on like a runner's torch from generation to generation, until Gaelic speakers gave the hill its present name. On the other hand, Tinto is remote from the main areas of Gaelic hill names in the Borders. Most of these are found in Galloway south and west of the Nith; while there are a few marginal Gaelic hill names in the Pentlands. This distribution – and

Tinto, a landmark throughout Lanarkshire and beyond, is crowned by one of the largest Bronze Age cairns in Scotland – but is the name Gaelic or Cumbric? See p33, [Generics, din]

Tinto's closeness to the **Broughton Heights** with their several Cumbric names – might suggest that the first part of the name is the Cumbric *din*, a hill fort (as in Tinnis Castle near Stobo).

In an old book on the Pentlands, author Will Grant speculates that it comes from two Pictish words *teine* and *tom*, respectively a fire and a hill, but the words are in fact Gaelic not Pictish, and the Gaelic alternative of *teinnteach* meaning fiery seems to fit the modern name better. In the 14th century it was known as Kaerne de Tintou (cairn of Tinto) and as Tintock. The local name, still used, of **Tintock Tap**, is further evidence for *teinnteach*: however the suggestion that the pinkish colour of its summit felsite rock, or the deep purples of its northern screes, could be the origin of 'fiery' is rather fanciful.

The huge Bronze Age cairn on top (known as **The Dimple**) is one of the largest in Scotland and certainly suggests ancient use – the boulders shielding the ecosystem from scorching. The eastern shoulder and top of the hill is called **Scaut Hill** on the map, ostensibly from the Scots word *scawt* meaning scabbed: could it be a slight corruption of Scaud Hill, which would mean scorch hill, or indeed the 'glimmering of light'? (There are several examples of **Scawd Hill** or Law in the Borders). The top, The Dimple, is probably a euphemism for nipple, for just south of the top is the **Pap Craig**, literally the breast crag, its mammary profile being distinctive from many points.

CHAPTER NINE

MOUNTAIN CHARACTERS

Highland mountain names often contain characters, people or professions, as mountains elsewhere do. One of the most famous peaks in the Swiss Alps is the Eiger, on whose black north face scores of mountaineers have perished. In translation it means, The Ogre, appropriately. It is part of a famous trio of peaks in the Bernese Oberland together with the Monch (the monk) and the Jungfrau (the maiden) with the man of God separating the black rock of evil from the pristine white snows of innocence. Do they have Scottish namesakes?

Monks, Maidens and Ogres

In the Scottish Highlands we too have monks, **Beinn Mhanach** near Tyndrum, and indeed a priest in **Càrn an t-Sagairt Mòr** near Braemar. We have a maiden in **A' Mhaighdean** in the north-west, and indeed a pair of damsels in **Na Gruagaichean** in the Mamores, with its two finely counterpoised tops (although it was once known by its singular name A' Gruagach). But we have no clear-cut Ogres in spite of the many dark and sinister figures haunting Highland legend, though there are several pretenders.

Prime among the candidates for the title must be **An Riabhachan** above Glen Cannich, which can be translated straightforwardly as the brindled, greyish one, but in Gaelic An Riabhach Mòr can also mean The Devil, though it does seem a harsh name for this innocuously grassy hill. Grey rather than black is the colour Gaelic often associates with dark things, as in Am Fear Liath Mòr (the Big Grey Man) of **Ben Macdui**, the neck-bristling presence which has, driven several lone climbers to flee the mountain in mortal terror. **Sròn an Tàchair** above Kinloch Rannoch is the promontory of the ghost, and travellers were reputed to feel the hairs on their necks rising as a presence descended.

Ben Donich in the **Arrochar Alps** might appear to be literally evil mountain, from *dona*, evil or vile, although it has also been suggested that it is from *donn*, brown. The local minister, in the New Statistical Account of the early 19th century, argued that it was named after Saint Donnan (whom the six villages on the west coast called Kildonan commemorate). This is unlikely: however there is a religious slant in a more recent suggestion that it is from *domhnach*, with the meaning of church (land). The river flowing south-west from the hill is the Donich Water, with Inverdonich (i.e. mouth of the Donich) at its foot, and the parish church nearby in Lochgoilhead.

Not far away there's a **Beinn an t-Seilich** (from *seilch*, a water-monster rather like a giant snail) on the east shore of Loch Fyne. In any event not nice creatures to meet on a dark night. In the Mamores, **An Gearanach** (the complainer) and its neighbour **An Garbhanach** (the rough one) sound more like a couple of hungover hikers than a dangerous duo.

Beauty and the Beast

There are hills whose name appears to be highly complimentary, like **Beinn Alligin**

(darling peak?), **Beinn Èibhinn** (delightful or amusing mountain), and **Càrn a' Choire Bhòidheach** (cairn of the beautiful corrie); but beauty appears to be outnumbered by beasts. The word *beiste*, literally beast, appears in several names. The Bealach na Bèiste (pass of the beast) near Belig in Skye is said to be the spot where a much-feared water horse (*each uisge*) was killed by a MacKinnon, cut down in its maiden-seizing prime.

Devil's Ridge, The Mamores: an English soubriquet for a sharp ridge between two Gaelic mountains. See also p124, [Cairngorms, The Devil's Point]

The Devil

The devil himself was a stravaiging man, featuring in Gaelic in Bod an Deamhain (the Devil's Penis, politely translated for Victorians as **The Devil's Point**) in the Cairngorms, and in **Meall Diamhain** in Assynt. In English or Scots he pops up in the Devil's Kitchen above Loch Callater, his now-straightened Elbow above Braemar, his Cauldron by Comrie, his Beeftub and Barn Door near Moffat, his Putting Stane in the Carsphairn Hills, his Thrashing Floor in Galloway, his Bite on Feughside, his Burdens in the Lomonds, his Staircase above Glen Coe, and his **Ridge** between Sgòrr an Iubhair and Sgùrr a' Mhaim in **The Mamores**.

187

Most of these are relatively late names: the Devil's Beeftub below **Hart Fell** for instance was known as the Marquis' Beefstand until well into the 19th century. Hell, his centrally heated home – though it was supposed to be dark and cold in Gaelic lore – is *iutharn* (or *ifrionn*, from *i* plus *fuar*, cold) in Gaelic – although **Beinn Iutharn Mhòr** in the Grampians is more probably from *fubharainn*, from *faobhar* plus *roinn*, meaning sharp edged – as indeed is **Sgòr Iutharn**, above Culra, also known as **Lancet Edge** from its distinctive shape. *Fh* at the start of a Gaelic word is not pronounced: and *faobhar na beinne* is a common expression meaning simply the sky-line of the sloping part of a hill, as opposed to *fàire na beinne* the flat top's sky-line.

Witches and Crones

In Scots the word for an old woman can also mean a witch, implying a degree of overlap. The word is *carline*, as in **Carlin's Cairn** in Galloway: there is a tale that it was named in honour of a miller's wife who sheltered the persecuted Robert the Bruce, hiding him in a sack of meal. When he became king he granted her this land, and the cairn was erected to commemorate the deed. The **Carlin's Loup**, a giant rock at Carlops, is by tradition the witches' Cape Canaveral, a launch pad with a broom-stick-like bush sprouting from the cliff face!

In Gaelic the word for an old woman is *cailleach*, appearing in the several hills called **A' Chailleach** Some of these mountains perhaps commemorate the legendary Cailleach Bheur who wandered the hills, calling the deer hinds to her with her siren-like voice in order to milk them. But she was a 'wild old woman' rather than a dangerous witch.

The **Sgrìob na Cailleach** or Hag's Scrape on Jura's **Beinn an Òir** is said to have been made during a flypast by the powerful Goddess of Storm, Beithir (as in **Beinn a' Bheithir**). This tale echoes the legend attached to **The Whangie** cliff near Glasgow, said to have been split off its backing hill-slope by a flick of the devil's tail. The resultant 'window' between the hill and the cliff may be the origin of the name from *uinneag*, window.

There are two Munros called **A' Chailleach**, one in the Monadh Liath and one in the Fannaichs in Ross-shire, as well as other lesser examples. One, the **Ceum na Caillich** nick on Arran's rocky ridge, is usually translated as the Carlin's Leap or **Witch's Step**, a libel by English-speakers on little old ladies everywhere and particularly those many who have crossed this gap with no problems! The sexism implicit in the minds of the men who equate old women with witches is revealed too in the hill-name of **Beadaig**, a petulant female, although as a Skye name it may have had a similar-sounding Norse original name.

Darby and Joan

Joan's Darby is the *cailleach's bodach* (old man), and one such pair face each other above Glen Einich in the Cairngorms. Legend has it that when no mortal is looking this **A' Chailleach** and **Am Bodach** hurl boulders playfully at each other across the gulf – a second courtship, or perhaps a second childhood? Another two examples of Am Bodach, old man, frown over Glen Coe and in the Mamores: there are nine Am Bodach hills altogether, and 15 A' Chailleachs, mirroring the greater longevity of

women, perhaps! In a pre-industrial society where survival to a ripe old age was unusual, the old were respected, so it was natural to name a few peaks after them. Interestingly in Iceland there are several mountains called Kerling (including the highest peak in the north), meaning old woman (as in Scots *carline*), often paired with a nearby Kerl (an old man), as at Grimmstadir.

Commoners and Kings

In the hills of southern and central Scotland hill names rarely bear the names of people other than the landowners and others of high station. This tendency to syco-phancy is to be found in the several **Laird's Hill**s, the two **Earl's Hill**s and the **Earl's Seat**, the Ochils' **King's Seat** and the Lomonds' **Bishop Hill**. There are in fact 42 hills beginning with King's, 19 with Laird's and 12 with Earl's, but hardly any have been linked to specific kings, lairds or earls. Representing the ordinary people there is only a **Hunter's Hill** in the Sidlaws, a **Thief's Hill** in the Kilpatricks and a **Priest Hill** in the Lammermuirs.

In the Gaelic Highlands by contrast there are few high-status names, with but one large hill named after a king in **Càrn an Rìgh** in the remote eastern Grampians. This may refer to King Malcolm Canmore who in the 11th century hunted at Braemar and resided at Blair Atholl, passing and re-passing Càrn an Rìgh half way between: or to Kenneth MacAlpin two centuries earlier who had united the Picts and Scots tribes into a powerful kingdom. However Pont's late 16th century map shows it as Bin Chromby or Chroby (perhaps from *crom*, crooked): and James VI hunted on the hill in the 1590s and it may be a name given at a later date to commemorate him. If it was named after one of these kings, the fact that it does not name the specific one suggests the name was given some time after the event when the individual was forgotten. Alternatively, and more prosaically it may come from *ruighe*, a shieling, or the broad slope at the foot of a hill.

Sròn na Bàn-righ in Glen Feshie, promontory of the Queen, is the hill where Mary, Queen of Scots, sat to personally supervise the execution of her order to fire the woods below, a punishment for the Marquis of Huntly who – putting green before queen – had enquired after his trees' health before asking after hers. **Creag Rìgh Tharold** (properly Creag Righ Harailt) is a low hill on Speyside named after King Harold, the Viking, defeated here – and perhaps buried on the hill. King Nech-tan of the Picts was noted in **Dunechtan Hill** but Gaelic has few hill names for the 'high-heid-yins', and far more for ordinary people. Significantly one of the few found is in the English language, in the Duke's Chair above Glen Geldie, named after the Duke of Leeds who hunted the Mar estate in the 19th century.

Craftsmen and Musicians

The best-known craftsman in the hills is surely **The Cobbler** at Arrochar, a direct translation of the old Gaelic name An Greasaiche Crom the crooked shoemaker, from the shape of the summit rock. There's a less well-known craftsman, the tanner, a translation of Beinn an t-Sudaire north-east of Kirkcudbright, horribly anglicised to **Bentudor** on the Ordnance Survey map. **Beinn a' Chlachair**, stonemason's

mountain, lies above the Laggan valley. It is an ironic name, for the peak is too far from valley and village to be practical for a mason's work. The droll significance of the name will be appreciated by any walker who has climbed it from the *bealach* on the east and stumbled along its ridge strewn with rocks angled this way and that, like the jumbled mass of ice floes that piles up on a winter lochan.

In the Làirig Ghrù (another jumbled mass of rocks) one particularly large stone is the Clach nan Tàillear the tailors' rock. Here three tailors saw out one old year's eve but failed to see much more of the new year, snuffed out by exposure as they struggled to fulfil a bet that they could dance a reel the same Hogmanay night both on Speyside and on Deeside. Not even the doctor in **Meall Lighiche** above Glen Coe could have helped them that night! Perhaps one of the musicians at the dances was related to the **Càrn an Fhìdhleir** (the fiddler – sometimes anglicised to Càrn Ealar) above Glen Feshie, or **Uchd a' Chlàrsair** (the harper). Perhaps too the lament for their sad deaths could be played by the piper in **Stob a' Phìobaire**, the alternative name for the summit of **Buachaille Etive Beag**. Near the Munro Càrn an Fhidhleir is another, **Càrn an Fhìdhleir Lorgaidh**, where Richard Perry in his book In the *High Grampians* says in droving days,

> ... the Speyside boys would be met by the Atholl boys and the two sets of drovers would foregather and make merry with the fiddle.

Pastoral yes, but probable no, given the topography.

Hunters and Hunted

Hunting was a natural activity in the hills, and has left an echo in names. Thus we have **Sgùrr nan Conbhairean** above Loch Cluanie, peak of the keepers of the hounds (probably Fingalian hunters), and **Creag an Leth-choin** above Glenmore, the crag of the lurcher, a hunting dog.

Herdsmen and Shepherds

Cattle-herding (not to mention cattle-thieving) was an important part of the Highland economy, before the black cattle and the humans were driven out in the Clearances. Across Glenmore from Leth Choin we find **Meall a' Bhuachaille** (hill of the herdsman. More famous, at the junction of Glens Coe and Etive we have **Buachaille Eite (Etive) Mòr** and **Beag**, big and little herdsmen of Etive. They are sometimes translated as 'shepherd', which may be true in the Biblical sense of watching over the glens. But given Gaeldom's reaction to the hated Clearances that introduced the cheviot sheep, – 'Woe to thee, O land, for the Great Sheep is coming.' – shepherd seems less likely than herdsman. The word for sheep, *caorach*, appears only in a few peaks like **Beinn nan Caorach** near Glenelg, whereas words for cattle appear in several names like Ben Lui (calf), Làirig an Laoigh (pass of the calf) in the Cairngorms, and **Bidein a' Choire Sheasgaich** (fallow cattle). So 'herdsman' is the more apt translation of the Glen Coe Buachailles. Indeed the neighbouring glen Coire Gabhail (possibly corrie of the booty, also known as the Lost Valley, but probably forked corrie), a hanging valley high above and invisible from the main Glen Coe, was

Buachaille Etive Mòr, the big herdsman of Etive. See also p141, [Central Highlands, Buachaille Etive Mòr and Beag]

perhaps so-named from the hiding there of cattle, legitimate or stolen, from other raiding clans.

On lower hills throughout Scotland the word *buachaille* often appears in corrupted form in hills like **Tillybuckle Hill** (Angus), **Tarabuckle** in Glen Clova, **The Bochel**, **Barnbougle Hill** and **Barnbauchle Hill**. On these lower hills, often in the Borders where sheep-farming is long-established, *buachaille* almost certainly is the shepherd.

Herdgirls and Claimers

Cattle were taken up in summer to the high pastures or shielings in the hills. In the Cuillin of Skye, **Sgùrr na Banachdich** is from Gaelic, *bananaich*, or *banaraich*, a milkmaid, for it was the custom in the Highlands for young people to take the cattle to the shielings and stay with them. The Gaelic word for these spots is *airigh*, which can be found in names like Letterewe's **Beinn Àirigh Chàrr** (the mossy shieling hill): almost right at the summit is a lovely green sward, a real *àirigh*. On this peak is a crag named **Martha's Peak**, or Spidean Moirich, and tradition has it that a herdgirl of that name fell down the north-east cliffs to her death while trying to retrieve the spindle for her thread. Skye's **Sgùrr Mhàiri** (Mary's Peak) on Glamaig, was also named after a herdgirl who died here while on pastoral duty, seeking a lost beast. In Angus, the hill **Boustie Ley** is probably from *buailteach* (the summer sheilings) of (Glen) Lee, where the cattle were pastured by herdgirls.

In the east too there are herdgirl names on the hill. Seton Gordon, collector of the lore of the Cairngorms, relates that one of these shieling milkmaids spent her time, while wandering the heights with her herds, searching for the semi-precious Cairngorm stones, and by repute her collection is buried in **Ciste Mhearad** or Margaret's Chest, one of the clefts on the ski side of Cairn Gorm. However another tradition, related in the Scottish Mountaineering Club guidebook, is of a maiden jilted by her lover MacKintosh of Moy who wandered deranged through the range until she died at this *ciste*, or coffin. Fortunately there is a second Ciste Mhearad, nearby in Glen Feshie, so both legends can keep their credibility with a *ciste* each.

Arable farming, the people's mainstay, gets scant mention, although **Shilling Hill** near Muthil was where the corn was husked, or 'shilled' (in Scots); formerly it was Tom Chatha, knoll of the husk. The hills **Sgùrr nan Ceathreamhan** (hill of the quarters) and **Meall an Tagraidh** (hill of the pleading or claiming) refer to a concern with portions of land. Meall an Tagraidh was disputed by the laird of Locheil although it stood in Glengarry's land. Locheil argued that since a burn rising to the west but running north almost circumnavigates the hill before flowing south, thus the hill was inside his watershed.

That such boundaries were important is indicated by the existence of four hills, in different parts of the Highlands, called **Càrn na Crìche** boundary hill. In the Borders **Threep Hill** near Langholm is from the Scots *threap*, a quarrel, suggesting a boundary dispute. **Càrn nan Trì-tighearnan**, hill of the three landlords, between Spey and Findhorn, suggests a more amicable arrangement. Hill tops by their nature could be neutral meeting places: **Tòrran na Tighearnan** lay at the junction of three Wester Ross estates, Dundonnel, Gairloch and Ardess, and it is said that the three landowners could meet for lunch and discussion, each sitting within his own land.

Warriors and Watchers

Like the Arthurian rock holding fast the sword Excalibur, weapons are embedded in hill names like **Slioch** (spear), **Sgùrr nan Saighead** (arrows) and **Beinn a' Chlaidheimh** (sword). Weapon-wielders are found in **Cairn Toul's Stob Coire an t-Saighdeir** (soldier) and, a few kilometres away, **Càrn an Fhir-Bhogha** (archer's cairn). One

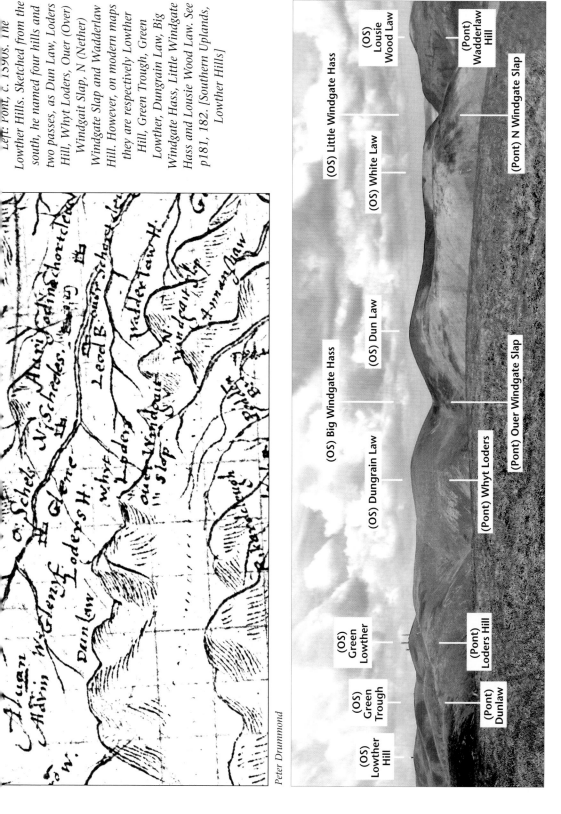

Left: Pont, c. 1590s. The Lowther Hills. Sketched from the south, he named four hills and two passes, as Dun Law, Loders Hill, Whyt Loders, Ouer (Over) Windgait Slap, N (Nether) Windgate Slap and Wadderlaw Hill. However, on modern maps they are respectively Lowther Hill, Green Trough, Green Lowther, Dungrain Law, Big Windgate Hass, Little Windgate Hass and Lousie Wood Law. See p181, 182. [Southern Uplands, Lowther Hills]

Peter Drummond

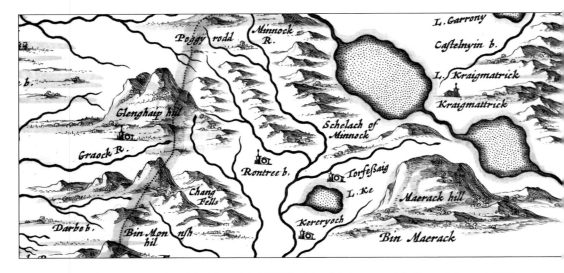

Above: Blaeu, 1654, Carrick. The high hill The Merrick is named both as Maerack Hill and Bin Maerack, indicating that the full original name was Beinn Meurach, See p182, [Southern Uplands, The Merrick]

Below: Blaeu, 1654, Galloway (north is right). Bennellury Hill and Maerach Hill (right of centre) are Benyellary and The Merrick. Schelach of Meannock (top right) appears to be a farm name, which perhaps is the source of the modern hill name Shalloch on Minnoch. Bin Meanach Hill, Suachtoun Hill and Meal Tuaichtan are now lost names – for their suggested successors, see p184, [Southern Uplands, Shalloch on Minnoch]

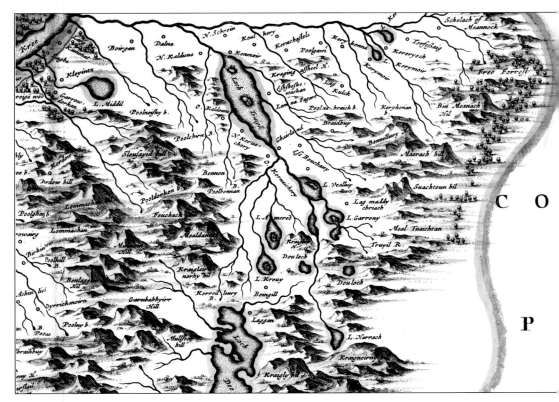

particularly nasty warrior, Sigurd the powerful, who plundered the Strathoykel area, met a deserved end that is celebrated in a hill name. Riding home with the head of a victim dangling from his horse, its tooth pierced his skin and he soon died of septicaemia (the medical term for sweet revenge), and was buried on **Cnoc Skardi**. Few tears were shed over him, unlike at **Creag a' Chòinneachan** nearby, the crag of lamentation, where the story is that Montrose lost a battle in 1650 and a slaughter followed: the Reverend Burn states however that the name simply means mossy.

Slioch, probably the spear. See also p110, [North-West Highlands, Slioch]

Lookouts were vital to military success and in this context in the far north, the name of **Ward Hill** or **Warth Hill** perhaps means a watch or guard hill (from *varð* or *varða* in Old Norse) and there are many of them in the Orkneys, Shetlands, and on this north coast. Far to the south the threat came from the English, and this is the reason for the several **Watch Knowes** and **Hills**, and **Watchman Hill**, all in the Borders. Almost on the Border near Dumfries is **Beacon Hill**, where warning fires could be lit, while just south of the line in Norse-speaking Lakeland is Wardlaw Hay hill, whilst near Dunbar **Knockenhair Hill** is *cnoc na h-aire*, knoll of the watch. The Gaelic *fàir* means sky-line or horizon ridge or simply hill, while *faire* means watching, and indeed the word on its own can simply mean a watch-hill – pre- modern radar stations. **Hill of Fare** on Deeside, and **Farrmheall** in the north, are examples.

In the much fought-over country near Oban, full of forts, crannogs and *dùns*, lie several hills called **Cnoc na Faire** (knoll of watching) and **Deadh Choimhead** literally good watching (hill), the latter prominent enough to have a later trig point built on it. Offshore on the island of Luing is **Binnein Fhurachail** attentive or watchful hill. Low Hebridean islands needed vantage points both for defence and for safety of

their seamen, and for instance Barra's **Ben na Scute** at its south-west tip is from *sgudachd*, watching.

Càrn an Fhreiceadain cairn of the watch, is probably named from deer-watchers who used it as a lookout – a few metres west from its summit you will find their flag-stone shelter, its doorway facing west over the Monadh Liath mosses. There's also a **Cnoc an Fhreiceadain** overlooking the Pentland Firth. A low hill beside Bo'ness on the Firth of Forth is known as **Tidings Hill**. In the autumn, when the local whaling boats were due back from a summer in the dangerous waters of the North Atlantic, their families used to walk up it in the evening to get the first glimpse of their returning menfolk, and to be first to run with the glad tidings to the town.

Church and Clerics

The Christian religion played an important part in clansmens' lives, and there are two hills called **Beinn na h-Eaglaise** in the north-west, mountain of the church. One stands above Arnisdale and its little chapel, the other on the shores of Loch Torridon rises above the lochside hamlet of Annat – throughout Scotland the name Annat signifies an ancient parent church cell from which missionary work was done. By Loch Linnhe is **Beinn na Cille**, mountain of the cell or chapel, above Cille-Mhaodain, the cell of early Irish missionary Mhaodain. Throughout Scotland's Lowlands are hills with names like **Mounthooly**, **Mounthoolie** or **Huly Hill** … but they are gentle hills, from the Scots *huilie*, <u>not</u> holy hills!

Càrn an t-Sagairt Mòr (sometimes spelt as it is pronounced Cairn Taggart), big hill of the priest, was named after Padruig, a Braemar priest, who led his flock out to Loch Callater to pray for an end to a severe frost that gripped the land well into May. As they prayed, the ice at the Priest's Well melted along with nature's iron heart, clouds gathered over the hill, and the thaw set in. The locals named that hill after him in gratitude. Elsewhere, **Beinn Mhanach** (hill of the monks) at the lonely head of Loch Lyon was named after those monks who set up a community at the foot of the hill in the distant past. **Mannoch Hill** near Nethan was formerly *cnoc nan manach*, monks' hill, and nearby is a translation, **Priest Hill**.

In the Cairngorms there's a **Cnap a' Chlèirich** (cleric), poised pulpit-like above the huge eastern corrie of Beinn a' Bhuird and its Clach (stone) a' Chlèirich. There's a 'pulpit' of a less conventional kind in the far north on the shores of the Pentland Firth. Here, just offshore, is Neave Island (from the Gaelic *naomh*, holy) where a community of missionaries had their base. Sallies to the shore had met with assault and murder, so on the Sabbath they *shouted* their services across the 200 metres of sea to the faithful gathered on a knoll, known as **Cnoc a' Phobuill**, knoll of the congregation. Another small island Berneray has a **Beinn a' Chlaidh** (burial), whose sandy-soiled graveyard was supposedly blessed by St Maelrubha.

Many Scottish places have saints' names, from St Andrews to East Kilbride. There are many small knolls with saintly names, often from the dedication of chapels or hospices which stood at their feet, including **St Mungo's Hill** near Huntly, **Magdalene Hill** near Perth, or **St Catherine's Hill** in Aberdeen. But the only moun-tain that has claimed this honour is **Farragon Hill** above Loch Tummel, allegedly

after St Fergan, fourth Abbot of Iona, who worked the Pitlochry area: however W.J.Watson has argued that it is from *fothir na h-eagan* meaning under the notches, there being a Beinn Eagach, notched hill, a little to the north-east of it.

Above Arrochar the hill **A' Chrois** (the cross) has no known religious significance, and its name may come from the way the deep gully on its face is intersected by a broad ledge. The mountain was originally known as Feòrlan or An Fheòirlainn, literally a farthing's worth of land. Perhaps the portion was doled out by the begetter of the high peak in the north named **Sgùrr nan Ceannaichean**, peak of the merchants or shopkeepers. The similar name Bac nan Ceannaichean, a shoulder of **Sgùrr a' Mhaoraich**, was allegedly named after two peddlers murdered in a local bothy and buried nearby.

Family Names

Beinn Chaluim near Tyndrum is the Scots first name Calum (or Malcolm), and may have been named in honour of St Columba (Colum Cille) by the monks of Glen Lyon, themselves remembered in Beinn Mhanach nearby. **Sgòrr Dhònuill** (properly Dhomhnaill) above Ballachulish is from Donald, the descendants of whom as the MacDonald clan were massacred in nearby Glen Coe one black night. There are also two peaks called **Sgùrr Dhòmhnuill** in the west – one of them the most striking peak in Ardgour – reflecting the importance of Clan Donald who ruled the isles and the west for centuries after the death of Somerled in 1164.

As Lords of the Isles (and much of the south-west), many of whose lands were no-go areas for the Scottish crown, they could afford to name two or three peaks after the clan family name. The Reverend Burn says that Sgòrr Dhomhnuill and nearby **Sgùrr na h-Ighinn** (daughter) was where a father, one Donald, and his daughter got lost in mist then were found again, but he quotes no sources and the tale has the air of a folk-etymology. The MacDonalds' mortal enemy the Campbells also have a hill 'plaque' in **Càrn Chailein** above the moors of their Argyll lands, at the site of inter-clan slaughter where one Colin, a clan chieftain, died. Another much humbler Campbell is named in the Argyllshire hill **Stùchdan Dùghaill** after Duncan Campbell, shepherd, who died in a blizzard here in 1881.

The name of a clan as such appears in **Bidein Clann Raonaild** in the north, but it is neither very high nor distinctive. Other sons (*mac* in Gaelic) immortalised in hill names include the MacDuff clan who owned the Mar estate, including Scotland's second highest mountain **Ben Macdui** (for long thought to be the country's highest, hence the prestige of naming it after the family), and **Mullach Coire Mhic Fhearchair**, peak of the corrie of Farquhar's son, a top as geographically remote as its origin is obscure.

Many of the origins of personal names on mountains are lost to us, swept away in the ebb of time. **Creag Mac Ranaich** for instance above Killin was named after a robber, now long forgotten – certainly his hill has good summit fortifications against arrest, with crags buttressing it. But who do hills like **Creag Pitridh** (Petrie's crag) commemorate? Is **Leum Uilleim**, William's Leap, above Corrour Station on Rannoch, a record of the passage of William Caulfield, roadmaker extraordinary

under General Wade, and builder of the nearby Devil's Staircase over to Kinlochleven? In the north-west, who was Farquhar's son whose Mullach and Coire lie eight or nine kilometres apart?

Beinn Fhionnlaidh, Glen Etive. There are two peaks of this name – the other has a tale attached

And who were the Elizabeths in **Càrn Ealasaid** or Creag Ealasaid? Hardly any hill names are feminine, either, in personal names or in occupations. There are some, such as **Ceann na Baintighearna** above Balquhidder; lady or wife of the owner, Campbell of Breadalbane. **Jean**, **The Cobbler**'s Wife, is of course a later English name, a fancy rather than a factual figure. **Sgùrr na Bana-mhòrair** near Loch Torridon, the peak of the lady, commemorates a poor soul whose cruel lord punished her for some trespass by making her stay on the bleak summit, fed only by shellfish brought to her.

Beinn Fhionnlaidh – there are two – is Finlay's hill: the southern one is in Glen Etive; the northern one bears the name of a notorious gamekeeper of MacKenzie's Gairloch estate in the 1580s, who – on discovering an intruder (a MacDonald) on the tops, killed him with his bow and arrow, thus precipitating a clan feud that spattered blood across a quarter-century until land transfers stopped it in 1607. You can find the full tale, with the gory details of the revenge attacks, in Ian R.Mitchell's *Scotland's Mountains before the Mountaineers*.

Fairies and Fingalians

There are other hill names relating to groups rather than individuals. **Schiehallion** (probably from *sìthean Chailleann*) translates as the fairy hill of the Caledonians, the long-lost Scottish tribe. At over 1080m it's rather a large fairyhill. *Sìthein* are

normally more delicate knolls, such as Handa Island's **Sìthean Mòr** (124m) or the knolls that give Glenshee its name, but it is the shape that counts. Near Aberfoyle, **Fairy Knowe** and **Doon Hill** are two hillocks where the fairies are reputed to have seized and imprisoned the Reverend Robert Kirk, a 17th century Gaelic scholar, as punishment for his book investigating them, *The Secret Commonwealth*. His spirit, it is whispered, is locked in a pine tree on the summit. Another fairy trick and one used by modern retailing is to play music to lure you in. Glen Ey's **Cnoc Chadail** (sleep) was one such place where a man was enticed by the music. He entered, set down his sack of meal, and awoke seven years later. Returning home, he found his children had grown up. The fairy knoll was, at least, his explanation for missing out on their teenage years …

The Fingalians, the followers of Finn MacCool, recur in Gaelic legend and in peaks from **Feinne-bheinn Beag** and **Mòr** below Loch Hope to **Sgòrr nam Fiannaidh** above Glen Coe, the peak of the Fian warriors. Across Glen Coe is the black dripping gash of Ossian's Cave, named after Fingal's son who was a famous bard of the Celts. Not far away is **Beinn Lora**, a mountain reputedly one of the portals of Bealach Banruinn Fhionnghail, the pass of Fingal's Queen, the other portal being the sea.

We move more concretely into history with **Stob Coir' an Albannaich** a few kilometres away across Glen Etive, peak of the corrie of the Scotsman – the Scots were of course 'Irish immigrants' at an early stage! Over to the east the legendary Fionns surface in **Beinn Bhrotain**, named after a large mastiff with which they hunted. **Torinturk** near Loch Etive, **Tòrr an Tuirc** and **Càrn an Tuirc** are all boar's hills where they hunted, and Dùn a' Diarmaid near Glen Shiel, and **Tom Dhiarmaid** by Glenshee, are after Diarmaid o' Duibhe, a Celtic hunter. A Skye tradition says that Diarmaid is buried together with Grainne and two of his hounds, on top of **Beinn Tianavaig** which was supposedly called Guilbheinn in the days before the Norse invasions. The name **Ben Gulbin**, occurring in several places in the Highlands, is a Fingalian hallmark. (See **Ben Gulabin** in Cairngorms chapter.)

Over in Argyll **Sliabh Ghaoil** is literally the darling hill, locally translated as the Mount of Love. On its slopes, according to legend, the Fionn warriors caught up with the eloping lovers Diarmaid and the beautiful Grainne. Unfortunately for him, she was still the legally-wedded wife of Fionn MacCumhaill, a chief, who then devised a trap for his wife's lover in which he perished poisoned by a boar's bristles. The same way that he died, in the other legend, in Glenshee!

Spaniards and Sassenachs

From Glen Shiel rises **Sgùrr nan Spàinteach**, Spaniards' Peak, which commemorates the 200 Iberians captured here in 1719 during a Jacobite rising against the British goverment. Catholic allies in Spain had ventured this force as a token of their support, landing them at the head of Loch Duich to join a Jacobite force. However these white-coated soldiers fled at the first challenge from the British redcoat armies, retreating in disorderly fashion up the hill to surrender the next day in the Coire nan Spàinteach. It may be that those Spaniards who fell in battle are buried on the hill.

CHAPTER TEN

NATURAL WORLD

All over Scotland there are hill names dedicated to the natural world. Birds of the air, and beasts of the field and hillside, mix with flora and serpents, weather and rocks, in words English, Scots, Gaelic and Norse. The Gaelic areas have the lion's share of these, with nearly a quarter of the Munros and many of the lower hills having nature-based names.

Nature has always occupied a core part of Gaelic culture, and so in the Highlands and Islands' hill names wild birds and animals, deer and cattle predominate, while by contrast in the Borders hills the domesticated sheep grazes, the tops both literally and in names. This difference is to be expected. The lower and gentler southern hills were long ago tamed by the shepherd's crook, while in the sterner and environment the hunting of wild animals and birds went hand-in-hand with the rearing of the hardy 'black' cattle to eke a living from the land. The incoming Sassenach landowners, and the anglicised descendants of clan chiefs, brought in the hated sheep which drove the people off their ancestral land. As a Gaelic poet wrote 200 years ago:

> *An iad na caoirich cheann-riabhach,*
> *Rinn aimhreit feadh an t-saoghail*
>
> Was it the grizzly-faced sheep
> That turned the world upside-down?

Later these landlords turned the wide open spaces into Killing Grounds for gilded guns to bag stags and shoot 'vermin' (including, at that time, eagles). Both these developments were quite foreign to Gaelic culture, for while they hunted creatures for food, they lived in balance, with them: slaughter for its own sake was unnatural: Donnchadh Bàn Mac an t-Saoir (Duncan Bàn MacIntyre), arguably the greatest Gaelic poet, and himself a hunter, expressed this view of nature 200 years ago in his poem *Cead Deireannach nam Beann* Final Farewell to the Hills:

> *'S aobhach a' ghreigh uallach*
> *Nuair ghluaiseadh iad gu farumach*
> *'S na h-èildean air an fhuaran*
> *Bu chuannar na laoigh bhallach ann*
> *Na maoisleichean 's na ruadh-bhuic*
> *Na coilich dhubh is ruadha*
> *'S e'n ceòl bu bhinne chualas*
> *Nuair chluinnt' am fuaim 's a' chamhanaich*
>
> Joyful was the proud flock,
> Strutting, full of spirit,
> When the hinds were at the spring
> How graceful were the speckled fawns
> The does, the red roe-bucks,
> The blackcocks and the red grouse,

No sweeter music was ever heard
Than their calls, heard at sunrise.

Another famous Scottish literary figure, Sir Walter Scott, who overlapped Donnchadh Bàn in lifespan, took a quite different approach to nature, romanticising its beauty, without the real appreciation of it that comes from the struggle to make a living from it that Donnchadh Bàn knew. It was no accident that Scott the romantic dwelt in the heart of the southern Borders, where nature had been largely tamed by man and his sheep: romanticism about nature was not appropriate in the wild Highlands.

Berries

The hill on Hoy in the Orkneys called **The Berry** is probably a direct descendant of the Old Norse *berg*, a hill. In southern Scotland there are several straightforward **Berry Hill**s, as well as a **Goldenberry Hill** in the Renfrew Heights and a **Nutberry Hill** in the Borders – both exotic fruits, the one being a Cape gooseberry (clearly unknown in the Borders) – and the other not known even to botany. This is because they are corruptions of Old English *burh*, a fort; **Bizzyberry Hill** (Montis de le Bissybery in 1452) near Biggar has an ancient fort on top, as do **Gallowberry** near Blyth Bridge, and **Arbory Hill**s – this latter, above the M74, was Garaberry on Blaeu's 1654 map.

In the Highlands there are some true berry hills, like **Meall nan Subh** (hill of the berries, or raspberries) near Loch Lyon. There's a ridge of blackberries in **Druim Ruighe nan Smeur** on Deeside, whilst **Meall nan Oighreagan** near Cannich is hill of cloudberries. Cloudberries fruit more readily the further north they grow – in Scandinavia they're a common jam fruit – and it's not surprising to find other hills with this name, like **Beinn nan Oighreag** above Glen Lochay. In the north-east **Everon Hill** is from a Scots word *averin*, this same berry.

These berries would have been part of the autumn diet, and it is surprising to find no bilberry or blaeberry – in Gaelic *braoileag* – hill, for it grows plentifully. Many a walker of today has been caught purple-fingered in the evening sun, and it certainly was part of the Gael's diet – as well as a dyestuff and, apparently, a cure for dysentery; the Border hills manage a **Blaeberry Hill** in Eskdale. Buachaille Etive Mòr has the rock-climb Crowberry Ridge, English-named after the shrub much favoured by ptarmigan, and growing on its ledges. In the far north-west lies **Beinn nan Cnàimhseag** the mountain of bearberries. Berries are often associated with nuts, and although **Chnò Dearg** (probably Cnoc Dearg) above Loch Treig literally means red nut (*cnò dearg*), it is quite probably an Ordnance Survey error for Cnoc Dearg (red hill). However **Sgùrr a' Bhraonain** near Loch Hourn is probably earth-nut (or pignut) peak, from a type of root-tuber.

Birds

Birds were of course a source of food, as the name of **Beinn Eunaich** near Dalmally (fowling mountain) indicates. A short crow's flight away lies **Meall nan Eun** peak of the birds, while a migration away in Torridon **Beinn an Eòin** is peak of the bird

(named Bin Eoin on Pont's map). Meall nan Eun has slabby sides useless for nesting or perching, but on the flatter grassy top on a wet August day I was surprised by the sheer number of small birds, pipits and wheatears, bobbing around on every available boulder and even on the summit cairn.

On Speyside is **Tom an Eòin** knoll of the bird, and legend has it that whenever the stolen bell of Insh church, sited on it, was rung in its far-off home, it pealed 'Tom-an-Eòin' as a rebuke to its captors!

These bird peaks were probably so-named from the relative density of breeding birds on them. On the little isle of Colonsay, rich in birdlife due to the tree-planting efforts of an early improver, is **Càrn an Eòin** and at over 750m in the hills east of Glenshee the lonely Loch nan Eun echoes to the playground shrieks of the gulls who have bred there for decades, as at Loch nan Stuirteag (loch of the seagulls) near Cairn Toul. Elsewhere hillsides were simply B&B calls for the birds, where they rested or roosted: **Meall nan Spàrdan** in the west means just that. **Marsco** on Skye was possibly seagull mountain to the Norsemen, while **Meall nan Faoilean** on Staffa is its Gaelic equivalent. Another sea-bird, *sgarbh* the cormorant, appears to be a generic name for a hill in Islay, with hills **Sgarbh Dubh** and **Sgarbh Breac** in the north.

The two classic birds of the high tops are the grouse – exploding from the heather with motorbike staccato – and the ptarmigan, discreetly belching as it cranes snake-like over boulders at you. The ptarmigan (*tàrmachan* in Gaelic), habitant of the very highest plateaux, has rightly had the fine **Meall nan Tàrmachan** ridge above Loch Tay named after it, as well as the **Ptarmigan** shoulder of Ben Lomond (and another on a hill in Knoydart). Meall nan Tàrmachan was named Kaillach Rannach in MacFarlane's Manuscripts of the 17th century, and by Pont in the 1590s as Kreig na-Gheyrach, apparently taking the mountain's name from the most westerly top, now named **Creag na Cailleach**.

The grouse by comparison appears to have been overlooked apart from a mere shoulder in Torridon called **Meallan na Circe-fraoich** (little hill of the grouse). Its Gaelic names are *cearc fhraoich* or *coileach ruadh*, literally heather hen and red cock, and unless the Fannaich's peak **An Coileachan** (little cock) counts, it has been forgotten in the honours. It was the Norse who gave it airspace in the three peaks named **Oreval** (moorfowl fell) on Harris and South Uist.

Another bird fond of the summits is the raven, distinctive both for its acrobatics and its eerie croaking in the mist, and it has crags named for it like **Creag an Fhithich** on **Ben Lawers**. The raven is the adopted bird of Clan Dougall, and it's interesting that in the clan's heartland around Oban, there's a Creag an Fhithich and a **Creag nam Fitheach** within a short distance. The Norse named **Krakkaval** on Lewis after the crow, probably the raven member of that family, since it was considered sacred to Odin in Scandinavia – hence another, **Beinn Cracavaig** on Eriskay. **Càrn a' Chlamhain**, cairn of the kite near Glen Tilt, is not to be confused with **Creag a' Chalamain** near Glenmore; dove's crag.

The southern Cairngorms have bird-hills too: there is **Tom Bad na Speireige**

Meall nan Tarmachan, hill of the ptarmigan. See also p155, [Southern Highlands, Ben Lomond]

(sparrowhawk), Coire na Feadaige (plover), the Munro **Càrn a' Ghèoidh** (goose) and **Tom na Riabhaig** (lark) near Loch Callater.

Some birds are more timid than others, **Beinn Enaiglair** in Ross has been interpreted as the hill of the timid or fearful birds from *eun eagal*, although the Reverend Burn claimed it should be *beinn aon a chlàir*, all in one piece; although it might more plausibly be from *eunadair*, a fowler or gamekeeper – a man, certainly, to make the birds fearful. **Bonxa Hill** in Shetland refers to the bonxies, local name for the great skuas, the bovver boys of the bird world who attack other birds for food. Staying in the northern isles, Birsay in the Orkney group has two neighbouring hills **Starafiold** and **Starling Hill**, the latter being a translation of the Norse former.

Cattle

While bird and animal hunting may have provided food intermittently, the rearing of domesticated animals was the mainstay of the Highland economy. In particular the keeping of the so-called 'black' cattle (in reality as often brown, fawn, grey or dappled) for dairy produce, and later for sale to the Sassenachs for beef. This trade has faded away over the last 150 years, but has left its memorial in the hill and corrie names. **Druim nam Bò** is ridge of the cattle: **Meall Greigh** of **Ben Lawers** is herd hill and **Beinn a' Chuallaich** above Rannoch Moor, on one of the great drove roads, is mountain of herding.

A calf or fawn in Gaelic is *laogh* – and also means, significantly, dear one. **Ben Lui** is from this word. One well-hoofed drove route was the Làirig an Laoigh in the

Cairngorms, the pass of the calf, easier going for the beasts than the higher and stonier Làirig Ghru a few kilometres west. In the north flank of **Cairn Gorm** itself is Coire Laoigh Mòr, which once echoed to their lowing, and above Loch Monar lies **Bidein a' Choire Sheasgaich**, corrie of the barren cattle, referring to the farrow cattle (those kept temporarily without calf at udder or womb) that grazed there. This very distinctive peak was known in MacFarlane's Manuscripts as simply 'the high hill of Bhearnish'.

Cattle were liable to theft, to the extent that it was a young men's pastime to make raids on other clan's herds, and in the west there are five mountains called **Creach Bheinn**, hill of spoil or plunder. In Glen Coe the famous Lost Valley – so-named because it is a glacial 'hanging valley' lost to view from the main glen – was where the MacDonalds hid away their still-hoofed hamburgers! At the eastern mouth of Glen Coe stand **Buachaille Eite (Etive) Mòr** and **Beag**, the big and little herdsmen of Etive; the old names were **Stob Dearg** and **Stob Dubh** (red and dark peaks), and perhaps the 'herdsman' was an ironic name given by the wary drovers edging their herds past here.

Dairying

In the earlier centuries when these cattle were kept for their milk and hides, transhumance was practised. While the men went fishing in the summer, and the women tended the crops, the young girls took the cattle to the high summer sheilings (*airigh*) for summer pasturage. (Butter and cheese were of course made on the hill, at the shieling pastures.) **Beinn Ìme** near The Cobbler in Argyll is the butter mountain – a name long predating the European Union – while on the other side of The Cobbler the Buttermilk Burn churns its way down to Loch Long. **Beinn Smeorail** in the north is its Norse counterpart. Speyside's **Craig a' Bhainne** is the milk crag while Rannoch's **Meall na Meòig** is the whey hill. Small islands offshore were also used for summer pasture, as Staffa's **Meall nan Gamhna** (hill of the stirks) indicates.

Although the cowherds had time to dally – **Caisteal Samhraidh** (summer castle) above Glen Lyon being probably a sunny belvedere to lie on – milkmaids who tended the cattle in the shielings faced certain risks. Both **Martha's Peak** and **Sgùrr Mhàiri** (Mary's Peak) in the Red Cuillin commemorate two who died in falls while on pastoral service. A more frequent if less serious risk was that posed by the visits of young men to these lonely spots, and Gaelic poetry is full of references to amorous encounters of the shieling kind. As Donnchadh Bàn recalls in his *Final Farewell*:

> *Fhuair mi greis am àrach*
> *Air àirighnean a b' aithne dhomh*
> *Ri cluiche, 's mire, s' manran*
> *'S bhith 'n caoimhneas blàth nan caileagan*

> I spent a part of my youth, in the shielings I knew well … playing, frisking and flirting, among the warm kindliness of the girls

Could **Beinn Èibhinn**, delightful mountain, be named from such sweet memories?

Deer

If the eagle was king of the skies, the stag, long before painter Landseer, was monarch of the mountain. **Beinn Damh** in Torridon is one of many stag mountains. **Sgùrr Èilde Mòr** in the Mamores is for its female companion the hind, *eilid*, while **Beinn nan Aighenan** has the same meaning (from *aighean*). Near Ben Nevis is **Sgùrr a' Bhuic** peak of the buck, the young deer, and there is also **The Buck** (locally known as Buck o' the Cabrach) in the east. Near Cannich, **Càrn na h-Earbaige Bige** refers to the young roe as does **Craignarb** hill in the east, and the roe's colour is apparent in **Meall nan Ruadhag** (red roe) above Loch Ness.

Another *eilid*, **Meall na h-Èilde** above Glengarry was, according to local naturalist Edward Ellice, so-called from its provision of good feeding and shelter from the westerly gales for the nursing hinds. Red deer are conservative animals, returning to their traditional calving areas time and again. Above Glen Coe the peak **Stob Coire Altruim** is from *altrum*, nursing or rearing, and nearby runs the Làirig Eilde Mòr, big pass of the hind. **Am Biachdich** and **Meall Tionail** mountains are respectively the feeding place (from *biadhtach*) and hill of the gathering place – the latter is a common name, and may refer also to the gathering of cattle or sheep. According to the Reverend A.E.Robertson, Sgùrr Thionail, a ridge running north from Sgùrr a' Mhaoraich, was 'the sheep gathering point'.

Ben Vuirich near Killiecrankie and the Quoichside duo of **Gàirich** and **Gleouraich** are from *buirich*, *gàirich* and *gleadhraich* for roaring, shouting and uproar, from the stags' autumn rut.

Deer hunts and Dogs

Beinn Chabhair probably means antler mountain (or just possibly hawk, from the obsolete *cabhar*) while **Ben Wyvis'** pointed **An Cabar** is simply the antler (one of several in the area), as are the hills **Croic-Bheinn** and **Crock**. **Beinn Oss** near Tyndrum may be from *os*, a stream outlet – there is a lochan in its southern corrie – or more likely from *os*, a stag or an elk, an animal that was hunted to extinction in *c*.1300. No such fate attended the red deer, whose numbers now exceed the human population of the Highlands, in spite of hunting, for in the age before the high-velocity rifle, dogs and traps and simpler weapons were used to cull rather than slaughter the deer.

Hunting was part of every man's yearly round. Strath na Seilge in Ross is from *sealg*, the hunt. **Meall nan Con** is peak of the dog, whilst **Sgùrr nan Conbhairean** above Glen Shiel is peak of the keepers of the (hunt) dogs; there are legends relating to the Fingalian hunting dogs being kept here. **Creag an Leth-choin** above Glenmore means lurcher's crag: a lurcher is a hunting dog, a formidable cross between a greyhound and collie. But on the occasion that led to this name, several of the lurchers plunged to their deaths over the cliff while in foaming pursuit of a stag all the way from Ryvoan. The nearby Lurchers' Gully – over which ski promoters and conservationists have had dog-fights – is a translation of Coire a' Leth-choin. Another lurcher appears in **Bac an Leth-choin** near Loch Maree: the dog commemorated had

tracked the wounded Neill MacLeod up it, allowing his master to shoot him on top – the top is named **Druim Càrn Niall**. The nearby peak of **Càrn Eilrig** is from an elrick (in Gaelic *iolairig*), a natural V-shaped notch in the hillside into which the deer were driven to be trapped and killed. (There is however a legend that any deer resting on the Càrn itself were deemed to be in a sanctuary and could not be slaughtered.) **Elrick Hill** near Aberdeen comes from the same word, and has a similar pass at its foot.

There's another fearsome if fantastic legend associated with hunting dogs on **Creag nan Caisean** near Foss in Perthshire. It tells of a large party of hunters, ghillies and their dogs who paused to rest on its top. The ghillies encouraged two of the dogs to fight; the excitement of the fight sucked in the ghillies and then their masters and the other dogs, and the whole episode ended with the dogs, ghillies and hunters (who were brothers) tearing each other's throats out, leaving but one half-brother as survivor and witness to this bloody tableau. The word *caisean* in Gaelic means short-tempered person or quarrel, and the hill's name is a wild understatement *if* the legend is true!

Deer-killing was to be a double-edged sword for the Gaels. It provided them with an important source of food through the centuries, but when the 19th century industrialist landlords discovered the joys of organised deer-hunting for their rich friends, they speeded up the clearances and evictions to create people-less, tree-less deserts called deer forests, the empty quarters that now dominate the high ground. **Bruach na Frìthe** in the Cuillin is from *frìth* meaning both deer forest and, aptly, wilderness, and in the Southern Highlands **Auchnafree Hill** is hill of the field (*achadh na frìthe*) of the deer forest.

Eagles

In Gaelic mythology the seagulls (*stuirteag*) were believed to be the spirits of the good on earth, their black caps being worn to expiate sins. But *if* they were Heaven's angels on earth, surely the Lord of the sky was the eagle, in Gaelic *iolair*. Yet curiously few summits bear the bird's name. Partly this reflects the fact that they nest lower down, in the pines or for security on remote crags, generally below 750m. Thus there are several instances of **Creag na h-Iolaire** for instance at 500m on Mull, and in Glen Shiel a shoulder called **Sgùrr Nid na h-Iolaire**, peak of the eagle's nest. In the Trossachs **Meall na h-Iolaire** barely reaches 600m. In Galloway, **Benyellary** is in fact Beinn na h-Iolaire.

But while the eagle nests lower down it hunts and soars high over the tops, and the Gaels did recognise the significance of the bird with a special alternative word *fior-eun*, literally the 'true' or 'notable' bird: and above remote Glen Pean is a top called **Meall an Fhìr-eòin**. Yet the absence of its name from any of the high peaks on mainland Scotland seems to be an omission by the Gaels, when even the rather prosaic Norse found space for **Arnaval** (eagle fell) on both Skye and South Uist, maybe inspired by the white-tailed sea eagle of the Hebrides which also soared over their ancestral Norwegian fiords. However, **Mount Eagle**, an unprepossessing tree-covered ridge in the Black Isle, is probably a corruption of *monadh na h-eaglais*, hill of the church.

Goats

Far better suited than the sheep to the terrain (and to the people) was the goat, *gobhar*, whose name occurs throughout the Highlands, as in **Stob Ghabhar** in the Black Mount or **Sgòr Gaibhre** facing it across Rannoch Moor. Coire na Minseag (properly Coire nam Minnseag) near Glen Lyon is the she-goat corrie. Edward Ellice, in his account of Glengarry, noting a Goats' Crag above Aberchilder says they were extensively kept for milking. Like all economically valuable goods, they were subject to theft. A 16th century raid by the rapacious MacDonalds on Glen Garry carried off 1302 goats and 763 kids – in the circumstances, of these semi-wild creatures, a prodigious feat of counting let alone thieving.

Heather, Peat and Moor

Heather, *fraoch*, is commoner on the actual slopes than in names, and while there are a few hills called **Fraoch Bheinn** in the west, there is only one Munro-high mountain with it, **Mullach Fraoch-choire**, although the Corbett **Fraochaidh** is almost that height. This is probably because heather does not grow much above 900m because it needs a substantial growing season free of snow cover, and so does not reach the summits: significantly both these hills are in the milder west, and the highest one's names reflects the corrie not the summit. In southern Scotland some examples of the common name **Black Hill** refer to heather. Moors blanketed with bog are found stretching almost to the summits, especially in the eastern plateaux,

Stob Ghabhar, goat peak. Feral herds still roam in Galloway and Torridon and on Ben Lomond

as names like **Càrn Bhac** (peat bank), **Bac nam Fòid** (banks of peat, above Loch Hourn) and **A' Chòinneach** (the moss) show. The two hills called **Sgùrr na Lapaich** are peak of the bogland.

Ben Chonzie (alias Ben y Hone) in Perthshire is a terrible anglicisation (often pronounced as it is spelt in English) of the gentle Gaelic *beinn na còinnich* (mossy mountain). It appears to be named Hill of Turret (after the Glen below) in Pont's map. **Meall an Lundain** above Derry Lodge is the hill of the green mossy spot, the ground referred to making it a favourite grazing spot for deer, and **Maoile Lunndaidh** in the west has a similar meaning. **Conic Hill** at the foot of Loch Lomond has little to do with its shape and everything to do with pidgin Gaelic, from the same word *còinneach*. **Waggle Hill** in the north-east is from the Scots word *waggle* meaning a quagmire, suggesting one's probable movements across its shoogly surface. Meanwhile in the heart of the Cairngorms the **Mòine Mòr** (A' Mhòine Mhòr, big peat bog) is no idle warning.

Horses

Of some importance in the Highland economy was the horse, which ran free on the hills unlike today's corralled creatures. It is believed that the summit of **An Sgarsoch** above Glen Geldie was where they were brought to a great annual horse market. (An Sgarsoch's name is sometimes given as meaning the place of sharp rocks, from its grey hairpiece of scree, unusual in these flat-topped hills). The horses' place in the name pantheon is in hills like **A' Mharconaich** the horsy place above Drumochter. Sgùrr nan Each and the popular Beinn Each near Callander are both horses' mountains, as is Beinn Eich in the Luss Hills.

Around Kintail in Wester Ross is an intriguingly 'horsy place': here there are foals (in **Sgùrr an t-Searraich** – on the Five Sisters and **Beinn an t-Searraich**), a mare (in **Sgùrr na Làire Brice** – and in **Beinn Làir** further north), another mare above Glenelg (in **Beinn a' Chapuill**), a mane (**A' Mhuing**, the long ridge running west from Biod an Fhithich), and Norse and Gaelic horses (in Rosdail near Glenelg and in **Sgùrr Leac nan Each** on The Saddle). **The Saddle** itself (An Dìollaid in Gaelic) is so-named from the yoke-shape of its 1000m summit slung between two peaked tops – like its English little cousin Saddleback, and its distant relative the Sattelhorn in the Swiss Bernese Oberland – and completes the equestrian connection in this area. The concentration in this western seaboard area may be due to the Norse influence, for the Norse word *hross* occurs throughout the Western Isles, as well as in place names like Rosdail and Rois-bheinn. The Vikings did use horses, and may well have introduced new strains to the local people.

Elsewhere in the Highlands the word *dìollaid* has passed into general use for a saddle between two hills like the An Diollaid on **Ladhar Bheinn**'s western shoulder. **Saddle Yoke**, a spur of **Hart Fell**, perfectly describes the shape of its delightful top. It was apparently mapped in 1775 by M.J.Armstrong as Caripheran Yoke, the specific referring to Carrifran Glen nearby, although it may have been the name then for what is now Carrifran Gans hill.

In contrast to the horses which gave their name to hills, Arkle and Foinaven are

two hills which gave their name to two famous racehorses. In the Borders, **Riding Hill** in upper Tweeddale might appear to refer to the Common Riding, the annual practice of marking out of local boundaries on horseback: but the old name on Blaeu's map is Dridderdon, from which Riding is probably a corruption: the suffix -don probably relates to the hill-fort on its slopes, from Cumbric *din* or British *duno*, hill-fort.

Insects

The southern hills are the home of two insect hills, **Golloch Hill** in the Ochils from the horny goloch or earwig (from the Gaelic *gobhlach*, forked), and **Midge Hill** near Camps Reservoir although it was simply Mid Hill on Roy's 1755 map. It is curious then that in the Highlands where the true midge dines out (on people) there are no hills dedicated to its Gaelic name of *meanbh-chuileag*, literally tiny fly – but then, even Donnchadh Bàn could not bring himself to mention it in his 'Final Farewell'! The closest hill name is **Meall Cuileige** above Glen Moriston, hill of the fly.

Landscape

The Gael had an eye too for the stiller, geologically-creeping aspect of nature, the shape of the land. Adjectives like *eagach* (notched – as in the **Aonach Eagach**, running like a corrugated fence along Glen Coe) and *cas* (steep – as in Coire Cas of Cairngorm), *fada* and *geàrr* (long and short as in **Beinn Fhada** and **Geàrr Aonach**), *garbh* and *leacach* (rough and slabby) are all accurate for their particular hills. *Garbh* (rough) is common (**Meall Garbh** hills abound) while the word for smooth appears in Speyside's **Càrn Sleamhainn** and fat or stout is found in the score of hills called **Meall Reamhar** in the Southern Highlands. A more unusual word for fat, perhaps in the sense of rich soil, appears in **Mèith Bheinn** in South Monar. And in the same vein, **Duncryne Hill** overlooking Loch Lomond (*dùn cruinn*, rounded hill-fort) is usually known by the unflattering name Dumpling Hill.

Mòr and *beag* (big and little) are widely used, usually to distinguish two proximate hills like **Aonach Mòr** and **Aonach Beag**: sometimes the 'wee one', the *beag*, is actually higher than the bigger *mòr*, as in the two just named, but the *mòr* may well be bulkier, or nearer the local village and therefore higher-looking in the view. *Meadhon* (often pronounced as in the several **Ben Vane**s) means the middle or intermediate peak, so **Aonach Meadhoin** above Glen Clunie is between the higher **Sgùrr a' Bhealaich Dheirg** (red pass peak) and the lower **Sgùrr an Fhuarail**. **Ben Mannoch** in the east is from the same word, while **Beinn Stumanadh** is the 'modest' hill alongside Ben Loyal. In the Borders **Drochil Hill** is the Scots-named dwarfish or dumpy hill.

Tarsuinn, transverse or oblique, is commonly used of hills whose axis runs counter to the grain of the land. Thus **Beinn Tarsuinn** in the Letterewe forest, a west-east running hill, is set at right angles to the long north-south ridge running up to **Beinn a' Chlaidheimh** (sword). Another hill that ends a long ridge, but in this case is simply set apart from it, **Cruach Innse** appears to be the 'island' heap, standing 'offshore' from the Grey Corries chain; but *innse* can also mean meadow where

cattle can be grazed, and this was on a drove road.

Finer details of the landscape are picked up in names like **Beinn Sgritheall** (or Sgriol, maybe related to *sgriodan*, scree – it pours its stone shoots down towards Loch Hourn), **Càrn na Caim** above Drumochter (cairn of the curve, from the narrow bending corrie Cama Choire on its east flank) and **Cairn of Claise** (cairn of the ditch or hollow, or green grassy place). **Beinn nan Imirean** is ridged mountain, **Meall na h-Aisre** the defile hill, **Meall na Leitreach** slope hill, and Fireach is simply 'sloping'. Among other descriptions are the precise **Bràigh Coire Chruinn-bhalgain** height of the corrie of the rounded blisters, the imaginative **An Tunna** in Arran, meaning the barrel – there are two of them, one at either end of the main mountain chain, both just over 300m high. **Croit Bheinn** is probably humped mountain.

Berneray's **Sand Hill**, translated from the Gaelic *gaineamh*, is a marram-covered sand dune, an ideal site for the burial ground upon it: while **Meall Gaineimh** at the east end of Loch Avon has huge spreads of granite grit, like sand, on it. The Cuillin's **Sgùrr nan Eag** is peak of the notches, its rocky teeth-gaps. Other descriptions are almost superfluous, like the two mountains called **Sgùrr nan Coireachan** in the west, for there can hardly be a Highland mountain (after millennia of ice-sheets) without a gouge of corries on its flanks. Others should not be taken too literally; **Càrn Ghluasaid** is hill of movement, apparently from the slippage of its screes, while nearby **Aonach air Chrith**, ridge of trembling, perhaps causes you to shake in your boots.

Subjective feeling rather than objective description might seem to account for **Càrn a' Choire Bhòidheach** on the **White Mounth**, cairn of the beautiful corrie (but it has good grazing on it and the shepherds would have loved it), and Gleouraich's ridge called **Sròn na Breun Leitir** the nose of the filthy or rotten slope. **Beinn Sgreamhaidh** in Sutherland is loathsome hill. And what tale lies behind **Luinne Bheinn** often translated as the angry peak, or sometimes as the hill of mirth or melody? Perhaps it is from *luinne* suggesting the swell of the sea, a fine description of its shape; when the adjective precedes the noun it indicates a poetic turn of phrase, and 'sea-swelling mountain' conjures up a lovely picture of this peak: as does **Moruisg**, big water!

Beinn Heasgarnich near Glen Lyon is often translated as peaceful or sheltering mountain, from *seasgairneach*. Its main ridge runs north-south and would be a barrier to the strong westerly winds, for cattle sheltering in the glen of its main burn. It is interesting that, close by, are two hills **Sgiath Bhuidhe** and **Sgiath Chùil**, *sgiath* being a wing, and expressing the 'sheltering' idea well in the crook of their wing-shaped north-south ridges. The mountain may be the source of a little mystery, for in an 1872 guidebook is listed, among Scotland's principal peaks, one Ben Feskineth at 1075m in Perthshire. The peak has never since been heard of, but the height and county are identical to Heasgarnich's!

The Border hills convey little of the landscape bar the frequent references to subsidiary features like *coomb* (a corrie), *cleuch* (a gully), *hope* (a valley), and *craig* (a cliff). However, there are some more interesting names: **Steygail Hill** is from *stey*,

steep, and *gail*, a gable (England after all has a Great Gable); **Shankend** is the expressive name for a slope running from high to low ground, like the Gaelic *sròn*; and **Spango Hill** is apparently from *spangie* or *spanghue*, a Scots word for leaping frog-like up in the air. **Taberon Law** near Broughton draws upon the resemblance to a tabron, a drum. The Norse on the other hand in their naming of Hebridean hills did go in for topographical description. Peaks like **Breaclete** (broad rock), **The Hoa** (high), **Reieval** and **Roneval** (smooth and rough fells), and **Sletteval** (flat fell) occur in several places, for the Norse were primarily seafarers naming peaks for maritime identification purposes, appearance being all-important.

Sheep

Sheep were kept by the earlier Gaels, in small numbers. But the introduction of large-scale sheep farming by the 19th century landlords was the means of impoverishing the people and evicting them from their ancestral lands. As Donnchadh Bàn laments in his *Final Farewell:*

> *'S a' bheinn is beag a shaoil mi*
> *Gun dèanadh ise caochladh*
> *O'n tha i nis fo chaoraibh*
> *'S arm thug an saoghal car asam.*

> I hardly thought
> That the mountain would ever change,
> But now it is under sheep,
> The world has cheated me.

The ecologist Fraser Darling has argued that, amongst its other sins, the sheep's grazing destroyed the rich natural vegetation of the hills, found now only on a few inaccessible ledges. Scarcely surprising then that not many hills bear the creature's name, in complete contrast to the hills of southern Scotland. The name is only borne by lesser hills like **Beinn nan Caorach** by Loch Hourn (although it is a gendarme-type rocky hill en route to Druim Fada and most un-lamblike), and **Meallan nan Uan** little hill of the lambs in Strath Conon. **Soval**, a Lewis hill meaning sheep fell (from the Norse) represents the more ancient breed of sheep brought by the Vikings, a beast that did not trample livelihoods underhoof as the later Cheviots did on the mainland.

The wet boggy conditions of the west Highlands do not make it ideal terrain for the sheep, exposing them to the risks of footrot, ticks and the like: the peak **Spidean Mialach** above Loch Quoich in the wettest part appears to mean literally lousy peak, perhaps from *mial-caarach*, the sheep-louse. In fact it was probably named long before sheep moved onto the hill, and comes from an obsolete meaning of *mial* for any animal, probably deer. Reverend A.E.Robertson noted in the late 19th century that its 'green grassy corries afforded splendid shelter and pasturage for the deer'. Over time *mial* changed its meaning to louse, and its name was therefore something of a puzzle; apparently the Glengarry people created a 'folk etymology' to the effect that it had come from *spidean neulach*, cloudy peak, and that their ancestors

changed it to the similar-sounding *spidean mialach* to distinguish it from the many other 'cloudy' peaks in this the wet west.

Close to Spidean Mialach is **Beinn Mhialairigh** from the same word *mial*, while **Sturdy Hill** in Kincardine may well be from Scots *sturdy* (Gaelic *stùird*), a sheep brain disease producing dizziness (mad sheep disease?). But it is significant that none of the highest peaks bear the sheep's name.

There are two hills in southern Scotland called simply **Sheep Hill**. But there are several **Lamb Hills** or **Rigs** – and the **Lammermuir Hills** themselves may come from 'lamb' – as well as **Ewe Hills** and **Hog Hills**, a hog being a yearling sheep. The ubiquitous **Wether** (or sometimes **Wedder**) **Hills**, **Laws**, and **Dods**, of which there are at least a dozen, are named from a wether, a castrated ram: and hill-points **Wedder Lairs** in the Lammermuirs, as **Hoglayers** in the Lomonds of Fife, refer to the lairs or scoops where the wethers weather the storms. Unlike the magnificent Swiss peak the Wetterhorn (the 'weather peak') at the northern edge of the Bernese Oberland, our many Wether Hills have neither the height nor the position to indicate the outlook by catching the first of the cloud. **Bught Knowes** in Eskdale refers to a sheepfold, while the intriguing **Minny E' Hill** south of Sanquhar may indicate a place where lost lambs were rejoined with their mothers, a practice called *minnie*.

Shells

Several Highland peaks appear to be named from shells, surprisingly in view of their general distance from the sea. **Beinn a' Chreachain** has been translated as peak of the clamshell: but lying as it does at the head of Glen Lyon it would be a fish out of water so far from the sea. In fact, the word *creachan* or *creachann* originally did mean a clam or scallop shell, and by analogy with a bare exposed rocky-ribbed top led to the word being used for hills like this too. **Am Faochagach** in the Deargs, **Faochag** above Glen Shiel, and **Faochaig** above Glen Elchaig all translate as whelk or periwinkle, or in the case of the first-named, abounding in whelks. Their original Ordnance Survey spellings were Am Fraochagach, literally the heathery or berried place or Fraochag, the cranberry, which might suggest that *faochag* was a later corruption since heather and berries are commoner than shells on mountains. However, *faochag* also means whelk-like in a whorled or ribbed style, by analogy with the shell: and all three mountains are characterised by just such a ribbed appearance, Am Faochagach by solifluction lines across the summit and eastern shoulder, and Faochaig by distinctive hummocks on the ridge, while these peaks are grassy rather than heathery, suggests the shell-likeness is indeed the true meaning.

Sgùrr a' Mhaoraich at the head of Loch Hourn apparently from *maorach*, shellfish, and its peaked and ribbed shape could resemble a shell. In an early Scottish Mountaineering Club Journal it was referred to familiarly as 'The Whelk' and the Reverend A.E.Roberston said its name derived from the fossil shells found on its summit, although this is geologically improbable. Its local name (and old Ordnance Survey name) is Sgùrr a' Mhorair, the peak of the landowner. A shoulder of this hill is **Bac nan Canaichean**, bank of bog-cotton, although **Meall Onfaidh** nearby is hill of the sea's fury.

Shrubs and Flowers

Flora in hill names include the broom, as in Deeside's **Tom Bealaidh** (though surely not as well-known as Glasgow's Broomielaw), the bramble (Glen Doll's **Dreish** from *dris*), and the holly (**Sgùrr a' Chuilinn** above Glen Shiel). Flowers are rare, but there are hills with names like **Leac na Buidheag**, slab of the buttercup, and even thrift (the sea-pink) in **Sgùrr na Fearstaig**. This plant grows not only on sea coasts but also mountain tops, favouring very exposed habitats where other plants do not dare to spread, and that's why there's another **Sgùrr na Feartaig**, a few kilometres away. **Meall an t-Seamraig** above Loch Lochy is the hill of the shamrock, while **Beinn Lurachan** is garlic mountain. **An Geurachadh** is the agrimony herb, **Cnoc Bad na Conaire** willowherb knoll, **Meall Copagach** docken hill, and **Creag Rainich** ferny crag. Plants in the southern hills include bent, a coarse grass, in the Ochils' **Bentie Knowe**, some **Peat Laws**, **Turf Law**s and **Broom Hill**, and two hills which seem to refer to crops: **Carrot Hill** in the Sidlaws and **Corn Law** in the Ochils (though the latter may be a corruption of *corum* meaning little round hill). **Rispie Hill** and **Rashy Hill** are covered in coarse grass and rushes, respectively.

Snakes

Modern landowners sometimes fix 'Beware of adders' signs on gates to deter hill-walkers – the 21st century equivalent of 'Here Be Monsters'. Perhaps it was an earlier landlord who named hills like **Meall Nathrach Mhòr** above Rannoch Moor, hill of the big adder – nasty-sounding, but a mere wriggle compared to the ominous **Beinn a' Bheithir** at Ballachulish which might translate as mountain of the prodigiously large serpent!

Trees

Peeping like rotted molars from the gaping peat hags are bleached tree stumps, the remains of the great Caledonian Forest that covered the Highlands centuries ago before man and climate laid waste to it. Today, depending on exposure to the wind, the treeline reaches up only to about 600 metres. But several hill names include trees, usually from plants growing on their lower slopes. The ancient Highland tree cover was mainly of pine, birch and oak, in Gaelic *giuthas*, *beith* and *darach*.

The last-named of this trio, the oak, prefers the fertile soils in the river valleys; it therefore appears rarely in hill names, with exceptions like **Meall na Doire Darach** above Kinlochleven. Within, sight of this hill is **Sgòr an Iubhair** in the Mamores, the peak of the yew tree, often associated with churchyards (and it can be clearly seen from the old graveyard in Glen Nevis) but a tree which grows wild in the milder west.

Not far away in Glen Coe, **Stob Coire nam Beith** represents one of the few birches in names, and another one is in **Barbay Hill** (*bàrr beithe*) in the Cumbraes. But the birch, like the oak, grows in lower spots, and tends to huddle with its own kind: in contrast trees that grow both high, and as loners, get noticed more. So it is that the rowan (or mountain ash), *caorann* to the Gaels, has a veritable copse of mountains named for it – the many instances of **Beinn a' Chaorainn**, **Sàil Chaorainn**, and **Creag Chaorainn**. Sometimes planted as a lone tree by a crofter

Beinn a' Chaorainn, hill of the rowan. There are over a dozen hills named after this tree

seeking protection against evil spirits, sometimes germinating in a rock crack (hence the Creag examples) from a bird's dropping, this rugged individualist contributes a striking splash of blood-red berries to the blues and golds of autumn, and a worthy name for a mountain. **Sgùrr a' Chaorachain** in deepest Monar is peak of the rowan-berried place. It is also virtually the only tree of note in the southern hill names, with **Rowantree Hill**s in both the Renfrew Heights and the Lammermuirs.

The pine – not the modern narrow-shouldered regiments, but the beautiful free-branching Scots pine – is a hardy individual that can grow alone on a slope. In the Fannaichs the hill **Beinn Liath Mhòr a' Ghiubhais Lì** is the big grey hill of the coloured pine, a name that speaks almost orientally of its beauty. The beautiful Glen Derry is encircled by a scattering of such lonesome pines riding shotgun high up on the slopes like outriders. Ironically for this lovely forest of ancient pines, Glen Derry – which gave its name to Derry Cairngorm above it – is named from *doire*, a thicket. The pine itself is named in the Cairngorms in Glen Geusachan – although the glen is now bare of pines – and in **Càrn a' Phris-Ghiubhais** (cairn of the pine thicket),

an outlier of the famed Rothiemurchus pines. The Scots pine is found more in this eastern part of the Highlands since it prefers sandy, drier soils. On the north side of Derry Cairngorm lies **Càrn Etchachan**, named from the corrie between; it is probably derived from *aiteann*, the juniper, whose wind-dwarfed shrubs green the stony corrie floor. South of Derry Cairngorm is Coire Craobh an Òir, corrie of the tree of gold, beneath which a crock of gold was supposedly buried. And in Glen Luibeg is Preas nam Mèirleach, thicket of the robbers, where thieves lay in wait for the drovers passing through the Làirig Ghrù.

The destruction of the Scots pine forest is not all in the distant past. Above Loch Arkaig is **Druim a' Ghiùbhsaich** ridge of the pine, whose northern slopes are still scarred by the charcoaled remains of a great Caledonian pine forest here, burnt down in the last war by commandos training at nearby Spean Bridge, the trees' bleached bones not yet covered by new plantations.

Meall na Feàrna near Callander is the alder hill, while **Fafernie** is *feith feàrnaidh*, bog of the alder. The alder is a tree that loves damp soil, and in wet Knoydart it's no surprise to find **Stob an Uillt-Feàrna**, peak of the alder stream. **Spirebush Hill** in the Lammermuirs is from a *spire*, Scots for a small tapering tree (usually pine) used to grow paling wood.

Weather

The weather in its unpleasanter form manifests itself in the names of the westerly Ayrshire hills of **Windy Standard** and **Cloud Hill**, and **Misty Law** in the Renfrew Heights. (*Standard* appears to be a hill generic in the south-west, with two

Fuar Tholl, cold hollow – formerly known as Beinn Leac Dearg, hill of the red slab. See p106,
[North-West Highlands, Fuar Tholl]

213

Windy Standards, a Black Standard and two The Standard hills.) Above Lauder **Scoured Rig** evokes a windswept top, while shelter beckons leeward of the intriguing **Windshield Hill** near Moffat. As for the hill shoulder above Megget Water called **Dead for Cauld** ... And in the southern hills there are dozens of **Windy Hill**s and **Windy Law**s, while Windie Edge is a common name for an exposed farmhouse.

The weather dominates life more in the north. There, mountains can provide shelter from the westerly gales or funnel them down on you, as in a spring Cairngorm 'roarer'. They can rip open the clouds' rain-laden bellies, or break them up to let the sunshine through. So we find hills that are called misty (**Beinn a' Ghlo** from *glo*, a veil of mist, and **Beinn Cheathaich**) or wind (**Sgòr Gaoith**), wet (**Maoile Lunndaidh**), and cold *fuar*, as in **Fuar Tholl** by Glen Carron, and **Meall Fuar-Mhonaidh** and **Fourman Hill**) from cold *monadh* or hill-mass. **Cnoc Braonach** by Lochinver is knoll of drizzle, and **Brat Bheinn** on Jura is literally the veil or mantle mountain, perhaps from its cloud cover. **Cnoc na Fuarachad** on the Atlantic shore of Skye's Sleat peninsula is the coldness hillock.

Not all the weather names are gloomy, though, for there are several small hills called *grianan* – like the shoulder **An Grianan** above Glen Lochay – meaning the sunny spot or hillock. And comfort might be sought in the names of **Caisteal Samhraidh** over Glen Lyon, the summer castle, and **Beinn an Dòthaidh** above Bridge of Orchy, literally mountain of scorching.

Wild Animals

The wild boar, which followed the elk (**Beinn Oss**) into extinction in about 1400, lives on in peaks like **An Torc** The Boar of Atholl, which with its partner **The Sow of Atholl** hogs the western skyline at Drumochter, and **Càrn an Tuirc** at Glenshee. **Beinn Ulbhaidh** above Strathoykel is the 'wolfy' mountain; the last wolf is supposed to have been killed in 1700 by MacKintosh of Moy in Inverness-shire. Hunted too – but too wily to be exterminated – was the fox, *sionnach* or *madadh ruadh* (literally red dog). **Druim Shionnach** above Glen Shiel and **Sgùrr a' Mhadaidh** in the Cuillins are but two of several hills where pads the sly beast, and **Càrn na Saobhaidhe** in the Monadh Liath (there are six of this name there) is the cairn of the fox's den. Foxes nest in boulder-tumbles, so they are spoiled for choice in the Highlands, which is why there are several spots called **Creag a' Mhadaidh** (although these could possibly have been wolf lairs as well). The fox was not always seen as the villain of the countryside – this is the view of the later sheep-farmer – and to the Gael dispossessed by these bleating animal cuckoos, their predators might be smiled on. Donnachadh Bàn was moved in his *Song of Foxes* to cry:

> *Mo bheannachd aig na balgairean*
> *A chionn bhi sealg nan caorach*
>
> My blessing to the foxes
> Because they hunt the sheep

Small wonder then that the fox's name appears quite often in hill names. However, although *madadh* is also a dog, the name of **Dog Hillock** above Glen Clova

is not a translation, for a 'dog hillock' is a north-east Scots name for a hill covered in long grass. In this Clova hill's case, it's in contrast to the nearby **Sandy Hillock**. There was a name Dog Hillock in the Ochils, extant up to the early 19th century, probably a translation from the adjacent Maddy Moss.

Cnap an Dhòbrain in Glen Avon is otter hillock, **Meall nam Maigheach** is hare's hill and there are several wild cats in spots like **Beinn a' Chait** by Atholl and Lochan nan Cat on Ben Lawers. Wild cats are apparently as populous as foxes, preferring similar rock-strewn habitats – but being less bold they are very rarely seen, except by the sharp-eyed Gaels who gave these names. However **Cat Law** and the **Hill of Cat** in Angus are deceptive: the old name Carnecaithla (1458) might suggest cairn of the battle (from *cath*). And the **Cat's Back**, a low crouching hill by Strathpeffer, is a local name from its arched shape, and certainly not a translation of its Gaelic name Cnoc Farril (possibly hill of watching, from *faire* or *cnoc far-eiligh*, high stone-place from the vitrified fort on top).

In southern Scotland the hare is one of the few wild animals apparently mentioned, in the **Hare Hill**s and **Law**s. In Scots, however, a *hare stane* is a boundary stone or marker – from hair meaning grey or hoary (with age) – and the several Hare Laws or **Harlaw**s are probably from this meaning.

Swansong

The wide range of nature names on the hills indicates a deep concern for the environment. The bitterness that the Gaelic people felt at the Clearances was not just at the loss of home and livelihood, but also at being torn from the natural world they had been so intricately a part of. This bitterness was expressed so clearly by Donnchadh Bàn, in his lament:

> Mo shoraidh leis na frìthean
> O' s mìorbhailteach na beannan iad,
> Le biolair uaine 's fìor uisg,
> Deoch uasal, rìomhach, cheanalta:
> Na blàran a tha prìseil,
> 'S na fàsaichean tha lìonmhor,
> O' s àit a leig mi dhiom iad,
> Gu bràth mo mhìle beannachd leo.

> Farewell to the deer forests – they are marvellous mountains,
> With green watercress and pure spring water,
> A noble, beautiful, royal drink;
> To the moorland that is precious,
> And the many lonely places,
> This is my land that I have left,
> A thousand blessings be with them for ever

Today's nature reserves and the general 'green' movement towards conservation may be fighting a rearguard action for wild life and wilderness in the Scottish countryside, but the rich heritage of nature names is part of this legacy that is worth studying and preserving.

Other Common Gaelic Words

This list of some Gaelic words commonly-used in place names is confined to words not examined in the text of the book. For example, all the colour words (*gorm*, *glas*, etc) will be found in the main index. For a fuller list, the Ordnance Survey publish a booklet called *Place-names on maps of Scotland and Wales* containing a fuller list of Gaelic, Scandinavian and Welsh name elements.

Please bear in mind that the spellings on maps, etc may not always be exactly the same as those in this glossary due to the corruption of names over time (e.g. – *baile* often becomes *bal*), or to the inaccuracies of the OS surveyors. The letter *h* may well appear as a second letter (e.g. – *bhaile* is the same in meaning as *baile*). I have included anglicisations after Gaelic words in brackets (e.g. – *ach* is an anglicisation of *achadh*).

A

abhainn river
achadh (ach, auch) field
ail rock
àiridh high pasture, shieling
allt stream
àth ford

B

bac bank
bad place, copse
baile (bal) farm, township
bàthach byre
beag (beg) wee, small
bealach (balloch) pass (in hills)
beàrn pass, gap
blàr, *blair* plain
bò, *bà* cow, cattle
both cottage

C

cadha steep slope, pass
cam bent, crooked
camas (camus, cambus) bay, river bend
caol (kyle) narrows
caora sheep
cas steep
cath battle
clach stone
clais narrow valley, gap, ditch
coille (coyle) wood
coire corrie, cwm, cirque, hollow
corran point shaped like a hook
craobh tree
croit croft, small farm
crom curved
cù, *coin* dog, dogs
cùil nook

D

dà two
dail (dal) field
damh deer
deas south
dìollaid saddle, pass
dobhar water
doire copse, wood
drochaid bridge

E

each horse
eadar between
eag cleft, notch
eaglais church
ear east
eas waterfall
eilean island
eun, *eòin* bird, birds

F

fada	long
feadan	small valley
fear	man
feàrna	alder
fèith	bog, moss
fraoch	heather
fuar	cold
fuaran	spring, well

G

gabhar	goat
gaineamh	sand
gall (gaill)	stranger, foreigner
gaoth	wind
garbh (garve)	rough, stony
geàrr	short
gil	gully
giuthas	pine, fir-tree
gleann (glen)	valley
gobhal (gavel)	fork, prong
greigh	herd

I

iar	west
inbhir (inver)	river-mouth
innis, innse	isle, meadow
ìochdar	lower part
iolair	eagle

L

lag (lagg, laggan)	hollow
làirig	pass
leac (leck)	stone, slab
learg	slope, hillside
leitir (letter)	steep slope
linne	pool
loch; lochan	lake; small lake/tarn
lòn	marsh, pool, meadow
loisgte	burnt, charred
lùb, lùib	bend

M

machair	seaside meadow
magh (moy)	plain

(continued)

meadhon	middle, central
meanbh	small
mòine	moss, bog
mòr (more)	big
muilinn	mill

P

pait	hump, knoll
poll	pool, pit
preas	wood

R

raineach	ferny
ràth	fort
reamhar	fat
ros	headland
rubha (rhu)	sea headland

S

saighead	arrow
sgoilte	split
sgriogalach	bare mountain top
sleamhuinn	smooth
sloc, slochd	hollow
srath (strath)	valley

T

tairbert (tarbert)	isthmus, narrow neck of land
tigh, taigh	house
tìr	land
tobar (tibber)	well
toll	hollow
torc	boar
tràigh	beach
tuath	north

U

uachdar	upper part
uamh	cave
uan	lamb
uisge	water

Bibliography

General Books

Allan, Elizabeth
Burn on the Hill, Beauly 1995

Bennet, Donald
The Munros, Glasgow (reprinted 2006)

Brown, Hamish
Climbing the Corbetts, London 1988

Dorward, David
The Sidlaw Hills, Kirriemuir 2004

Ellice, Edward
Place-Names of Glengarry and Glenquoich, London 1931

Fraser, Ian
The Place-names of Arran, Glasgow 1999

Forbes, Alexander
Place Names of Skye and adjacent islands, Paisley 1923

Jakobsen, Jakob
The Place-Names of Shetland, Lerwick (reprinted 1993)

Johnston, J.B
Place-Names of Scotland, Edinburgh 1934 (reprinted 1976)

Julyan, Robert
Mountain Names, Seattle 1984. (American and world mountain names)

MacBain, Alexander
Place-Names, Highlands and Islands of Scotland, Stirling 1922

MacIver, Duncan
The Place-names of Lewis and Harris, Stornoway 1934

MacLean, Charles
The Isle of Mull – Place-Names, Meanings, Stories, 1997

Milne, Rob and Brown, Hamish
The Corbetts & Other Scottish Hills, Glasgow 2002

Mitchell, Ian R
Scotland's Mountains before the Mountaineers, Edinburgh 1998

Mitchell, Ian R
Timothy Pont and Scotland's mountains. In The Nation Survey'd, ed. Cunningham, Ian 2001

Mitchell, Ian R
The View from Timothy Pont in Scottish Mountaineering Club Journal 2002

National Library of Scotland
Website for Pont and Blaeu maps <*www.nls.uk/maps/*>

Nicolaisen, W.F.H
Distribution of Certain Gaelic Mountain Names in *Transactions of the Gaelic Society of Inverness, 45* (1967-8)

Nicolaisen, W.F.H
Scottish Place-names, Edinburgh 2001

Scottish Place-Name Society
website *<www.spns.org.uk>*

Stewart, T.F
Gaelic-English Hill-Names of Perthshire, 1974

Taylor, Simon
The Place-Names of Fife, Volume 1, 2006

Watson, Adam and Allan, Elizabeth
The Place-Names of Upper Deeside, Aberdeen 1984

Watson, Adam
The Cairngorms, Glasgow 1992

Watson, Angus
The Ochils: Place-names history, traditions Perth 1995

Watson, W.J
The Place-names of Ross and Cromarty, Inverness 1904 (reprinted 1976)

Watson, W.J
The History of the Celtic Place-Names of Scotland, Edinburgh 1926

Watson, W.J
Scottish Place-Name Papers, Edinburgh 2002

Whaley, Diana
A Dictionary of Lake District Place-Names, Nottingham 2006

Will, C.P
Place-Names of North-East Angus, Arbroath 1963

Yeaman, W.J
Handbook of the Scottish Hills, Arbroath 1989

Gaelic Dictionaries

Dwelly, Edward
The Illustrated Gaelic-English Dictionary (reprinted by Gairm Publications, Glasgow 1988)

MacLennan, Malcolm
Gaelic Dictionary, 1925, (reprinted by Acair/AUP)

Scots Dictionaries

The Concise Scots Dictionary (AUP, 1985), draws on the ten-volume *Scottish National Dictionary*. See the website at *<www.dsl.ac.uk>* for the *Scottish National Dictionary* and the *Dictionary of the Older Scots Tongue* on-line

Index

SCOTTISH MOUNTAINEERING CLUB
SCOTTISH MOUNTAINEERING TRUST
Prices were correct at time of publication, but are subject to change

HILLWALKERS' GUIDES

The Munros	£22.00
Munros GPS data sets – from SMC website	£10.50
The Corbetts and Other Scottish Hills	£22.00
The Cairngorms	£18.00
Central Highlands	£18.00
Islands of Scotland Including Skye	£20.00
North-West Highlands	£22.00
Southern Highlands	£17.00

SCRAMBLERS' GUIDES

Skye Scrambles	£18.00
Highland Scrambles North	£18.00

CLIMBERS' GUIDES

Scottish Winter Climbs	£24.00
Scottish Rock Climbs	£24.00
The Cairngorms	£24.00
Ben Nevis	£21.00
Glen Coe	£21.00
North-East Outcrops	£21.00
Arran, Arrochar and Southern Highlands	£15.00
Highland Outcrops	£17.50
Lowland Outcrops	£21.00
Northern Highlands North	£21.00
Northern Highlands Central	£24.00
Northern Highlands South	£24.00
Skye	£24.00
The Islands	£24.00

OTHER PUBLICATIONS

Hostile Habitats – Scotland's Mountain Environment	£16.00
The Munroist's Companion	£16.00
Ben Nevis – Britain's Highest Mountain	£27.50
The Cairngorms – 100 Years of Mountaineering	£27.50

Visit our website for more details and to purchase on line:
www.smc.org.uk

Distributed by:
Cordee Ltd, (t) 01455 611185 (w) www.cordee.co.uk